Other titles by the RCC Pilotage Foundation

Atlantic Crossing Guide: Second Edition
ISBN: 0 229 11828 3
Published by Adlard Coles

North Brittany Pilot: Fifth Edition Revised
ISBN: 0 229 11696 5
Published by Adlard Coles

Far Horizons: Extracts from the Royal Cruising Club Journal
ISBN: 0 229 11822 4
Published by Adlard Coles

Atlantic Spain and Portugal
ISBN: 0 85288 110 X
Published by Imray Laurie Norie and Wilson

The Atlantic Islands: Azores, Madeira, Canary and Cape Verde Islands
ISBN: 0 85288 139 8
Published by Imray Laurie Norie and Wilson

North Biscay Pilot

Brest to La Gironde

K. Adlard Coles and A. N. Black
Revised by the RCC Pilotage Foundation
Edited by Nicholas Heath
Fourth Edition

ADLARD COLES
8 Grafton Street, London W1

Adlard Coles
William Collins Sons & Co. Ltd
8 Grafton Street, London W1X 3LA

Partly based on
Biscay Harbours and Anchorages, Vols I and II,
by K. Adlard Coles, first published in 1959 and 1960

As North Biscay Pilot
Revised by Professor A. N. Black
Second edition 1977
Reprinted with amendments 1978
Third edition 1982
Revised by the RCC Pilotage Foundation
Reprinted with amendments 1985
Reprinted with amendments 1987
Fourth edition 1990

Distributed in the United States of America
by Sheridan House, Inc.

Copyright © RCC Pilotage Foundation 1982, 1985, 1990
Chart illustrations by Jennifer Johnson

British Library Cataloguing in Publication Data
Coles, K. Adlard (Kaines Adlard), *1901–1986*
    North Biscay pilot: Brest to La Gironde. – 4th ed.
    1. Western France. Coastal waters – Pilots' guides
    I. Title II. Black, A. N. (Archibald Niel), *1912–*
    III. Heath, Nicholas IV. RCC Pilotage Foundation
    623.89′2944

ISBN 0–229–11808–9

Printed in Spain by Graficas Velasco, Toledo

The RCC Pilotage Foundation

In 1976 an American member of the Royal Cruising Club, Dr Fred Ellis, indicated that he wished to make a gift to the Club in memory of his father, the late Robert H. Ellis MD, of his friends Peter Pye and John Ives who were both prominent members and as a mark of his esteem for Roger Pinckney, a past Commodore of the Club. An independent charity known as the RCC Pilotage Foundation was formed and, with the approval of Dr Ellis, the funds provided by him were transferred to the foundation.

At the request of K. Adlard Coles, the Foundation undertook the 1980 revision of the *North Brittany Pilot* and was then asked by Professor A. N. Black to revise the *North Biscay Pilot*. The RCC Pilotage Foundation gratefully acknowledges the gifts by the authors of the copyright of both these famous pilot books. It is the intention of the Foundation and the publishers to revise them at appropriate intervals so that the valuable work of the original authors will be kept up-to-date for the benefit of cruising yachtsmen. The Foundation has also undertaken new books, *The Atlantic Crossing Guide*, the *Atlantic Islands Pilot*, and *Atlantic Spain and Portugal*. Other projects will follow.

The Foundation is deeply indebted to Nicholas Heath for the enormous amount of meticulous work and many miles of travelling in France by land and sea that have gone into the preparation of this edition of the *North Biscay Pilot*.

Preface

The history of pilotage books on the Biscay coast for yachtsmen is a long one. The first was Frank Cowper's *Sailing Tours – Falmouth to the Loire*, one of a set of volumes he published at the end of the nineteenth century. Anyone who can lay hands on a copy will find in it a fascinating contrast to the situation described in the present volume. He was surprised to find a French naval vessel in almost every port he visited, but eventually realised that the French navy had hit on the only reasonable explanation for his eccentric behaviour – that he was a spy. Then came H. J. Hanson's great work, the *Cruising Association Handbook* but, as this covered the British Isles and much of north western Europe, the space devoted to this coast in the earlier editions was necessarily limited.

After the World War II, the race programme of the Royal Ocean Racing Club normally ended with a race to a port in the Bay of Biscay. Most owners and crew members had then to make fast passages to get back to work as quickly as possible. Only a few, of whom the late Adlard Coles was one, were able to finish the season with a comparatively unhurried cruise home. This enabled him, often accompanied by his wife alone, to make a thorough exploration of this coast and he realised the need for a detailed pilotage book.

The result was two volumes of *Biscay Harbours and Anchorages*, published in 1959 and 1960. The careful preparation of these volumes, with the selection of just that information which yachtsmen required, encouraged many British yachtsmen to visit this excellent cruising ground. After about ten years *Biscay Harbours* was in need of up-dating due to the many changes which had occurred in that time. As Adlard Coles himself was not able to find the time for the work involved, I undertook the task. Robin Brandon was then preparing his *South Biscay Pilot*, so the name was changed to the *North Biscay Pilot*, to avoid confusion, and the work was published as a single volume. Despite the change in name and format, the layout, and indeed much of the text, that had proved so successful was maintained.

An up-dated reprint was published in 1977, with much new information. It could not fairly be called a new edition, because it was not preceded by the check of all the ports which this would have implied. It is increasingly difficult for one author to find the time to do all the work involved in a complete revision. When the introduction of the IALA buoyage system made a full new edition necessary Adlard Coles and I gladly handed the responsibility for this to the RCC Pilotage Foundation. The Foundation will be able to use the resources of the Club to maintain the usefulness of a book which it has given us much pleasure to produce in our more active cruising days.

A. N. Black

Acknowledgements

Most of the charts in this book have been updated from those in previous editions, which were almost all based on the official French charts, with the kind permission of the Directeur du Service Hydrographique et Océanographique de la Marine. Exceptions were based on Admiralty Chart 3427, with the permission of the Hydrographer of the Navy, and ECM Chart 547, with that of Editions Cartographiques Maritimes.

The present edition is the result of a survey, lasting three months, in *Capelan*, a bilge-keel ketch drawing 1.1m, during which (except for Pouliguen and Pornichet, which were covered by others) it was possible to observe and photograph the approaches to all the harbours and to enter the majority in order to investigate the facilities available at the time. The editor was able to make contact with a large number of yachtsmen of many nationalities who were most helpful with information and many of whom offered to correspond in the future, to advise of the changes that are taking place so rapidly in the area. He is particularly grateful to Paul Dane (RCC) and to Hamish Simpson Lawrence (Clyde CC) for researching specific harbours more thoroughly, at his request, during 1989.

All the colour photographs are new, as are most of the black and white photographs, though some have been retained for their continued usefulness and their nostalgic value.

The charts have been redrawn by Jennifer Johnson and it is hoped that the reintroduction of colour will make them as useful in the cockpit as were Hasler's charts in the original *Harbours and Anchorages of the North Coast of Brittany*, the white areas indicating deep water.

In conclusion I am bound to echo the words of the previous editor, Lt. Col. C. A. Biddle, and say that it would be presumptuous to attempt to improve on the work of K. Adlard Coles and Professor Black except when changes have made revision unavoidable; those who have used previous editions of the Pilot know how much is owed to them. It would be difficult to list all the sources from which information has been obtained, still more the individuals who have contributed. To all are due the thanks of the RCC Pilotage Foundation and its editor.

N. E. Heath 1990

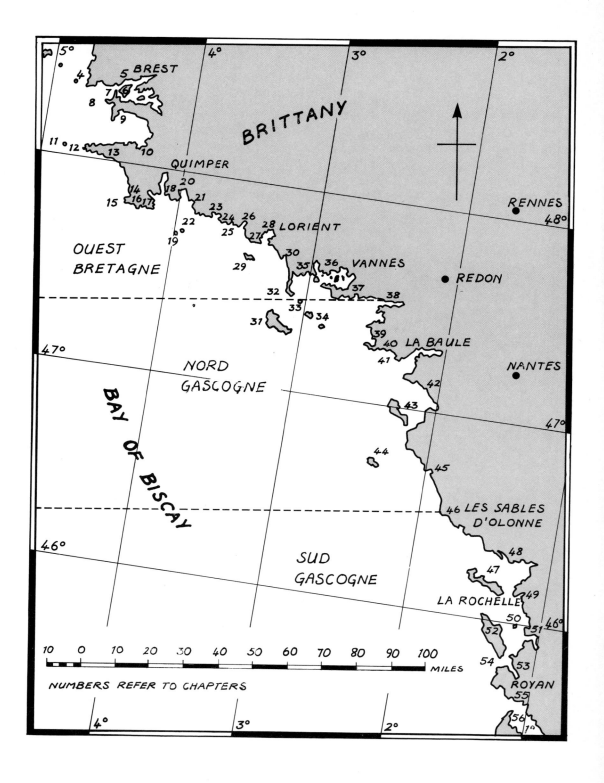

BRITTANY

BREST 5

4

7 6
8
9

11 12
13 10
QUIMPER
20
14 18
15 16 17 21
23
22 24 26
25 27 28 LORIENT
19
30
35 36 VANNES
29 32
31 33 34
37 38

OUEST
BRETAGNE

RENNES
48°

REDON

39
40 LA BAULE
41
42

NANTES

43

NORD
GASCOGNE

BAY

44

47°

45

OF

46 LES SABLES
D'OLONNE

48
47

SUD
GASCOGNE

BISCAY

49

LA ROCHELLE
50
52 51 46°
54 53
ROYAN
55
56

47°

46°

5°
4°
3°
2°

47°

46°

4°
3°
2°

10   0   10   20   30   40   50   60   70   80   90   100

MILES

NUMBERS REFER TO CHAPTERS

Contents

Late corrections

This book has been corrected up to Admiralty Notices to Mariners 30 Sept 89; as it went to press the following further changes were noted.

ANM

89.2019   Rade de Brest, page 36. South of Marine Museum: port-hand light-beacon with topmark, Oc(3)R 12s in position 48°22.74'N 4°26.45'W.

89.3206   La Vilaine entrance, page 212. Beacon tower off Pte de Kervoyal is lit Dir Q WR 8–6M. Tréhiguier light (Oc(4)R 12s) and leading line discontinued. No. 1 (stbd) channel buoy moved to slightly east of old position. No. 2 (port) buoy remains in old position N of Petit Sécé. It is not clear whether the buoys 4, 5, 6 and 8 are now lit.

89.3634   Pointe de Penmarc'h, pages 76, 77, 80. Menhir tower light amended to Fl(2)WG 6s, 19m, 8–5M

Charted depth errors

Grey/blue on the charts represents drying areas. Depths marked in these areas should be under-lined to show the drying height but in several cases this is not the case. (This is obvious on page 291 – 'Ile d'Aix' – where the Anse de Saillant dries 4m and none of the figures in the drying area has been underlined.) On all charts it can be assumed that a grey/blue tinted area dries and that the figures represent drying heights.

1 Cruising in South Brittany and Biscay

A small yacht heading for the Bay of Biscay will pass Ushant, usually passing inside through the Chenal du Four. After she has rounded Pointe de St Mathieu, the Rade de Brest lies to the east, providing in itself a magnificent cruising ground. Next comes the Baie de Douarnenez, a fine big bay, having however only two secure harbours.

Bound south, a vessel will next pass through the Raz de Sein. Here, as in the Chenal du Four, the tidal streams are strong and in bad weather the seas are dangerous, but once through the channel the Bay of Biscay is entered. The tidal streams are weaker and the weather becomes progressively warmer the further south one sails. Between Penmarc'h and La Rochelle there are three granite islands, Ile de Groix, Belle Ile and Ile d'Yeu, each of which has a harbour and minor anchorages. To the north and east of these islands, the mainland coast offers the variety of harbours and anchorages which makes it so attractive to the cruising man. There are anchorages in deep water and shallow, fishing harbours, busy ports, sophisticated holiday resorts, yachting centres, estuaries and rivers with peaceful reaches.

The first busy sailing area to be reached is the large bay from Loctudy to Concarneau, sheltered by the Iles de Glénan with their enormous and famous sailing school. Thence some passage-making leads to Quiberon Bay, another sheltered area, very popular with French yachtsmen. Here, between the yachting centres of La Trinité and Le Croisic, there lie all the anchorages in the Morbihan ('the little sea'), Penerf and the beautiful river La Vilaine. To seaward there are the little islands of Houat and Hoëdic, and to the west Belle Ile with the crowded harbour of Le Palais and another, less active, at Sauzon. In this area one could spend a month exploring and sailing in shelter even in bad weather.

Shallow draught yachts which do not wish to make the passage down Channel and through the rough waters of Four and Sein can come through the Breton Canals. The usual exit from these is to La Vilaine, but it is also possible to go on to Nantes and come down the Loire. The real canal enthusiast, if his draught is small enough, can turn aside at Redon, where he is almost at sea, and after another hundred locks, emerge at Lorient.

Beyond Le Croisic is the Loire, the southern boundary of Brittany. The coastal scene changes, rock reluctantly, but never entirely, giving place to sandy shores. The character of the harbours changes too; there are not so many harbours in which a yacht can lie afloat and come and go freely at any state of the tide. For this reason the best time for cruising in this region is when the tides are taking off from springs to neaps. It is then possible to leave near the morning high water and arrive in time for the evening one. On this part of the coast there are two large islands, Noirmoutier and Ile d'Yeu. Noirmoutier offers interesting anchorages, and one marina. Port Joinville is the only good harbour on Ile d'Yeu.

Another passage leads to the area round Ile de Ré and La Rochelle. La Rochelle is a historic city with two fine old towers guarding the entrance to one harbour and a vast new marina. Ile de Ré is low and sandy. St Martin, the capital, has a secure harbour with a wet dock. This area is the end of the popular cruising ground, but a few ports down to the entrance to the Gironde have been included for the benefit of those using the Canal du Midi, which connects with the Mediterranean.

The cruising area which this book covers is a fascinating and varied one. For many British yachtsmen, the difficulty lies in the time taken to get there and return within the span of a summer holiday. A good plan is to work the yacht down Channel in weekends before the real holiday begins. Then make a direct passage from there to the South Brittany coast. The English Channel is fairly wide here, say 120 miles to Ushant, and it is about the same distance on to Belle Ile.

Ushant is not a nice landfall in bad weather and in fog it is horrid; in thick weather it is better to keep offshore, outside all the dangers. However in summer really bad weather is uncommon.

Winds
Winds in the north of Biscay are variable, but westerly winds (SW to NW) are most frequent in the summer months, especially in July and August. In spring, early summer and late autumn, winds between N and E are also common. There is some indication that the climate is changing; the strong westerlies of the last few decades seem to be dying away. The Bay of Biscay has a reputation for gales, but in summer from May to September winds of force 7 and over are recorded only about once in 25 days. Most summer gales are associated with depressions passing to the northward, with backing winds followed by a veer to the W or NW. At intervals of several years, very severe short storms may occur, which may be missed by the forecasters. Beware of a sudden fall in the barometer in muggy, thundery weather, with poor visibility.

Land and sea breezes near the coast are common in settled summer weather. Especially in the southern part of the area they result in the *vent solaire*. After a noonday calm a westerly sea breeze sets in. This goes round to NW and by evening to N, and finally about midnight, or a little later, it settles in the NE, when it sometimes blows very freshly, causing quite a rough sea, and continues until 0800.

Another feature of this part of the Bay of Biscay is that if a NE wind starts to veer to S in the morning, and only goes as far as S and then backs to the NE, the NE wind may be accompanied by strong squalls.

Visibility
Fog, mist or haze is quite frequent during the summer. There is visibility of under 5 miles on about one day in five, but real fog, reducing visibility to less than $\frac{1}{2}$ mile, averages only one day in twenty. The coast is so well marked by beacons and towers that navigation in poor visibility is possible, but thick fog is very unpleasant if it occurs when one is sailing in narrow tidal waters.

Currents and tides
When navigating in light weather and fog, the tidal streams are of great significance.

Small-scale tidal charts only show the main streams, but in coastal waters there are local variations and eddies. The local set can be estimated by examination of pot buoys, which are numerous on this coast.

Note

Swell

Swell is a factor which sometimes has to be reckoned with on the NW and W coasts of France. It appears to run higher in some parts than others, and is notable in the vicinity of Ushant and NE of Le Four. In the Bay of Biscay itself swell seems to be less frequent as the weather is better, and the swell ranges from gentle undulations to waves of considerable height, though it is rarely so uncomfortable as between Ile Vierge and Ushant, where the strong tidal streams are an added complication.

A large swell will break heavily on bars and in shallow water, with the result that the approaches to some of the harbours, such as Bélon, Le Pouldu and Etel, are dangerous even in fine weather if there is a ground swell. Swell can break intermittently and dangerously on rocks rising from deep water, even when there is apparently a safe depth over them.

Another characteristic of swell is that when it enters a narrowing inlet it tends to increase in height and steepness. It funnels up the entrance and will surge into anchorages which one would expect to be sheltered from the direction of the swell. For this reason, anchorages open to the Atlantic, such as those on the west side of Ile de Groix, Belle Ile and Ile d'Yeu should be used only with caution, in settled weather, with an offshore wind and in the absence of swell. Furthermore, if ground swell manifests itself in calm weather (and it can arrive with little warning, originating in disturbances far out in the ocean), a vessel should leave the open anchorage before it builds up to possibly formidable dimensions, when no anchor will hold. French fishermen take swell seriously, and none should know better. The French weather forecasts for shipping include forecasts of swell (*la houle*).

Type of yacht – draught and drying out

The North Biscay coast suits all types of yacht, large or small, deep-keeled or shallow draught.

For large yachts there are plenty of deep-water anchorages and most of the shallower harbours can be entered near high water, and the yacht can dry out against a quay. Before doing so it is best to make local enquiries, as the bottom in parts of some harbours is rough or rocky. To ensure taking the bottom with the yacht at the correct angle against the quay, which need not be great, it is usual to put all movable weights on the landward side of the yacht. In addition it is a wise precaution to shackle the main halyard to a bollard on the quayside and set it up as the tide falls. By this means the mast is stayed to the quay and the yacht cannot fall outwards, but do not forget to release the halyard when the tide rises. Good fenders are needed, as quay walls are often very rough; they should be hard and not squashy or they will be squeezed flat and the yacht will lean heavily inwards.

The yacht *Cohoe III*, in which Adlard Coles carried out his many surveys, had a draught of 1.8m (6ft). She had a fairly long straight keel, which was an advantage when drying out alongside a quay. Yachts with very cut-away forefoots rest bow down at a considerable angle, which is not necessarily dangerous, but decidedly uncomfortable. The modern racing yacht with short fin keel and separate skeg does not usually lie comfortably against a quay.

French fishing vessels and most small French yachts are equipped with legs. Not only can they dry out against a quay more safely, but they can dry out anywhere in any sheltered anchorage if the bottom is smooth and hard. Legs are a great asset to cruising on the Biscay coast. Best of all is a bilge-keel yacht that can take the ground. She can explore many parts that are impossible for keel yachts, and can often find a snug berth inside the local moorings while her deep-keeled sister is rolling farther out.

Where reference is made in the text to a 'yacht which can take the ground,' it is implied that she does not need the outside support of a quay wall.

A very large number of French yachtsmen sail dinghies or small yachts that are launched from trailers and the launching facilities are good nearly everywhere. It is quite easy, therefore, to trail a boat out and spend a happy holiday on this coast exploring its nooks and crannies, rocks and sands.

Navigating among rocks

The coast of Brittany and North Biscay is famous for its rocks, which to a stranger may cause some apprehension. This will be especially the case if he is accustomed to mud pilotage, as on the east coast of England. He will soon come to realise that although it is much more important to avoid hitting the bottom, the large number of landmarks, natural and man-made, make it easy to know exactly where one is: if one knows exactly where one is, one has no reason to run aground. It is usually easy, by sliding a ruler over the chart, to find your own transits to keep out of trouble.

Beacons and towers are permanent, although occasionally damaged by gales, but complete reliance should not be placed on buoys, which may drag their moorings during gales, though in practice I have never found one out of position. Many of the rocks and shoals shown on the charts are not dangerous to moderate draught yachts, except in bad weather, when they cause the seas to break. Much depends upon the state of the tide. A useful tip is to estimate the rise of tide at the time when a harbour is to be approached, and then to put a pencilled circle on the chart round each rock or shoal which will not have a safe depth of water over it, remembering that tides do not always rise exactly as predicted. It is often surprising to find how few they are, so that pilotage is simplified by concentrating on the ones which are dangerous.

A common feature of a rocky coast is the extension of a pronounced headland in the form of a reef continuing seaward under water. For this reason, when approaching an inlet between two promontories, never cut across one of the promontories to the entrance, unless the chart indicates clear water. Approach from seaward with the middle of the inlet well open, allowing for the probable extension of the promontory under water.

4

If there is a big swell the seas will probably break over sunken rocks which are dangerous, and it may be necessary to avoid rocks which are covered by water of a depth equal to several times the yacht's draught. In strong streams the presence of rocks may be indicated by rips, or in smooth water by circles of oily-looking water. Even in deep water an uneven bottom causes a disturbance on the surface if the current is strong, so the oily circles do not always denote danger. In parts of Brittany the water is very clear, and if a member of the crew stands forward he can often see underwater rocks.

Rocks can be dangerous in light weather to yachts not equipped with reliable auxiliary power. In such circumstances the danger is greater than in rough conditions, if the tide is setting towards them. There is a theory that if a yacht is drifting becalmed, the stream will set her safely past rocks on one side or the other. This may be true of steep isolated above-water rocks, but it is certainly not true of underwater ledges. Great care must be exercised when navigating in calm weather near rocks; a good kedge with a very long warp must be ready for use.

Some harbours, such as the Ile de Sein and St Guénolé, have many rocks in the approaches. These present no great difficulty to the experienced cruising man, but as a mistake could have serious consequences, a newcomer to these coasts may prefer to limit his cruising on the first occasion to the better known and more easily accessible harbours. The more difficult anchorages should only be attempted in settled weather with clear visibility and preferably at neaps. The transits and landmarks should be identified with certainty *before* the yacht enters the danger area of rocks.

It is a good idea to check the yacht's position regularly by reference to natural features. New beacons can be built, or one mistaken for another, the large white building can be rendered inconspicuous by a larger whiter building, but nobody replaces or removes headlands or islands. Above all keep the identifications going well ahead of the yacht; not only does this give more time if things do not 'add up', but minor headlands may be quite prominent when looked at along the coast, but insignificant and unidentifiable when seen from directly offshore.

Harbours
In artificial harbours formed by breakwaters, it is inadvisable to cross close off the end of a breakwater, as these are often built on rocks, or have rocks at their bases. When entering a strange harbour it is best to approach about midway between the jetties with the inner harbour open; see page 10.

Unless using a mooring or a berth at a marina there is generally no need to seek out the authorities on entering a port. They will often visit a yacht after she is berthed. Stay away from areas assigned to the fishing fleets.

Mooring
It may be worth mentioning some methods of mooring which are more common in France than in England. The first is lying close packed, side by side, with a mooring or anchor ahead and the stern pulled in to a quay or pontoon. If it is necessary to lay out an anchor ahead, one must note the direction in which the chains of those already berthed

lead, and lay the anchor accordingly. Sometimes there is a line of buoys to which to secure the bow. Sometimes the pick-up rope for the bow mooring is led back to the pontoon; this can be tricky, as one has to back into the pontoon before getting the mooring on board, unless one sends out a dinghy.

Another unfamiliar method of mooring uses a big-ship buoy. Each new arrival takes a bow rope to the buoy and a cluster forms. When this is full a second circle is sometimes formed, by anchoring and taking a line to the buoy.

Both of these methods call for a good supply of fenders. Both methods, and also more familiar methods, are made less comfortable than they might be because French yachtsmen hardly ever use springs in circumstances in which the English regard their use as normal. I have, indeed, been positively asked not to use them by my neighbour when we were moored head and stern to buoys.

Provisions

Ordinary provisions can be bought in all towns, most of which have a supermarket, and even in small villages there are shops which supply necessities and are nearly always open. Very small communities sometimes rely on a travelling shop, which is less convenient. Milk should be bought pasteurised, or it will not keep long. *Stérilisé* is similar to 'long life'. Groceries and meat are similarly priced to the UK, but it is wise to stock up with non-perishables before starting the cruise. Sea food, such as mussels, crabs and prawns, is good and reasonably priced when bought in the market, though lobsters, alas, command their price anywhere. Mackerel can be caught, though less easily than in the English Channel; they seem more sluggish and will not come if the yacht is travelling fast. French bread is delicious, but does not keep. A *baguette* can sometimes be given a second life after 24 hours if placed in a hot oven for a short time. If bread is required to remain edible for several days, ask for *Pain complet*, which is similar to a wholemeal loaf. Where there is a baker, bread will be available early, but there may be a delay where it comes by van to a *dépôt de pain*.

In the text, under *Facilities*, 'all shops' implies at least bread, grocer, butcher, cooked meats and usually ironmonger and 'droguerie' (paraffin, paints etc) as well.

Telephone cards

These can be purchased from a tobacconist/newsagent and from some café/bars. All the public telephones in Concarneau appear to require cards. These can be purchased from the Bar de Mouton close to the marina (fr44 and fr88 in 1989).

Water

There is a tradition that French water is suspect. The installation of a central piped water supply almost everywhere has changed this and brought other changes, too. The water towers, which have appeared in great numbers, are conspicuous marks for the navigator, but piped supplies everywhere mean that the taps in the streets, which used to be so convenient, have now gone.

The availability of convenient watering points is given in the text under the heading *Facilities*. Only rarely is the absence of a watering point specifically mentioned; if water is not mentioned under this heading it should be assumed that water may be difficult to find, except by courtesy from shops or cafés.

Fuel

It is no longer permitted for yachtsmen to buy the tax-free fuel available to fishermen, or the red-tinted diesel oil sold for domestic heating as 'fuel oil domestique' (FOD). It is, however, now exceptional for the numerous marinas not to offer both petrol and diesel oil from quayside pumps, though not all will operate outside the French holiday season. Where there is no marina, fuel may also be available from pumps, though the presence of a pump does not guarantee this: it may be for fishermen's supply only. In some ports it may be necessary to fill by can from roadside garages.

Petrol (essence) comes in two grades, 'super' and 'normal'. Prices are (1988) rather above those in UK, with a rather higher differential between grades. Diesel (gasoil, pronounced 'gazwahl') costs as much as that obtained from roadside filling stations. In 1988 diesel was around 80p per gallon in UK harbours and £1.70 per gallon in France.

Formalities

British yachts must complete and deposit Part I of Customs Form C1328 before departing from British waters for abroad. Parts II and III must be retained on board and dealt with on return.

When in France all visiting yachts must carry a Certificate of Registry on board. Very heavy fines may be imposed on defaulters. The British certificate can be that of the Board of Trade, or the Small Ships Register, administered by the RYA, RYA House, Romsey Road, Eastleigh, Hants (tel: 0703 644061). The status of yachts registered elsewhere should be established in advance.

Personal passports should be carried by all members of the ship's company. In practice they are likely to be required only for cashing cheques, for independent return to the UK by public transport and, in the case of the owner, for dealing with the Customs. The green card (Passeport du navire étranger) is needed to obtain duty free stores (although at some ports it is not asked for). To obtain it, report to the Customs with the ship's Certificate of Registry and the owner's personal passport. Although it is not otherwise necessary to report to Customs, doing so can be taken as legally equivalent to a formal declaration that the vessel is healthy and is not engaged in importing goods, being chartered, or otherwise infringing the regulations.

Few officials, except in marinas, speak English. To enforce the ownership regulations Customs visit yachts, even under way. A 'fiche' from them will simplify later visits. It is forbidden for one skipper to hand over to another in French waters, except between part-owners or immediate members of a family, including 'habitual concubines'. These regulations are intended to stop chartering in French waters by non-French organizations.

The French search and rescue organizations (CROSSCO, N of Pointe du Raz;

CROSSA, S of Pointe du Raz) operate an excellent passage surveillance service. Some harbourmasters require a form to be completed showing 'where from' and 'where to'. This information is passed on to CROSSCO/CROSSA. It is important that, if a yacht does not go where she has said she is going, the information should be reported quickly. Otherwise a futile search may be instituted.

Yachts arriving in French waters with goods on board that are dutiable in France must enter a port where they can be cleared by Customs, flying the 'Q' flag. Yachts arriving without dutiable goods can enter any harbour but *must not* fly a 'Q'. During its stay in French waters a yacht may be boarded on several occasions by Customs and the onus is on the skipper to prove that no regulations are being broken. During the first visit ask for *une fiche* and if the officers are satisfied you will be given one to show that the vessel has been cleared. Should you be approached at a later date, it is only necessary to show 'la fiche' to satisfy the intending boarders.

Yacht clubs
There are yacht clubs and sailing schools in most French harbours; they are invariably hospitable to visitors. Assistance or advice is always given readily, and showers are often available.

Laying up
In order to spend more time on the Biscay coast, it may be convenient to take a holiday late in the summer and leave the yacht in France for the winter. By taking an early holiday in the following year, the cruise can be continued and the yacht brought home again in time for the remainder of the season. When laying up the green card must be deposited with the local Customs Office.

Fishermen
There are many fishermen's dan buoys round the coast and sometimes well out to sea. They present a hazard, especially at night when under power, and a constant lookout is necessary. The buoys are usually in pairs, flying the owner's particular flag. If the pair can be identified, it is advisable not to pass between them when north of the Loire. South of the Loire a line of very small floats may be seen running between the larger dans. Their presence can be indicated on French charts by the legend: *Attention aux Orins des Casiers*. Do not pass between these pairs of dans!

In this edition, *metres* have replaced *feet*, *fathoms* and *cables*. Larger distances remain in *nautical miles*.

Chart datum

Datum in the sailing directions and in the plans reproduced in this book is the same as on French charts; soundings are reduced to the approximate level of the lowest predicted tides. This level is referred to as LAT (lowest astronomical tide). Although the actual lowest predicted tide can only occur near the equinox and will not, therefore, affect most yachtsmen, predicted tides nearly down to LAT can occur at any time. At such times exceptional meteorological conditions could result in tides falling below chart datum.

This datum is of the utmost importance when navigating in the Bay of Biscay, for it means, especially in Brittany, that at *mean low water springs* there may be 0.6m (2 ft) more water than is shown on the chart, and at *mean low water neaps* even greater depth. The height of MLWS and MLWN above datum is shown at the head of each chapter and under each plan, so that the appropriate figure can be added to the soundings shown on the plan or given in the text. British charts of the French coast adopt the same datum as the French charts on which they are based.

Heights

In the plans and sailing instructions in this book the French method of measurement has been followed which differs in some respects from British practice.

Rocks that uncover and drying patches

The heights are given above chart datum, being shown in underlined figures. In the text the word 'dries' is used. This is the same as British practice. On modern French charts, but not in this book, these figures are in italic.

Rocks that never cover

The heights are given above chart datum, being shown in underlined figures. In the text the word 'high' is used. British practice is to give these heights above MHWS. On older French charts these rocks are marked with the symbol 'T' over them; this must not be misread as representing a beacon. This convention is not used in this book.

Land heights

Heights on land, not underlined, are above mean tide level. British practice is to give these heights above MHWS.

Lighthouses

The elevation of the lights – not the actual heights of the structures – is given above MHWS. This is the same as British practice.

Sailing directions

The description of each port is set out in the same form, so that the reader will come to know where to look for the information he wants. It is written from the point of view of the master of a sailing yacht of normal size. If there is more than 3m (10ft) of water, the channel is described as deep, on the assumption that users of the book will not have a greater draught than this. Low bridges are treated as blocking navigation; although many motor yachts will be able to pass them unhindered, the upper reaches beyond them have not been inspected.

Beacons

There are many kinds of beacon and it is hard to find a descriptive terminology. British charts use 'Bn.' or 'Bn. Tr.' to cover this wide range. The scheme which has been followed as far as possible in this book can be set out thus:

Description on French charts	Appearance	Description in this book
Balise	A wood or iron pole beacon usually on ground which covers and uncovers, *or*	*Beacon*
	A modern version of the above, made of concrete, usually about 1m (3ft) in diameter, on a wider base. They resemble thin tourelles, *or*	*Concrete beacon*
	A built up beacon on shore, often of iron or masonry in the shape of a pillar.	*Masonry beacon*
Tourelle	A stone or concrete beacon, usually on ground which covers with the tide. Cylindrical or slightly tapered in shape.	*Tower*
Amer	A built up beacon on shore which may be of any shape, often painted white.	*Masonry beacon*
Mur blanchi	A wall painted white (sometimes specially built as a beacon).	*Wall beacon*
Pyramide	A slender conical beacon painted white (not a mathematical pyramid).	*Pyramid*

Beacons, concrete beacons and towers are commonly painted to conform with the buoyage systems (cardinal or lateral) and have the appropriate topmarks; the others are not. The word 'tower' is also used in a less restricted sense on occasion; there should be no confusion, since when it refers to a *tourelle* it will be followed by a note on the colour. The heads of breakwaters, forming a harbour entrance, are often marked with white paint, with a green triangle or red square indicating the side on which to pass them. When passing under a bridge there are similar marks to indicate the appropriate arch for the channel.

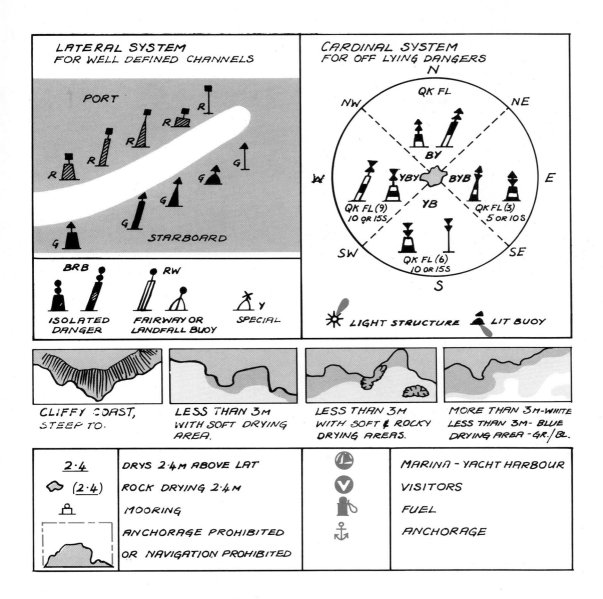

The key above shows the symbols for marks, limits and dangers used in the charts and plans in this book.

The cardinal system of buoyage is now well established and needs little explanation. Cardinal lights are all quick or very quick flashing white, memorable from a clock face: three flashes at 3 o'clock for E, six, with one long flash, for S, nine for W, and continuous, which may be thought of as twelve, for N. The conventional Lateral system is used for marking a channel, with red for port hand and green for starboard, marked from the entrance without regard to the tidal stream. Occasionally, as in the entrance to L'Aulne river, the red port hand buoys are conical instead of can shaped.

Isolated dangers with navigable water all round are marked by **BRB** beacons or buoys. Wrecks are now marked by lateral or cardinal warnings in the same way as any other obstacle to navigation. Fairway, Landfall, or Safe Water buoys are painted with red and white vertical stripes, with white lights and a single red spherical topmark, to show navigable water. The key shows the topmarks, which are significant in a poor light when the colours cannot be identified. The French describe their buoys as 'pylone' (pillar), 'espar' (spar), 'cylindrique' (can) and 'conique' (conical).

Each plan has been subdivided along the right hand and bottom margins into tenths of a minute of latitude and longitude. The use of identical units in each plan should give an immediate indication of the scale. A scale of metres is shown on the plan and the right hand margin can be used to measure off in cables. One division on each edge is numbered so that reference to other charts, notices to mariners, etc. is easily made.

Dry land is tinted grey, drying areas are blue/grey. In most cases, areas where the depth is less than 3 metres are shown blue and deep water is left white. This convention has been found to work well when the plan is being used in a poor light. For safety, keep in the white areas if possible. In a chart where the division between blue and white does not define the 3m contour, this will be indicated in the caption below.

Bearings
Bearings are expressed in degrees true, but in the text magnetic bearings in points are occasionally given to indicate an approximate direction of a course or object. Variation is at present $7\frac{1}{2}°$W in the north and $4°$W in the south of the area.

Lights
The descriptions of all the lights to be used in entering a port are collected into one tabulation to assist in identification. The heights are given in metres (m), and the range of visibility is given in miles (M). Where a light has sectors the limits of the sectors are shown only on the plan and the range given refers to the light of maximum range (white, or intensified sector).

The light from a lighthouse may become invisible at a long range for one of two reasons; the light may not be sufficiently bright, or it may disappear below the horizon (geographical range). The geographical range normally quoted is for a height of eye of 4.5m (15ft). From a typical yachting height of eye of say 1.5m (5ft) the actual visible range is about 2 miles less than the geographical range.

The distance at which a light is bright enough to be seen varies with the haze in the atmosphere; the term nominal range is used for this distance when the meteorological visibility is 10 miles, though a light may of course be seen at a greater distance. It is this nominal range (quoted in Admiralty and French light lists) which is quoted in this book. If the nominal range quoted is 15M or more it is likely that it will exceed the geographical range. Lights with a nominal range of 10M or less are relatively weak and may be difficult to identify among other lights on the shore.

The characteristics referred to in the text are for 1989, and are liable to alterations which will be shown on chart corrections and in the current List of Lights (for shore lights) and Pilot (for buoys).

Although the general practice is for coloured sectors to indicate dangers and white sectors the clear passages, this is not universal, and it should not be assumed that the white sectors indicate deep water over the whole sector at all distances from the light. Generally, if a light shows a white safe sector with red and green sectors on each side, the green sector is to starboard and the red to port, at least in the principal channel. To return to the white sector, show your green to a green light, your red to a red light, a variant on 'green to green or red to red, perfect safety'. This rule is not universal and should be checked for each light. Also narrow intensified sectors usually, but not always, fall within the safe width of the channel.

The French make considerable use of rhythmic lights, such as:

	Fl(2 + 1),	on French charts	F.2é.1é.
or	Oc(1 + 2),	"	F.10.20.
or	Oc(1 + 3),	"	F.10.30

Lights are often 'Directional'; that is, they show brightly over a very narrow sector, sometimes faintly outside the sector.

Radiobeacons
The descriptions of the radiobeacons are given with the lights; they comprise:
1. The call sign.
2. The frequency in kHz (formerly called kc/s).
3. The period of transmission and the cycle time; thus '1/6 min' means that the beacon has a cycle time of 6 min, during which it transmits for 1 min and is silent for 5 min.
4. The beginning of the first transmission in each hour, if transmission is not continuous; thus 'H + 1 min' means that the transmission begins at 1 min past each hour; if the cycle time is 6 min, transmission will also begin at 7, 13, 19, etc. min past each hour.

Tides

Tidal streams
The Biscay currents and tidal streams offshore are weak, but inshore they are sometimes strong, notably in the Chenal du Four, Raz de Sein, Passage de la Teignouse and the Morbihan. As is to be expected the streams tend to be faster off headlands.

The rates and even the directions of tidal streams may be affected by the wind, especially if it blows hard for a long time from one direction. In rivers and estuaries they may be affected by flood water from the land. They often run perpendicular to the coastline.

Tidal heights
The Admiralty Tide Tables give the most accurate predictions of tidal heights, but few yachtsmen carry them and the calculations are tedious.

Special tables (see page 322) have been prepared for this volume which give adequate accuracy, while being very much simpler to use. They are based on the principle that

HW and LW heights can be found by taking the mean tide level (MTL) of the port and adding or subtracting the half-range of the tide for the day at that port.

The appropriate half-range is found by adding two index numbers: one, for the day's tide (small near neaps, large near springs) and one for the port (small for a port with a small tidal range, and larger for one with a greater range). The index number for the day's tide is given in the tables in terms of the height of HW at Brest, the standard port used on this coast. The index number for each port is given, with the MTL, at the head of each chapter, and under each plan. Detailed instructions, and an example of the calculations, follow.

From the Nautical Almanac take the time and height of HW Brest. Note that in some Nautical Almanacs the times for Brest are as for Time Zone −1. From the chapter heading for the port take the time of local HW as compared with Brest, the port Index and the mean tide level (MTL).

1. Calculate the time of local high water.
2. Calculate the interval between local HW and the time when the tidal height is required.
3. Along the top of the tide table, pages 322–3, find the column with the nearest height of HW Brest (in metres).
4. Note the corresponding tide Index, add the port Index, and locate the column headed by the total. Another way of putting this is that the port Index tells you how many columns to move to the right.
5. Run down this column to the correct interval from local HW, calculated in 2. above, and read off the correction to the MTL. The answer will be in metres.

Example
Required the height of tide at La Trinité on 16 August 1989 at 1330 French double summer time (*Heures locales*) = 1130 GMT.

From an Almanac HW Brest (Time Zone −1) is at 1640 = 1540 GMT, height 7.1m.
From chapter 35: La Trinité; HW −0015 Brest, index 1, MTL 3.0m.
Working: Local HW is at 1540−0015 = 1525 GMT.
Interval from HW = 1525−1130 = 3h 55.

The table on page 323 has a column for 7.1m, giving a tide index of 13; where there is no column for the particular tide height, use the nearest column. Adding the port index of 1 to 13 gives a total of 14. In the column headed 14 for interval 3h 50 (the nearest to 3h 55) the correction to MTL is −0.7. Tide height will then be 3.0−0.7, or 2.3m. There may well be differences of 0.1 or 0.2m from the more accurate tables, but this simplified system with no interpolation is good enough for practical purposes.

The first 3 lines of the tables on pages 323–4 suffice to find HW and LW heights. Look up in the Almanac the height of HW Brest. Line 2 gives the corresponding tidal index, to which add the port index, taken from the chapter heading or below the plan. Corresponding to this total index, the fifth line (interval for oh oo) gives the half-range. Look up the MTL for the port, and add/subtract this half-range for HW/LW.

Weather forecasts

Forecasts broadcast by the French coastal stations are more detailed than those broadcast by the BBC and the English coastal stations. The form of the forecast is: the general situation followed first for the next 12 hours for each area general weather type, wind direction and speed in knots, state of sea (*calme* to 0.1m = 6 in., *belle* to 0.5m = 1½ ft, *peu agitée* to 1.25m = 4 ft, *agitée* to 2.5m = 8 ft, *forte* to 4m = 13 ft, *très forte* to 6m = 20 ft, *grosse* to 9m = 30 ft, *très grosse* to 14m = 45 ft, *énorme* the rest), swell (if necessary), visibility in miles; secondly for each area for the following 12 hours similar information in rather less detail; and finally the outlook. The forecasts are read slowly and repeated, so they are not hard to follow with even limited French. Some less familiar words: *brume* = mist, *coup de vent* = gale, *averses* = showers, *houle* = swell, *suroit* = south west, *noroit* = north west, *sudé* = south east, *nordé* = north east.

There are also forecasts broadcast by the national stations, including a special one for yachtsmen, during the summer only, on long wave.

The sea areas covered by this book are Ouest Bretagne (Brest to Quiberon), Nord Gascogne (Quiberon to Les Sables d'Olonne) and Sud Gascogne (south of Les Sables d'Olonne). The broadcasts are detailed below. The times are occasionally changed but are given on a leaflet issued annually and obtainable from harbour masters and marinas.

Coastal stations

Times are French Standard Time; add one hour for French Summer Time.
Brest–le Conquet 1673 kHz, 179m; 0833, 1733, 2253. (Areas Ouest Bretagne, Nord Gascogne, repeated by Quimperlé 1876 kHz, 159m; 0833, 1733.)
St Nazaire 1722 kHz, 174m; 0903, 1903. (Areas Ouest Bretagne, Nord Gascogne, Sud Gascogne.)
Bordeaux–Arcachon 1820 kHz, 165m; 0803, 1803. (Area Sud Gascogne.)
These bulletins are followed by notices about floating dangers, extinguished lights etc. Gale warnings are broadcast at H + 03 and H + 33 from Le Conquet, 1806 kHz, OH + 7 St Nazaire, 1687 kHz, and EH + 7 Bordeaux on 1862 kHz, where EH/OH are even/odd hours of GMT.

VHF stations

The following VHF stations transmit local forecasts at 0733 and 1233 Heures locales (French clock time) (GMT + 2 during French summer time):

Ouessant	Channel 82	St Nazaire	Channel 23
Le Conquet	Channel 26	St Gilles, Croix de Vie	Channel 27
Pont l'Abbé	Channel 27	La Rochelle	Channel 21
Nantes	Channel 28	Royan	Channel 23
Belle Ile	Channel 25		

Les Centres Régionaux Opérationnels de Surveillance et de Sauvetage (CROSS)
Forecast
[CROSS CORSEN] Ouessant. Announced on Ch 16 and transmitted on Ch 11 in French and English. Every 3 hours from 0150 to 2250 GMT. Covering Manche Ouest, Ouest Bretagne and Nord Gascogne.

   [CROSS ETEL] Announced on Ch 16 and transmitted on Ch 13, Heures locales: 0400, 0830, 1410, 1910. Covering Penmar'ch to Sables d'Olonne.

   [S/CROSS SOULAC] Ch 13 heures locales: 0800, 1100, 1430, 1800 (in winter), 1430 (in summer), 1900.

Yachtsmen's forecast
France-Inter 164 kHz, 1829m. Forecasts are given at the end of bulletins, starting at the advertised time; now, 0645, 2005 heures locales.

Severe passages
With some trepidation a few passages marked as *severe* have been included for the benefit of those who may wish to use them in suitable conditions. They are strictly only for those with some local knowledge and reliable auxiliary power, in fine weather and good visibility, at the correct time of tide. They are generally narrow and beset by fierce tides which could quickly lead to disaster. It is hoped that they will not be a challenge to the foolhardy, who must keep clear of them. One is tempted to add that the French impose heavy fines on foolhardy yachtsmen, but presumably anyone who is prepared to risk his yacht and the lives of himself and his crew is not going to be daunted by the prospect of tangling with the French police.

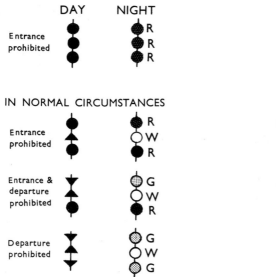

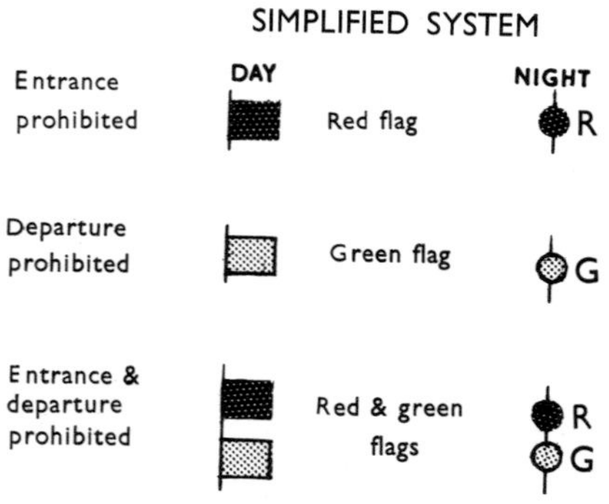

Figure. 2 SIMPLIFIED PORT SIGNALS

Figure. 1. PORT SIGNALS

16

Corrections

The editors would be glad to receive any corrections, information or suggestions which readers may consider would improve the book, as new impressions will be required from time to time. Letters should be addressed to the Editor, North Biscay Pilot, care of the publishers. The more precise the information the better, but even partial or doubtful information is helpful, if it is made clear what the doubts are.

Conversion tables

An approximate method of converting metres to feet is to multiply by 10 and divide by 3. The answer will be too great, but only by one part in 60, which can usually be neglected.

Feet	Metres	Metres	Feet	Naut. Miles	Kilo- metres	Gallons	Litres	Pounds	Kilo- grams
1	0.3	1	3.3	1	1.9	1	4.5	1	0.4
2	0.6	2	6.6	2	3.7	2	9.1	2	0.9
3	0.9	3	9.8	3	5.6	3	13.6	3	1.4
4	1.2	4	13.1	4	7.4	4	18.2	4	1.8
5	1.5	5	16.4	5	9.3	5	22.7	5	2.3
6	1.8	6	19.7	6	11.1	6	27.3	6	2.7
7	2.1	7	23.0	7	13.0	7	31.8	7	3.2
8	2.4	8	26.2	8	14.8	8	36.4	8	3.6
9	2.7	9	29.5	9	16.7	9	40.9	9	4.1
10	3.0	10	32.8	10	18.5	10	45.5	10	4.5
20	6.1	20	65.6	20	37.1	20	90.9	20	9.1
30	9.1	30	98.4	30	55.6	30	136.4	30	13.6
40	12.2	40	131.2	40	74.1	40	181.8	40	18.2
50	15.2	50	164.0	50	92.6	50	227.3	50	22.7
100	30.5	100	328.1	100	185.3	100	454.6	100	45.4

Port signals

The French authorities use two systems of signals to control the traffic into harbours. These are best explained by means of diagrams, which are based, by permission of the Service Hydrographique de la Marine, on those appearing in *Instructions Nautiques*.

By Day and Night three Green lights one above the other signify that the port is open but that there are obstructions in the channel and vessels must navigate with caution.

Figure 1 shows the International port signals used in large ports. *Figure* 2 shows the simplified system used in smaller harbours. Supplementary signals are sometimes used, in particular flag P of the International Code (Blue Peter) is often used to indicate open dock gates.

The traffic signals are not usually hoisted for yachts, and they should therefore be regarded more as a signal to keep out of the way of large vessels.

Charts

For the British yachtsman cruising in the Bay of Biscay the appropriate Admiralty charts are recommended. These cover the area well and are prepared with the conventions, abbreviations, soundings and compass roses with which he is familiar. General coverage is on a scale of $\frac{1}{2}$ in to the mile, although from Brest to the Loire there is coverage on a scale of 1 in or larger. They are particularly useful for passage making, and in addition some areas, such as the Rade de Brest and the Morbihan, are covered on a scale suitable for detailed exploration in yachts. They are obtainable, corrected to date of sale, from Admiralty chart agents, which means, in effect, that they must be obtained before leaving English waters. They can be kept corrected from Admiralty Notices to Mariners, published weekly and obtainable free (but not post free) from chart agents, or from the quarterly small craft summaries. A list of charts is given on pages 20 and 21.

Messrs Imray, Laurie, Norie & Wilson publish six coloured charts, nos. C35 to C40, covering the coast from L'Aberwrac'h to Les Sables d'Olonne. They include large scale insets of harbours. Monthly bulletins of corrections may be obtained from the publishers, and more charts are in preparation.

The most complete coverage is naturally by the official French charts. The general coverage is on a scale of 1 in 50,000, with generous overlaps between adjacent charts, but there are also large scale plans of many areas, such as the Glénan islands, which are of great interest to the exploring yachtsman, but are not covered by large scale British charts.

French official charts have no compass roses, so some form of protractor is needed. The Hurst Plotter, Douglas Protractor, the Sestrel Course Setting and Compass Conversion Protractor and the Harries Direct Course Finder provide solutions with a variety of compromise between cost and convenience. Although modern French charts are very easy to read, the older ones are very finely engraved, and a chart magnifier is helpful in reading them.

Editions Cartographiques Maritimes (ECM) publish a series of four-colour charts intended for yachtsmen. The standard scale is 1:50,000 with large-scale inserts. These charts show very clearly all features in which yachtsmen are interested, have legends which are also in English, and bulletins of corrections are available.

French official charts can be obtained from Kelvin Hughes, 145 Minories, London EC3N 1NH (telephone: 01 709 9076, telex: 887386); they should be ordered about two months in advance as delivery is sometimes very slow. They can also be ordered direct from Bureau des Cessions au Public, Service Hydrographique de la Marine, 29283 Brest Cedex. They may also be obtained, while cruising, at the authorised agents in the principal ports. These agents keep local charts in stock, but do not correct them after receipt. They usually require two or three days' notice to obtain ones of more distant parts. The French hydrographic office publish weekly notices to mariners, but they are very expensive. However they also publish, each April, primarily for yachtsmen, a summary of notices issued during the last 12 months affecting the French coast and adjacent waters. This summary entitled *Recueil des Corrections de Cartes, 199* – is not expensive, and enables one to correct one's French charts in time for a summer cruise.

Full lists of the abbreviations and conventional signs in use on French and British charts can be obtained but a short list of the more useful ones, arranged in parallel columns to serve as a glossary, is given below.

Lights and Beacons

F.	Fixed	F.*f.*	*Feu fixe*
Oc.	Occulting	F.*o.*	*Feu à occultations*
Iso.	Isophase	F.*i.*	*Feu isophase*
Fl.	Flashing	F.*é.*	*Feu à éclats.*
Q	Quick Flashing	F.*sc*	*Feu scintillant*
VQ	Very Quick	F.*sc.rap.*	*Feu scintillant rapide*
IQ	Interrupted Quick Flashing	F.*sc.d.*	*Feu scintillant discontinu*
Alt.	Alternating	F.*alt.*	*Feu alternatif*
Oc (2)	Group Occulting (e.g. 2)	F.*2o.*	*Feu à occulations groupées*
Fl. (2+1)	Group flashing (e.g. 2 flashes, then 1)	F.*2é.1é*	*Feu à éclats diversement groupés*
Dir.	Directional light	F.*d.*	*Feu de direction*
obsc^d	Obscured		*Masqué*
occas^l	Occasional	*occas.*	*Occasionel*
	Sector	S., Sect.	*Secteur*
dest^d	Destroyed	*détr.*	*Détruit*
vert^l	Vertical	V.	*Vertical*
hor^l	Horizontal	Hor.	*Horizontal*
Bn.	Beacon	*Bal.*	*Balise*
Tr.	Tower	*T*	*Tour*
Bn. Tr.	Beacon Tower	*T^{lle}*	*Tourelle*
Ro. Bn., R.C.	Radiobeacon	R.C., R.D.	*Radiophare Circulaire, Directionnel*

Colours (On French charts the colours of lights are in *italic*, but of the buoys, beacons themselves in Roman)

B.	Black		n.	*Noir*
Bu.	Blue formerly Bl	*bl.*		*Bleu*
G.	Green	*v.*	v.	*Vert*
Y.	Orange formerly Or	*org.*		*Orangé*
R.	Red	*r.*	r.	*Rouge*
W.	White	*b.*	b.	*Blanc*
Y.	Yellow		j.	*Jaune*
W.	Whitewashed		bli	*Blanchi*
Cheq.	Chequered			*à damier*
Vi.	Violet	*vio.*		*Violet*

Fog Signals

Fog Sig.	Fog Signal Station	*S^{al} br.*	*Station de signaux de brume*
Whis.	Whistle	*Sif.*	*Sifflet*
	Bell	*Cl.*	*Cloche*
	Siren	*Sir.*	*Sirène de brume*
Dia.	Diaphone		*Diaphone*
Reed.	Reedhorn		*Trompette*

Buildings and Miscellaneous

Cas.	Castle	*Ch^{au}*	*Château*
Cem^y	Cemetery	*Cim^{re}*	*Cimetière*

Ch.	Chapel		Ch^{lle}	Chapelle	
Ch^{y}	Chimney		Ch^{ee}	Cheminée	
Ch.	Church		$Egl., Cl^{er}$	Eglise, Clocher	
Conspic.	Conspicuous		Rem.	Ferme Remarquable	
CG	Coastguard				
Fm.	Farm		Sem.	Sémaphore	
F.S.	Flagstaff (signals)		$M^{t} S^{x}$	Mât de Signaux	
F.S.	Flagstaff		$M^{t} P^{on}$	Mât de Pavillon	
	Gable			Pignon	
Ho.	House		M^{on}	Maison	
L.B.	Lifeboat		St^{on} de sauv.	Station de sauvetage	
Mon^{t}	Monument		Mon^{t}	Monument	
P.A.	Position Approximate		P.A.	Position Approchée	
	Seamark			Amer	
	Summit		S^{et} Som.	Sommet	
Water T^{r}	Water Tower		Ch^{au} d'eau	Château d'eau	
	Windmill		M^{in}	Moulin à vent	
W^{*}	Wreck		Ep.	Epave	

Admiralty Charts

No.	Name	Scale, 1 in	No.	Name	Scale, 1 in
1104	Bay of Biscay	1 000 000	2353	Rade de Croisic to Presqu'île de Quiberon	75 000
2643	Raz de Sein to Goulven, including Brest		2358	Morbihan including Rivière de Crac'h	25 000
	and Ushant	145 000	3216	Approaches to La Loire	various
20	Ile d'Ouessant to St Nazaire	500 000	2989	Entrance to La Loire, and Approaches to St	
2694	The Channels between Ushant and the Mainland	50 000		Nazaire	15 000
3345	Chenal du Four	25 000	2985	La Loire, St Nazaire to Nantes	various
3427	Rade de Brest	30 000	2647	Les Sables d'Olonne to Bourgneuf	various
3428	Port de Brest	various		St Gilles sur Vie; Port Joinville	29 200
798	Baie de Douarnenez	various	2663	Ile d'Yeu to Pointe de la Coubre	200 000
	Douarnenez	various	2648	Pointe de la Coubre to Les Sables d'Olonne	various
2351	Anse de Bénodet to Chaussée de Sein	75 000		Port of Les Sables d'Olonne	25 000
	Port d'Audierne	24 000	2641	Pertuis Breton	50 000
2645	Ile de Groix to Raz de Sein	140 000	2746	Pertuis d'Antioche, with the Approaches to	
2352	Presqu'île de Quiberon to Anse de Bénodet	75 000		La Rochelle and Rochefort	50 000
3641	Loctudy to Concarneau	20 000	2743	La Rochelle; La Pallice	15 000
3640	Anse de Bénodet	various	2748	La Charente, Fouras to Rochefort	various
2646	Bourgneuf to Ile de Groix	140 000	2910	Entrance to La Gironde	various
304	Lorient Harbour	10 000	2664	Pointe d'Arcachon to Pointe de la Coubre	150 000

Charts by Editions Cartographiques Maritimes (ECM)

No.	Name	Scale, 1 in	No.	Name	Scale, 1 in
540	Argentan, Camaret	50 000	546	La Trinité, Le Croisic	50 000
541	Morgat, Ile de Sein	50 000	547	Le Croisic, Pornic	50 000
542	Brest, Douarnenez	50 000	549	Pornic, St Gilles, Ile d'Yeu	50 000
543	Audierne, Trévignon	50 000	1022	St Gilles, La Rochelle	100 000
243	Iles de Glénan	25 000	551	Ile de Ré, La Rochelle	50 000
544	Concarneau, Lorient, Ile de Groix	50 000	552	La Rochelle, Ile d'Oléron	50 000
545	Lorient, La Trinité, Belle Ile	50 000	553	Royan, Gironde entrance	50 000

French Official Charts, SHOM (Service Hydrographique et Océanographique de la Marine)

As with the BA charts these are listed in order following the coast from Ile d'Ouessant to La Gironde. Charts marked 'P' are available in the Spéciale 'P' Series, folded on thin, water-resistant and tear-proof material. When a new French chart is issued, replacing a similar one of the same area, it is given a new number, unlike British charts where the old number is reused. The charts listed below are a selection from the official catalogue of 1 January 1989. The date shown is the date of the édition 'P', or the date of the latest 'Grande Correction'. Titles and dates are not available for new charts (Jan 1989), and the area covered is given in brackets.

No.	Title	Scale, 1:	Date
7066 P	De l'île Vierge à la Pointe de Penmarc'h and Abords de Brest	150 000	1987
5287 P	De Portsall à la Pointe de St Mathieu, Chenal du Four et environs de l'île d'Ouessant	45 000	1987
6609 P	De la pointe de St Mathieu à Audierne, Goulet de Brest	45 800	1986
6542 P	Rade de Brest	30 000	1986
6099 P	Baie de Douarnenez	45 800	1986
7067 P	De la Chausée de Sein à Belle Ile	150 000	1987
7147 P	(Ile de Seine to Guilvinec)	50 000	new
7146 P	(Penmarc'h to Trevignon, with Iles de Glénan)	50 000	new
6649 P	Anse de Bénodet, ports de Bénodet et de Loctudy	15 000	1986
6679 P	Cours de l'Odet – de Bénodet à Quimper	20 000	1986
6647 P	Iles de Glénan partie Nord	20 000	1986
6648 P	Iles de Glénan partie Sud	20 000	1986
6650 P	Abords et port de Concarneau, baie de la Foret	15 600	1987
7031 P	De l'île de Penfret aux plateaux des Brivideaux – Abords de Lorient	50 000	1987
7032 P	De l'île de Groix à Belle Ile – Abords de Lorient	50 000	1986
7068 P	De la Presqu'île de Quiberon aux Sables d'Olonne	150 000	1987
7034 P	Golfe du Morbihan	25 000	1988
7033 P	De Quiberon au Croisic	50 000	1987
6825 P	De Croisic à Noirmoutier. Estuaire de la Loire	46 700	1986
5039 P	De la pointe de St Gildas au goulet de Fromentine, Baie de Bourgneuf	46 300	1986
7069 P	De l'île d'Yeu à la pointe de la Coubre – Plateau de Rochbonne	150 000	1986
6853 P	Du goulet de Fromentine à St- Gilles-Croix-de-Vie. Ile d'Yeu	47 000	1986
6523 P	De Saint-Gilles-Croix-de-Vie aux Sables d'Olonne, Ile d'Yeu (partie Est)	47 200	1986
6522 P	Des Sables d'Olonne à la pointe du Grouin du Cou	47 400	new?
6521 P	De la pointe du Grouin du Cou à La Rochelle, pertuis Breton, Ile de Ré	47 500	1986
6333 P	De l'île de Ré à l'île d'Oléron, pertuis d'Antioche	47 500	1986
6334 P	De La Rochelle à Rochefort, pertuis d'Antioche	47 600	1986
7070 P	De l'île d'Oléron au bassin d'Arcachon	167 000	1985
6335 P	De l'île d'Oléron à Corduan, pertuis de Maumasson	47 800	1986
7028 P	Embouchure de la Gironde – De la Pointe de la Coubre à la pointe de la Négade	45 000	1987
7029 P	La Gironde – De Mortagne-sur-Gironde au Bec d'Ambès, La Garonne et la Dordogne jusqu'à Bordeaux et Libourne (in 6 sections or 'cartouches' including Port de Pauillac and Port de Blaye)	45 000	1987
6470	Passes et rade de Lorient (may be superseded)	10 000	1987

21

3 The Breton Language

It is of interest, and sometimes actually of value to the navigator, to know the meanings of some of the commoner Breton words which appear in place names. Those who have cruised on the Celtic fringes of Britain will recognise some of them; the Irish *inish* corresponds to the Breton *inis*, and those who have cruised in West Highland waters will know the meanings of *glas* and *du*. I have no pretensions to a knowledge of Breton, but set down here the results of a few investigations.

The pronunciation is, or should be, more like English than French, with the final consonants sounded. The letters *c'h* represent the final sound of Scottish *loch* or Irish *lough* (but not English *lock*); there is indeed a word *loc'h*, meaning a lake or pool; *ch* is pronounced as in *shall*. The French books and charts do not always distinguish between these, and there may be some errors in this book in consequence. In France, as in England, mobility and the radio/TV are killing regional differences and *Raz* is now usually pronounced *Rah; Penmarc'h*, pronounced *Penmargh* a generation ago, is now often *Painmar* and *Bénodet* has gone from *Benodette* to *Bainoday* and collected an accent in the process. The most misleading example of this process is *porz*, which means an anchorage, possibly quite exposed and/or lacking all shore facilities, not a port. This gets frenchified into *port*, and the French word *port* does mean a port, and not an anchorage which is *anse* or *rade*.

A Breton glossary is hard to use, because initial letters are often mutated into others, following complicated rules, depending on the preceding word. I have tried to meet this by suggesting, after the relevant letters, other(s) from which the initial might have come. Thus suppose that one wants to find the meaning of *I. ar Gazek* (which is quite likely since *The Mare* seems to be the commonest name given to an islet). There is no word *gazek* in the glossary, but after G it says 'try K'; *kazek* means a mare; it mutates into *gazek* after *ar*. Mutations of final letters also occur, but these do not usually cause difficulty in finding a word.

al, an, ar	the	*karreg*	rock
arvor	seaside	*kastel*	castle
aven	river	*kazek*	mare
B (try P)		*ker*	house, hamlet
bann, benn	hilltop	*kern*	summit
baz	shoal	*koad*	wood
beg	point, cape	*kornog*	shoal
beniget	cut, slit	*koz*	old
benven	above-water rock	*kreiz*	middle
bian, bihan	small	*kriben*	crest
bir	needle, point	*lan, lann*	monastery
bras, braz	large	*marc'h*	horse

bre, brenn	small hill	*melen*	yellow
breiz	Brittany	*men*	rock
bri, brienn	cliff	*mor*	sea
C (try K)		*nevez*	new
D (try T)		*penn*	head, point
daou	two	*plou, plo*	parish
don, doun	deep	*porz, porzig*	anchorage
du	black	*poul*	pool, anchorage
enez	island	*raz*	strait, tide race
er	a, an, the	*roc'h*	rock
G (try K)		*ros*	wooded knoll
garv	rough	*ruz*	red
gavr	goat	*ster*	river, inlet
glas	green	*teven, tevenneg*	cliff, dune
gromil, gromilli	roaring	*toull*	hole, deep place
gwenn	white, pure	*trez, treaz*	sand, beach
hir	long	V (try B,M)	
hoc'h, houc'h	pig	W (try Gw)	
inis	island	*yoc'h*	group of rocks
karn	cairn		

The port of registration of fishing vessels may be identified by the letters on their bows, as follows:

AD	Audierne	LO	Lorient
AY	Auray	LS	Les Sables d'Olonne
BR	Brest	MN	Marennes
BX	Bordeaux	NA	Nantes
CC	Concarneau	NO	Noirmoutier
CM	Camaret	SN	Saint Nazaire
DZ	Douarnenez	VA	Vannes
GV	Le Guilvinec	YE	Ile d'Yeu
IO	Ile d'Oléron		

Charts: English BA 3345, 2694, 2643. Imray C36.
       French SHOM 5287 P, 7066 P. ECM Navicarte 540.

High water: −0005 Brest, Index 4, MTL 4.2m.
    MHWS 7.1m; MLWS 1.3m; MHWN 5.5m; MLWN 2.9m.

Tidal streams: The N stream begins about −0600 Brest, spring rates: 1 knot at 1 mile N of Les Plâtresses, $2\frac{1}{4}$ knots at St Pierre buoy (SW of Corsen), $5\frac{1}{4}$ knots at La Vinotière. The S stream begins about HW Brest, spring rates: 1 knot at 1 mile N of Les Plâtresses, $2\frac{1}{2}$ knots at St Pierre buoy, 5 knots at La Vinotière. At Les Vieux Moines the stream is rotary clockwise, spring rates: at −0100 Brest, N $1\frac{1}{4}$ knots; at +0200 Brest, SSE $3\frac{1}{2}$ knots; at +0500 Brest, SW $\frac{3}{4}$ knot; at −0600 Brest, WNW $1\frac{1}{2}$ knots. The streams are considerably affected by the wind.

Depths: The main channel is deep.

Lights:

   1. Le Four; Fl(5)W 15s, 28m, 20M. Siren (3+2) 75s. Grey tower.

Chenal du Four leading lights 158.5°.

   2. Front, Kermorvan; Fl W 5s, 20m, 22M. White square tower. Horn 60s.
   3. Saint Mathieu; Fl W 15s, 56m, 29M. White tower, red top.
      Rear leading light; Dir. W, 157.5°-159.5° 54m, 28M.
      Radio beacon, call SM 289.6 kHz 20M 1/6 H+02.
   4. Les Plâtresses; Fl RG 4s, 17m, 6M. White tower.
   5. Valbelle, By (port); Oc R 6s, 8m, 5M. Whistle.
   6. Basse St Paul, By (port); Oc(2)R 6s, 7m, 7M.

Chenal de la Helle leading lights 138°.

   2. Front, Kermorvan; Fl W 5s, 20m, 22M. White square tower. Horn 60s.
   7. Rear, Lochrist; Dir. Oc(2+1)W 12s, 49m, 22M. Eight-sided white tower, red top.
   8. Le Faix; Q W 16m, 9M. Tower (card N).
   9. Le Stiff; Fl(2)R 20s, 85m, 24M. Two white towers, side by side.
 10. Pourceaux, By (card N); Q W 7m, 8M.

Both channels

 11. Corsen; Q WRG, 33m, 12-8-8M. White sector 012°-015°. White wall and hut.
 12. La Grande Vinotière; Oc R 6s, 15m, 5M. Eight-sided red tower.
 13. Le Rouget By (stbd); Iso G 4s, 7m, 5M. Whistle.
 14. St Mathieu auxiliary; Q WRG 26m, 14-11-11M.
 15. Tournant et Lochrist, By (port); Iso R 4s, 7m, 5M.
 16. Les Vieux Moines; Fl R 4s, 16m, 5M. Eight-sided red tower.

Leading lights 007°

   2. Front, Kermorvan; Fl W 5s, 20m, 22M. White square tower. Horn 60s.
 17. Rear, Trézien; Oc(2)W 6s, 84m, 21M. Grey tower, white towards south.

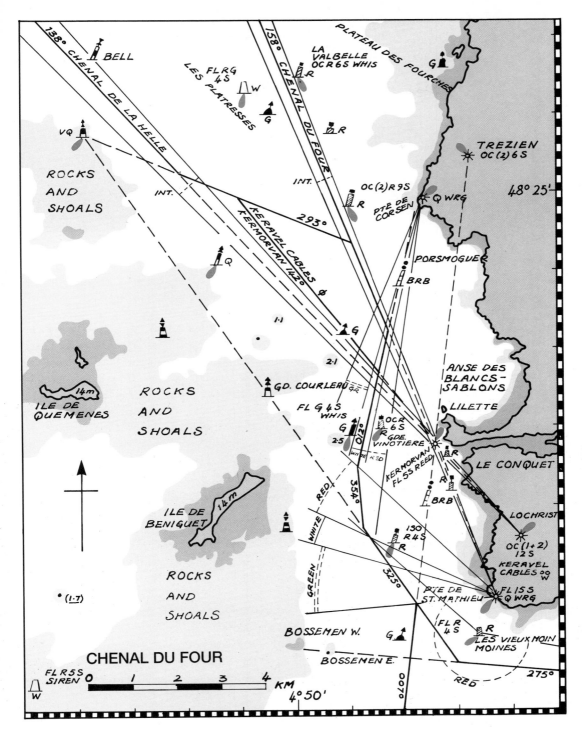

138° CHENAL DE LA HELLE

BELL

158° CHENAL DU FOUR

LES PLATRESSES FL R G 4 S
W
G

PLATEAU DES FOURCHES

G

LA VALBELLE OC R 6 S WHIS

R

VQ

ROCKS AND SHOALS

INT.

INT.

293°

R

OC (2) R 9 S

KERAVEL CABLES & KERMORVAN 142°

Q

TREZIEN OC (2) 6 S

48° 25'

PTE DE CORSEN Q W R G

PORSMOGUER

BRB

G

1·1

ROCKS AND SHOALS

2·1

ANSE DES BLANCS-SABLONS

ÎLE DE QUEMENES 14m

ROCKS AND SHOALS

GD. COURLEAU
G.R.

FL G 4 S WHIS
G
2·5

370°

WHITE RED

LILETTE

OC R 6 S
GDE. VINOTIERE

LE CONQUET

KERMORVAN FL 5 S REED

R

ÎLE DE BENIGUET 14m

354°

RED

WHITE

BRB

LOCHRIST

OC (1+2) 12 S

KERAVEL CABLES W

ROCKS AND SHOALS

• (1·7)

GREEN

325°

130 R 4 S
R

PTE DE ST. MATHIEU FL I S S Q W R G

275°

CHENAL DU FOUR

BOSSEMEN W.
G.

FL R 4 S
R
LES VIEUX MOINES MOINES

FL R 5 S SIREN
W

0   1   2   3   4 KM

BOSSEMEN E.

RED

0070

4° 50'

MLWS 1.3m; MLWN 2.9m; −0005 Brest, Index 4, MTL 4.2m
Based on French Chart No. 5287 with corrections. Depths in metres; right hand margin in cables

25

Les Vieux Moines light tower (red) with Pointe de St Mathieu lighthouse (red top), bearing 035° (p. 29)

The Chenal du Four is the channel normally used by small vessels bound coastwise for Bay of Biscay ports; it saves distance and avoids the larger seas and heavy steamer traffic outside Ushant. Those unfamiliar with the channel may think it presents special difficulties in navigation, but it is a wide, well-marked route, and anyone who has piloted his boat along the north coast of France as far as Ushant will find the Chenal du Four rather easier than some of the coastline that he has already passed. The difficulties lie rather in the facts that the strong tides and exposure to the Atlantic swell often result in steep seas, and the visibility is frequently poor. There are two other channels, the Chenal de la Helle, which is farther west and is also described here, and the Passage du Fromveur, SE of Ushant, noted for the strength of the tidal streams, which attain 9 knots at extreme springs. In rough weather the Chenal de la Helle is to be preferred to the Chenal du Four.

The roughest seas do not occur in the Chenal du Four, but in the approaches. Eastward, between Ile Vierge and the Four lighthouse, northerly winds often bring a considerable swell, and a strong weather going stream over an irregular bottom produces steep seas. With westerly winds, some shelter is found as the Chenal du Four is approached and the vessel first comes under the lee of Ushant and then of the inner islands and shoals. The seas drop as soon as the tide turns fair.

With a leading wind one will naturally arrange to pass the channel when the tide is favourable, but if the wind is ahead it is desirable to try to make the passage through the narrow part, where the tides run hard, at slack water. Coming from the north it is unfortunate that the tide turns in the Chenal du Four before it does in the English Channel, so that starting from l'Aberwrac'h, say, on the first of the SW tide, most of the tide in the Chenal du Four will have run to waste before one gets there. But one can cross the Iroise on the foul tide without difficulty, and reach the Raz de Sein as the tide turns fair again.

In fog or thick weather navigation is tricky in the Chenal du Four and on entry, the

Le Four lighthouse bearing about NE. Shoal water extends up to 1½ cables W of the lighthouse

moment is opportune for Murphy to interfere with the electronic aids. He has also, on two occasions, extinguished the light on a buoy which then appeared out of the night, sporting a large bow wave, as the present editor rushed (fortunately) past on the tide.

If the outer marks have been sighted, and the visibility is sufficient to enable the towers and buoys to be seen at a reasonable distance, pilotage is possible even if the distant landmarks and lighthouses are hidden in the mist. With poor visibility, however, it is better to remain either in harbour or out at sea. A VHF-equipped yacht can be talked through even in nil visibility by the English speaking radar station on Pointe St Mathieu, who listen on channel 16 and work on channel 12.

Coasting southward from Le Four lighthouse a fair offing should be given to Les Liniou and the Plateau des Fourches. The Chenal du Four may then be entered NE of Les

La Grande Vinotière light tower (red octagonal). Pointe de St Mathieu in the background, bearing 155°; Les Vieux Moines tower to the right

Plâtresses tower (white), with the lighthouses of St Mathieu (white circular tower, red top) and Kermorvan (white square tower) in transit, bearing 158°. The remaining transits and marks are shown on the plan on page 25. This plan has been simplifed by the omission of soundings, other than the 3m line, which shows the shoal areas. Except in certain parts, the area free from danger in normal weather is considerable; when it is rough the orthodox channel should be adhered to, as the overfalls are worse over an irregular bottom, such as the 3.7m patch SE of the Grande Vinotière.

If a vessel bound south is late on the tide she can avoid the worst of a foul tide by standing into the bay towards the Anse des Bancs Sablons, and again into the bay south of Le Conquet, but care must be taken to avoid the dangers.

Chenal de la Helle
Bring Kermorvan lighthouse to bear 138°, between the first and second houses from the right of five similar houses forming Le Conquet radio station. In good weather steer on this transit until Corsen lighthouse bears 012°, when steer 192° on this stern bearing. This transit leads across the Basse St Pierre (4.5m), marked by a buoy (stbd), which the transit leaves to port. In bad weather the shoal can be avoided, either by bringing the two white painted gables, resembling pyramids, of Keravel (near St Mathieu lighthouse) in transit with Kermorvan, bearing 142°, or more simply by leaving the buoy to starboard.

By night
The transits are shown on the plan. Bound south steer with Kermorvan (**2**) and St Mathieu (**3**) in transit, bearing 158°. Note that in a narrow sector each side of this transit St Mathieu shows a fixed white directional light as well as the flashing light that shows all round. For the Chenal de la Helle steer with Kermorvan (**2**) in transit with Lochrist (**7**), bearing 138°. To avoid the Basse St Pierre, if necessary, leave this alignment when Le Stiff light (**9**) comes in transit with Le Faix, bearing 293°, and steer 113° on this stern transit to join the Four Channel alignment.

In any case, when Corsen light (**11**) turns white steer in this sector, with the light astern, until the auxiliary light on St Mathieu (**14**) opens red. Then steer 174°, entering the red sector of Corsen until the Tournant et Lochrist buoy (**15**) is abeam, when the

Pointe de Kermorvan and the town of Le Conquet, bearing E

auxiliary light on St Mathieu will turn white and the light on Les Vieux Moines (**16**) will open. Then steer 145°, making sure that Kermorvan is brought in transit with Trézien (**17**), bearing 007° astern, before the green sector of St Mathieu auxiliary is left. If proceeding south, steer nothing west of the 007° alignment; if going east or SE steer to leave Les Vieux Moines (**16**) to port.

Bound north
Put the reciprocal courses on the chart and this will enable the above directions to be followed in reverse.

Anchorages
The following temporary anchorages are available under suitable conditions:

Anse de Porsmoguer
Good holding ground in sand in the pretty bay, with depths shoaling from 6m to zero. It is sheltered from N and E and popular for bathing. The village is about ½ mile to the north, but there are no shops there.

Anse des Blancs Sablons
This wide sandy bay is free from dangers except off the headlands on each side. The anchorage is anywhere, in from 9m to 1m on a sandy shelving bottom which dries out nearly ¼ mile from the shore, except on the west side, where there is 3m close to the rocks off Kermorvan. The peninsula protects the anchorage from the W and SW, and the land shelters it from the E and S. Yachts can work into this bay inshore against a foul tide, anchor there and slip round L'Ilette (off Kermorvan) when the stream becomes fair; note that there is a rock 200m east of this islet which is awash at chart datum. There is little stream in the bay, but often some swell. There are no facilities.

Le Conquet
There is a good anchorage in this inlet south of Pointe de Kermorvan. Leave the red La Louvre tower to port and go in as far as draught and tide permit. For a full description see *North Brittany Pilot*, published by Adlard Coles.

Anse de Bertheaume
This is a convenient bay, about 3 miles east of Pointe de St Mathieu, in which to wait before making the passage of Chenal du Four. It is sheltered from N and W, but exposed to the S and E. The Château de Bertheaume, on the SW corner of the bay, is itself fairly clean and can be passed at 100m; but 400m to the NE is Le Chat, an area of rocks nearly 200m across, with heads drying 6.6m and 7.2m. These are a particular hazard when they are covered near HW springs. Anchor in one of the two bays immediately north of Le Chat, going in as far as possible for shelter. Farther north and east the bottom of the bay is foul, with rocks. Village and shops are 1 mile. If anchoring, keep well to the south of the local moorings, or alternatively borrow an available mooring.

5 Brest, Marina du Moulin Blanc

Charts: English BA 2694, 3427, Imray C36
French SHOM 6609 P, 6542 P. ECM Navicarte 542.

High water: Standard port, Index 5, MTL 4.4m.
MHWS 7.5m; MLWS 1.4m; MHWN 5.9m; MLWN 3.0m.

Tidal Streams: Goulet de Brest. On the northern side the flood begins at −0535 Brest and runs E. On the southern side the flood begins at −0605 Brest, attaining 4 knots NE off Pointe des Espagnols and continues in a direction ENE towards the Elorn river. The ebb begins on the northern side at −0030 Brest, on the southern side at HW Brest. Within about 100m of the southern shore there are ENE and E eddies, which begin about +0100 Brest and continue until the flood begins. These eddies cause tide rips where they meet the main ebb from the Rade off Pointe des Espagnols.

Depths: Entrance channel dredged to 1.4m (1988).

Lights: Only the bys essential for Moulin Blanc are listed.
1. Point du Petit Minou; Fl(2)WR 6s, 32m, 19-15M. Grey round tower W on SW side, red top. Leading lights 068°; front Dir Q W same structure. Fog detector light; FG intens 036.5°–039.5° 420m NE.
2. Pointe du Portzic; Oc(2)WR 12s, 56m, 19-15M. Grey eight-sided tower. Leading lights 068° rear; Dir Q W same structure and Light; Dir 045°–050° Q(6)+L.Fl 6s, 54m, 24M.
3. Basse du Charles Martel; Q R, Lat Port by.
4. Fillettes; VQ(9) 10s, Whis, Card W by.
5. Roche Mengam; Fl(3)WR 12s, 8-5M.   RBR beacon tower.
6. Pénoupèle; Fl(3)R 12s, Lat Port by.
7. No. 2; Fl(2)R 6s, Lat Port by.
8. No. 1; Fl G 4s, Lat Stbd by.
9. No. 4; Oc R 4s, Lat Port by.
10. No. 6; Fl R 4s, Lat Port by (N of course).
11. Moulin Blanc; Oc(2)R 6s Lat Port by.
12. Buoyed channel to Moulin Blanc:
    MB 1; Fl G, MB 2; Fl R, Stbd and Port bys
    Fl G 2s, Fl R 2s. Marina entrance beacons.

General

Many yachts bound south stop the night at Camaret but avoid making the detour eastward to visit the Rade de Brest which is in fact an excellent cruising ground in its own right, reminiscent·of the Clyde.

Yachts are not very welcome in the commercial port but the Marina du Moulin Blanc, offering all facilities, makes a good starting point for an exploratory cruise of the area.

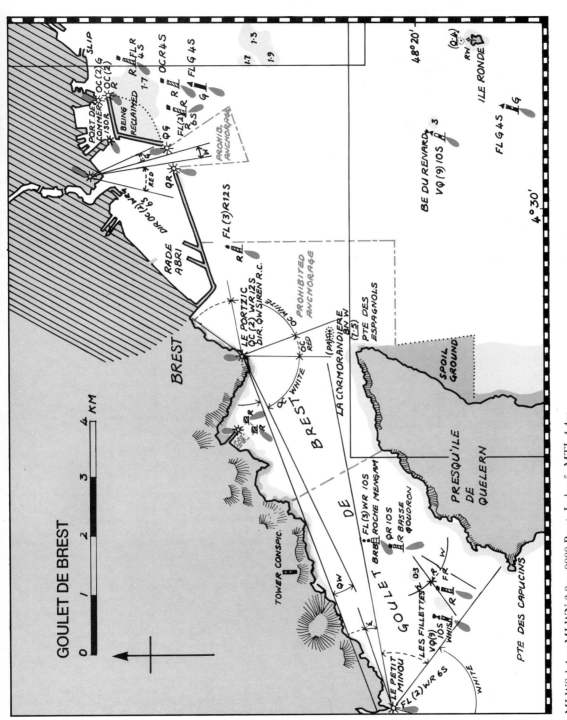

MLWS 1.4m; MLWN 3.0m; 0000 Brest, Index 5, MTL 4.4m
Based on French Charts Nos. 3799 and 6427 with corrections (Nos. 6609 and 6542 supersede). Depths in metres; right hand margin in cables

31

Moulin Blanc Marina from the S. The white roof of the Marine Museum provides a good landmark

Approach

The outer approach to Brest (Avant Goulet de Brest) is made with the twin lighthouses of Le Petit Minou (two adjacent white towers) in transit with the grey octagonal tower of Pointe du Portzic, bearing 068°. These lighthouses are on the north side of the Goulet de Brest. If the visibility is not good they may not be seen at first on rounding the Pointe de St Mathieu from Le Chenal du Four. However if Les Vieux Moines tower and Le Coq buoy are left to port, the Charles Martel port hand whistle buoy will be discovered close to the transit of 086° and the lighthouses should be in sight.

The outer approach from the SW, through the Chenal du Toulinguet, is described in Chapter 8.

On approaching Le Petit Minou, bear to starboard and pass up the Goulet on the northern side of the mid-channel shoals of Plateau des Fillettes. A west cardinal buoy marks the outer end and the BRB Roche Mengam beacon tower the inner end with two port hand buoys marking the northern limit of the southern channel.

When entering the Goulet from the SW, or on the ebb, the north coast of Presqu'île de Quélern is steep to with a useful eddy inshore. The central plateau is then left to port and La Cormoranderie (white beacon) with an unmarked wreck on the northeast tip of the peninsula left well to starboard.

Port of Brest from Goulet, Le Portzic Light far left

With the Pointe du Portzic abeam, a line of port hand channel buoys will be seen leading past the breakwaters of the Naval Base and the commercial port towards the bridge over the mouth of the Elorn river. The conspicuous white roof of the new Marine Museum, on reclaimed land at the inner end of the harbour, makes a good landmark for the marina.

By night
From the Chenal du Four after rounding Pointe de St Mathieu, or from the west, identify the leading lights (068°) of Le Petit Minou (**1**) and Portzic (**2**) and steer on this transit until Charles Martel buoy (**3**) is close abeam to port. Then bear to starboard to pass between Pointe du Petit Minou light (**2**) and Fillettes buoy (**4**). Identify Roche Mengam tower light (**5**) and, leaving it to starboard, steer about 070° to acquire Pénoupèle buoy (**6**). Leaving Pénoupèle close to port, steer 065° to follow the buoyed channel to Moulin Blanc buoy (**11**). Round the buoy, leaving it to port, and steer about 010° to locate the lights marking the narrow dredged channel. When MB 1 and MB 2 (**12**) have been identified, steer between them on 007° to enter the marina.

Coming from Camaret, steer north to enter the intense white sector of Portzic (**2**) (Q(6)+L.Fl 6s). Change to starboard and keep in this sector on about 047° until Roche Mengam tower (**5**) is abaft the beam to port, then turn onto 065° to acquire Pénoupèle buoy (**6**) and continue as above.

Entrance
The marina of Moulin Blanc is on the eastern side of the reclaimed land and, on passing the port hand buoy (Moulin Blanc) on the point, the small lateral buoys of the dredged channel into the marina will appear.

A central pier divides the marina into two halves. The Capitainerie is at the root of this pier and visitors' berths can be found in the northern half (see plan).

Pointe des Espagnols and La Cormorandière, bearing 120°

Facilities

The staff in the Capitainerie are most helpful (1988) and the marina is well equipped with water and electricity on the pontoons, a fuel berth by the Capitainerie, two wide slipways, a 14 tonne travel lift, 6 tonne crane and a large haul-out area.

There is a chandlery and there are engineers on site.

Showers are free and there is a launderette in the marina together with a bar/restaurant and a small food store.

Outside the marina is a restaurant/food store. The bus service into Brest is frequent and passes a large supermarket.

Brest has all the usual facilities of a large town and there are chandlers, sailmakers, a shipyard with marine engineer and Fournier, who can supply bonded stores, close to the Port de Commerce.

With local bus services, good railway connections and a twice daily air service to Paris (not Sundays), this commercial port and major naval base is a pleasant place with all facilities and is convenient for changing crews.

6 Rade de Brest

Charts: English BA 3427. Imray C36.

French SHOM 6542 P. ECM Navicarte 542.

High water: Standard Port, Index 5, MTL 4.4m.

MHWS 7.5m; MLWS 1.4m; MHWN 5.9m; MLWN 3.0m.

Tidal Streams: For the Goulet de Brest, see Chapter 5. The flood, beginning at −0605 Brest, in the south of the Goulet continues ENE to the Elorn and E towards Pointe Marloux. For the first half hour the ebb is still running out of the estuary of the Aulne and there are tide rips where the two streams meet off Pointe des Espagnols. Half an hour later, at −0530 Brest, the flood stream divides off Pointe des Espagnols, one branch setting E and ENE as before, with an eddy setting towards Pointe Marloux. The other branch sets S into the Baie de Roscanvel and SE towards the Aulne at $2\frac{3}{4}$ knots springs. The ebb stream from the Elorn begins at HW Brest and from the Aulne about 10 minutes earlier.

Depths: Given under the individual headings for the anchorages.

A peaceful mooring at Port Launay (see p. 44)

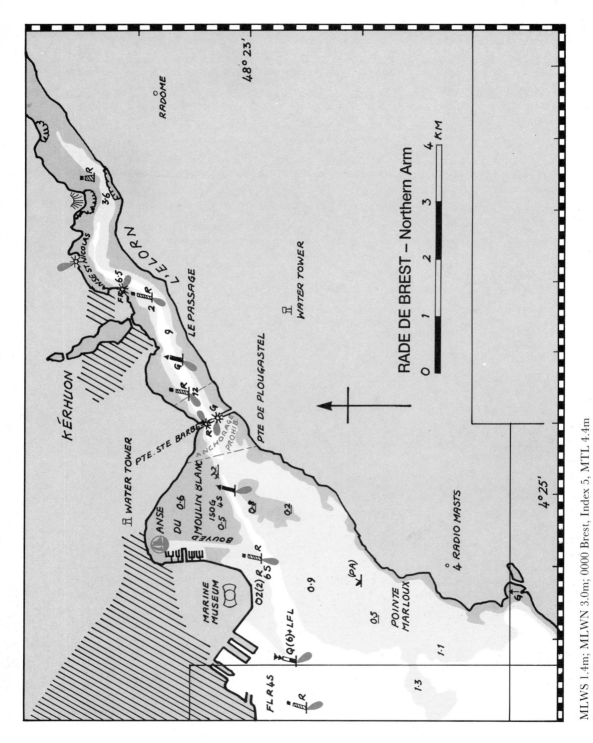

RADE DE BREST – Northern Arm

MLWS 1.4m; MLWN 3.0m; 0000 Brest, Index 5, MTL 4.4m
Based on French Chart No. 3799 with corrections (No. 6542 supersedes). Depths in metres; right hand margin in cables

36

General

The Rade de Brest provides an excellent cruising ground, with many anchorages, beautiful creeks and two rivers that present no problems to bilge-keelers and can, with due care, be enjoyed by owners of deep draught vessels. In bad weather it can be rough, especially with wind against tide, for there is often a fetch of 5 miles, but as it is sheltered on all sides it is free from the swell of the open sea. It makes an ideal place for a family cruise, or for filling in if caught by bad weather between the Four and the Raz.

Parts of the Rade are used for naval exercises, mining grounds etc. There are a few areas, marked on the charts, where anchorage, or even passage is prohibited. The Rade is entered by the Goulet de Brest as described in the previous chapter.

L'Elorn river

This not unattractive river leads up to the pleasant old town of Landernau. It offers an interesting run, particularly for bilge-keelers. As passage should be made near highwater and as the opening of the bridge must be arranged in advance, an overnight stay in Landerneau is to be expected.

The Moulin Blanc port hand buoy is one of the buoys marking the channel leading under the Albert-Louppe bridge and into the Elorn river. From this buoy the river is navigable at all states of tide to deep draught yachts for some 4 miles up to the port hand beacon St Jean. Above this point the river shallows but the channel, marked by rather small and widely spaced buoys, is navigable near high water to yachts drawing 2 metres for another 4 miles up to Landerneau where one can dry out against a wall. Half a mile below Landerneau a swing bridge was established in 1987. This can be opened on request by telephoning in advance (98 85 16 16).

From the Moulin Blanc port hand buoy a course of 070° leads to a starboard hand buoy 1 mile distant. Three quarters of a mile further on, take the northern arch of the Albert-Louppe bridge (minimum clearance 28m). The south bank of the river is thickly

L'Auberlac'h stone pier and moorings, looking NE. (See p. 43)

Ile d'Arun, an island at HW, looking NE. (See p. 43)

wooded with interesting rocky outcrops on the ridge. There are many houses in the town of Kerhuon on the north bank with deep water moorings inside the channel buoys. It should be possible to anchor in this stretch, or to pick up a vacant mooring on either side of the river up as far as St Jean. A dinghy landing can be made for supplies at Kerhuon on a slip, marked by a beacon with an orange top. At the eastern end of Kerhuon there is a wharf where the river curves north and then east again.

Landerneau. *Capelan* (with bilge keels) in good position below spire. Foul bottom and obstruction downstream

There are no channel buoys in this stretch but, keeping close to the yacht moorings, follow the curve round until the St Jean port hand beacon is passed. After this there is a straight unmarked stretch of the river. Keep in the middle and search with binoculars for the next of a succession of rather small green and red buoys marking the channel to Landerneau. From here on the channel winds in the river and it is important to follow the buoys closely in order to find a depth of 3m or more at HW neaps.

If the bridge is open, follow the straight channel into Landerneau. Passing the large sand-barge wharf to port yachts may dry out against a short length of wall with a slipway on the port hand side just below the roadbridge marking the end of the channel. If preferred one can negotiate the network of small boat moorings in the middle of the river and secure alongside one of the four ladders just below the bridge. Along the wall the bottom is hard and flat and there is 3m at HW neaps. Below the fourth ladder the bottom is foul with an obstruction caused by an overturned jetty (1988).

Facilities
Landerneau has all the facilities of a fair-sized market town and is the junction where passengers on the Morlaix–Brest line can change for Quimper and the south coast of Brittany.

Rade de Brest, southern section
There is an area where navigation is restricted and anchoring prohibited around Ile Longue, the French naval base. Entry is also prohibited to an area east of the Naval College inside a line bearing 160° from the Pen-ar-Vir N cardinal buoy to the shore. Except for a visit to Roscanvel, it is best to keep out of this section of the Rade.

Roscanvel
An important feature of the Baie de Roscanvel is the tidal stream. The flood stream begins to run S into the bay at −0530 Brest, but 1 hour later the stream, running S down

Landévennec Abbey, looking SW. (See p. 44)

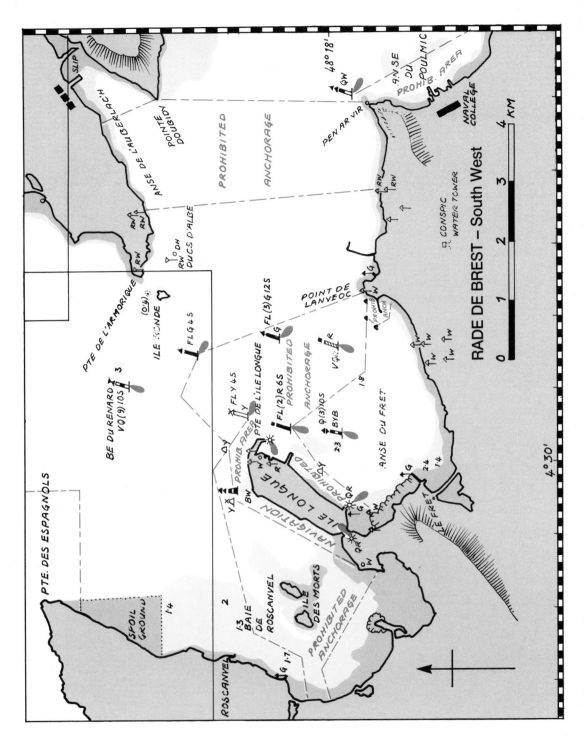

RADE DE BREST – South West

MLWS 1.4m; MLWN 3.0m; 0000 Brest, Index 5, MTL 4.4m
Based on French Chart No. 3799 with corrections (No. 6542 supersedes). Depths in metres; right hand

40

Guly Glas Lock, looking up river. (See p. 44)

the E side of the bay, sweeps along the S shore and causes an eddy up the west side towards Pointe des Espagnols. By −0200 Brest the stream is weak in the inner part of the bay, but the north-going eddy on the west side attains 1 knot at springs. The ebb stream is simpler. It runs from Pointe de l'Ile Longue towards Roscanvel and Pointe des Espagnols, leaving only a weak stream in the south of the bay.

The east coast of Presqu'île de Quélern offers good protection from winds from the north through west to the south east. From the Pointe des Espagnols to the village of Roscanvel there are several small coves with yacht moorings and a welcoming yacht club at Roscanvel which will loan a mooring on request.

Roscanvel has a double slipway, one running out east and the other south. It is a small holiday village, with village store, cafés and a restaurant, grouped round the village green. The church spire is not visible from the north-east on approach, but there is water at all states of tide fairly close to the slips. Anchor off the slips clear of any moorings. The eastern slip dries at LW and there are obstructions outside it. Towards LW approach the southern slip from the south and use the inside only. Further south anchorage is prohibited.

Rade de Brest SE section and L'Aulne river

The south-eastern portion of the Rade has more to offer for the explorer. There are many bays and inlets along the north shore as the river Aulne is approached. Navigation is restricted along the south shore, but there is a regular ferry service from Brest to the Port du Fret SE of Ile Longue, with a bus connection to Camaret.

The number of yacht moorings along the north shore suggests that the area is generally sheltered in the summer, although a strong south-westerly could cause trouble.

To avoid shallows north of Pointe de l'Amorique make for Le Renard E. cardinal buoy and then lay a course to leave the conspicuous islet Ile Ronde and two rectangular

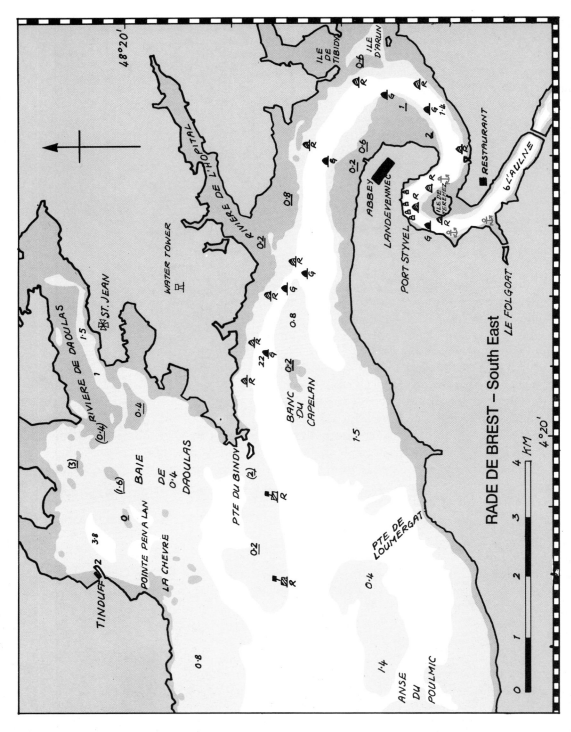

RADE DE BREST – South East

MLWS 1.4m; MLWN 3.0m; 0000 Brest, Index 5, MTL 4.4m
Based on French Chart No. 3799 with corrections (No. 6542 supersedes). Depths in metres; right hand

concrete 'Ducs d'Albe' 300m to port. If proceeding up l'Aulne, a course of 104° will lead to the outer port hand river channel buoy (numbered 4), from where on the remaining channel buoys can be located with binoculars. At present all the buoys are conical but are brightly painted in the correct lateral colours.

Anse de l'Auberlach

The hamlet of l'Auberlach lies at the head of a narrow bay running NE to the east of Ile Ronde. It has a short stone pier with a drying slip behind on which several fishing boats are hauled out. There are moorings and it is possible to anchor outside the pier with due attention to the vessel's draught up to a line from the pier to the opposite shore. At LW neaps there was 4m depth 100m off the end of the pier on this line.

Keep clear of an experimental fish farm in the middle of the bay, marked by small, unlit yellow buoys.

The plain-food restaurant 'Pic-nic' in the hamlet is open in July and August and is thoroughly recommended.

Tinduff

This is in an inlet on the west side of the shallow Baie de Daoulas, $\frac{1}{2}$ mile to the north of Pointe Pen a Lan. In the approach this point must be given a berth of over $\frac{1}{4}$ mile as there are shoals and La Chèvre rock (dries 3.1m) off it with another rock (drying 4.1m) closer inshore.

The bay may be entered with sufficient rise of tide and there is 2m off the end of the pier, which is sheltered from W and N with good holding. Keep clear of the experimental fish farm in the bay, marked by small, unlit yellow buoys.

There are no facilities ashore save for two cafés.

Rivière de Daoulas

This runs into the NE corner of the Baie de Daoulas. The bay is shallow and can only be entered at sufficient rise of tide. There is a bar at the entrance to the river but it is possible to anchor with complete shelter in 1.8m (mud) $\frac{3}{4}$ mile up river off the second slip.

There is a small village store at St Jean 1km up the hill. It is possible, but difficult, to proceed up river to Daoulas at springs, as the river dries 4.5m.

L'Hôpital river

The pretty entrance of this small river lies on the north of the entrance to L'Aulne. There is much local sailing activity here but, as the river dries, it must be visited at HW.

Faou river

Up stream of the entrance to l'Hôpital river, l'Aulne turns south into a large S bend. The mouth of Faou river is on the east bank of the curve. The bar dries 0.6m and lies between the Ile de Tibidy and the charming little islet of Arun. North of this islet is a pool with 0.4m below datum but further in the river dries. It is possible to go up to the quite large village of le Faou at springs but it is not very attractive and the river is said to be silting.

43

L'Aulne river

This is a beautiful river which winds between steeply wooded hills on either side and is quite comparable in charm with the Odet, though much less sophisticated. It is worth going out of the way to visit one of the quiet anchorages in this deeply sheltered river.

Keeping to the buoyed channel, described earlier, the river can be entered at all states of tide, with a minimum depth of 6m as far as the Térénez bridge. At high water a yacht may cut across the Banc du Capelan (dries 0.4m) providing that she is not so named!

On the south bank, inside starboard hand buoy no.7, at the start of the large S bend, is the drying jetty of Port Maria off which one can anchor beside the moorings at neaps, and the attractive looking village of Landévennec with the abbey of Penform on the promontory behind. There are mud banks on both sides of the river and it is best to keep in the buoyed channel which curves S, W and NW behind the headland, avoiding the shallows round Ile de Térénez.

In the middle of the S bend there are some large mooring buoys with a group of retired naval vessels attached behind which it is possible to land at Port Styvel (no port, see page 22) and walk up a path through the woods to Landévennec where there are shops, a hotel and the famous abbey, now restored.

From here on up the river winds between thickly wooded hills. The depth is 10m or more as far as the Pont de Térénez (headroom 27m) and the bottom is rocky. However there are several inlets where one can anchor out of the current, with soundings on mud. There are three on the starboard bank before the bridge with a good restaurant on the opposite bank. Channel buoys cease at the naval moorings, but there is enough water for deep draught yachts to go up with the tide, keeping to the outside of bends, and to the middle where the river narrows, another 12 miles to the lock at Guly Glas. At half tide, proceeding up river above the bridge it is possible to find a depth of 4m or more up to the lock. Beyond the lock the depth is 4m. Several high tension cables cross the river with more than adequate clearance for normal masts.

Trégarvan, about 2 miles above the bridge, is a reasonable anchorage; there are several local boats and a slip. There is also a landing at Le Passage, 2 miles further up. After that the banks become lower and reedy on one and then on both sides and there are no landings until the lock is reached.

The lock at Guly Glas operates from 2 hours before to $1\frac{1}{2}$ hours after high water. A popular transport restaurant by the lock was closed in 1988 but may reopen. The depth in the river above the lock is 3m or more. One mile above the lock, on the port side, is Port Launay, a long curve of quays, backed by old houses under high tree covered hills. Facilities are minimal but there is a pâtisserie, and small general store. A good hotel/restaurant de Bon Acceuil is a short walk upstream.

Most yachts passing through the lock carry on up to Châteaulin, which is a large town with banks, hotels, restaurants and shops. One can moor or raft alongside the quay. The canal from here to Nantes is closed. There are no facilities for masting, but a substantial length has been reopened for pleasure craft. Approaching the town on the starboard side a large hypermarket can be seen. Run the bow into the bank, secure to a tree and store ship with ease and economy!

7 Camaret-Sur-Mer

Charts: English BA 2643, 798. Imray C36.

French SHOM 6609 P. ECM Navicarte 540, 542.

High water: −0005 Brest, Index 4, MTL 4.2m.

MHWS 7.0m; MLWS 1.4m; MHWN 5.4m; MLWN 2.8m.

Tidal streams: In the bay of Camaret these are weak.

Depths: There are depths of 3m in the shelter of the outer breakwater and the inner harbour is dredged to 2m or more in a channel leading to the pontoon berths.

Lights:

1. North Mole. Head; Iso WG 4s, 7m, 12-8m. White pylon, green top.
2. South Mole. Head; Fl(2)R 6s, 9m, 5M. Red pylon.

General

For yachts bound south, after passing through Le Four channel, Camaret is the most convenient port of call. It was once a considerable centre of shell-fishing vessels of all sizes, but the activity seems to be declining. The town is built along the edge of the harbour and has figured in many wars. The old fort on Le Sillon, on the north side of the harbour, and La Tour Dorée were designed by Vauban and date from 1689. Five years after their construction the defences repelled with heavy loss a combined Dutch and English attack and in 1791 won a victory against five English frigates.

Rounding Pointe du Grand Gouin for Camaret. The breakwater head is far left. Do not be misled into steering for the green tower to the left of the sail – this is off the western root of the breakwater

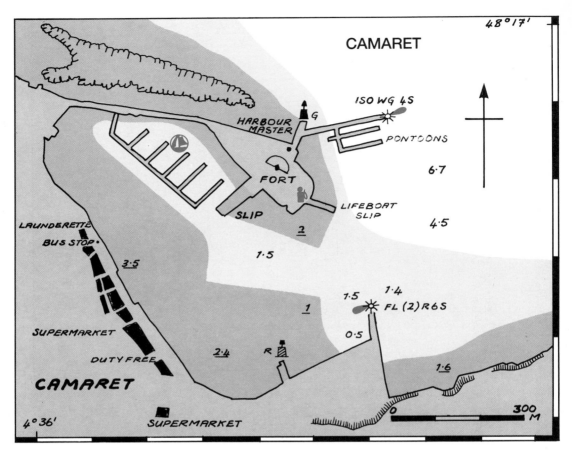

CAMARET

48°17'

ISO WG 4S

HARBOUR MASTER

G

PONTOONS

6·7

FORT

4·5

LIFEBOAT SLIP

SLIP

2

1·5

1·5

1·4

FL (2) R6S

1

LAUNDERETTE

BUS STOP

3·5

SUPERMARKET

DUTY FREE

CAMARET

2·4

R

0·5

1·6

4°36'

SUPERMARKET

0

300
M

MLWS 1.4m; MLWN 2.8m; −0005 Brest, Index 4, MTL 4.2m
Based on Admiralty Chart No. 3427 with corrections. Depths in metres; right hand margin in cables

Most of the inner harbour dries out but there is a dredged area with pontoon berths. There are 60 to 70 places for visitors on the pontoons behind the outer breakwater, though it is a long way from the town.

Approach and entrance

The Anse de Camaret is entered between the Pointe de Grand Gouin on the west and Presqu'île de Quélern on the east and the bay is clear of dangers. To the west the high cliff coast between Pointe de Toulinguet and Pointe de Grand Gouin has no dangers more than one cable from the line of the shore and the above water rocks. South-east of Pointe de Grand Gouin there is shallow water in the rocky corner of the bay, SW of a line from the point to the harbour entrance.

The long breakwater with a green beacon tower off its western end will be seen as soon

Camaret; inner pontoons

Camaret; outer pontoons

as it is opened up to the SSE of Pointe de Grand Gouin. Leave the breakwater to starboard to enter the harbour or to find a berth on the outer pontoons.

By night
Approach in the white sector of the light on the northern breakwater (**1**) and round it at a reasonable distance.

Anchorage
There are moorings but anchoring is forbidden in the bay south-east of the N mole in 3m or more.

It is convenient to berth alongside the pontoons connected to the south side of the N mole. However, they are exposed and damage may be suffered in strong winds. There is water and electricity on the pontoons.

An area in the inner harbour has been dredged and the pontoons extended providing twenty places for visitors on the outer pontoon. The berth on the elbow is reserved for the customs launch and is dredged to 3m. The depth reduces to 2m along the pontoon. On entering avoid the long shallow sloping slipway of the repair yard (see chartlet).

Yachts which can take the ground could anchor in many parts of the harbour after consulting the harbourmaster. There is good hard standing off the quays in the middle of the SW side of the harbour, with a stern anchor and a bow line to the quay.

Facilities
There are water and electricity on the pontoons and showers and toilets. Diesel can be obtained from a long hose on the lifeboat slip. Refuel at HW or at other states of the tide after inspecting the bottom.

There is a ship's chandler, ship builder and sail maker. All shops are available: two supermarkets, duty free shop, launderette, restaurants and bars.

There is a bus service to Le Fret where one can take the ferry to Brest.

8 Chenal du Toulinguet (passage notes)

Charts: English BA 798. Imray C36.
      French SHOM 6609 P. ECM Navicarte 540
Tidal streams: The S stream begins at +0015 Brest, the N at −0550 Brest, spring rates 3 knots. There is a cross tide at the northern end, the flood running to the E and the ebb to the W. To the S, between Les Tas de Pois and Cap de la Chèvre, the stream is weak, 1 knot springs, and runs almost continuously southwards.
Depths: As described here the channel has a least depth of 4.6m, though with care a greater depth can be carried.
Lights:
1. Le Toulinguet; Oc(3)WR 12s, 49m, 15-11M. White square tower and house.
2. Le Petit Minou; Fl(2)WR 6s, 32m, 19-15M. Grey round tower, white on SW side, red top.
3. Le Portzic; Oc(2)WR 12s, 56m, 19-15M. Grey eight-sided tower.

The Chenal de Toulinguet, which lies immediately west of the headland of that name, is a convenient passage for vessels bound south from Brest to Camaret, as it saves a long detour round the rocks and shoals outside.

On the east side of the channel is La Louve tower (card W), on the rocks off the headland, and on the west side there are the Roches du Toulinguet with a rock named Le Pohen, which is steep to and 11m high, nearest to the channel. The channel is over $\frac{1}{4}$ mile wide and carries a least depth of 4.6m. No directions are necessary other than to keep near the middle of the fairway between Le Pohen rock and La Louve tower. If proceeding SSE towards Cap de la Chèvre, note that the beacon on Le Chevreau was partially destroyed in 1987 and that the Le Bouc light tower, destroyed in 1980, has been replaced by a buoy (card W) 600m W of the rock.

By night
The passage is possible by night if there is enough light to see the rocks and La Louve tower at 100m. There are no lights for the narrows itself and use must be made of two safe sectors. In the southern sector, Le Toulinguet light (**1**) shows white, bearing less than 028°, and the Pointe de Petit Minou light (**2**) shows open of Pointe du Toulinguet, bearing more than 010°. In the northern sector Le Toulinguet light (**1**) shows white, bearing more than 090°, and the Pointe du Portzic light (**3**) shows open of the Presqu'île de Quélern, bearing more than 040°. This line passes very close to the rocks near La Louve tower, and it is desirable to keep Le Portzic light well open of Quélern.

From the south, enter in the southern safe sector and sail to its apex with Le Toulinguet light just turning red and Le Petit Minou light just shutting in behind Pointe du Toulinguet. From this point La Louve tower bears about 350° and Le Pohen about 270°. Steer to make about 310° to pass between them and into the northern safe sector.

Pointe du Toulinguet with La Louve (card E) tower, bearing 200°

From the north, enter in the northern safe sector, keeping Le Portzic light well open of Quélern as La Louve tower is approached. Once the tower has been seen, course can be shaped to pass through the channel, leaving the tower at least 200m to port, and out by the southern safe sector. From the apex of the northern safe sector, the course to steer is SW for 400m, thence SSE.

Les Tas de Pois from the NW. Yachts passing between rocks 1 and 2

Chenal du Petit Leac'h
From the south at night this channel may be preferred as Le Portzic light (**3**) can be held on a constant bearing of 043° to lead, with due allowance for tidal streams, between Pelen (card S) and Basse Mendufa (card N) (unlit) buoys to starboard and Petit Leac'h S cardinal beacon (unlit) to port. The channel is 600m wide with a depth of more than 10m.

Les Tas de Pois
There is no need to pass between these rocks, but as some may wish to do so, in good

weather only, the following notes may be helpful. There are five rocks, which may conveniently be numbered from seaward as follows:

1. Tas de Pois Ouest, 51m high.
2. La Fourche, 16m high.
3. La Dentelé, 44m high.
4. Le Grand Tas de Pois, 65m high.
5. Le Tas de Pois de Terre, 58m high.

Between **1** and **2** is the widest channel. A mid-channel course is clean. A rock dries 1.2m about 50m NE of no. 1 and there is a drying rock close to no. 2. Near LW it is therefore necessary to keep mid-channel, if anything closer to no.2.

Between nos 2 and 3 the channel is narrow but clean.

Between nos 3 and 4 keep closer to no. 3; there is a rock drying 0.6m close NW of no. 4.

Between nos 4 and 5 passage is only possible near HW; a rock dries 3.2m right in the middle of the narrow channel. Between no. 5 and the land there is no passage.

Anchorage
There is a snug anchorage in the Anse de Pen Hir, just inside Les Tas de Pois, in all winds but S or SE. There are no facilities ashore.

9 Morgat

Charts: English BA 798, 2643. Imray C36.
    French SHOM 6099 P. ECM Navicarte 542.
High water: −0010 Brest, Index 4, MTL 4.3m.
    MHWS 7.1m; MLWS 1.4m; MHWN 5.6m; MLWN 2.9m.
Tidal streams: Inside the Baie de Douarnenez the streams are very weak.
Depths: The old harbour dries; depths in the marina are 1.8m to 4.0m.
Lights:

1. Basse Vieille buoy (isolated danger); Fl(2)W 6s, 8m, 8M.
2. Pointe du Millier; Oc(2)WRG 6s, 34m, 16–11M. White house.
3. Pointe de Morgat; Oc(4)WRG 12s, 77m, 15–11–10M. White square tower, red top. House.
4. Morgat buoy (port); Fl R 5s.
5. Morgat old breakwater head; Oc(2)WR 6s, 8m, 9–6M. White and red metal framework tower.

Morgat is situated in the NW corner of the Baie de Douarnenez. It is a pretty, sandy bay, sheltered from the N and W by the land, and by the Pointe de Morgat on the SW, almost round to S. The village is a pleasant holiday resort with good beaches and the new marina makes it a popular port of call. It is more conveniently situated than Douarnenez as it is not so far east, and is nearer the Four channel and the Raz.

Approach

Cap de la Chèvre, 4km to the south of Morgat, has fangs of rock extending seawards on all sides, especially to the SW, where the bottom is irregular as far as the Basse Vieille whistle buoy. In westerly winds the approach from Cap de la Chèvre, provides pleasant sailing, completely sheltered by the land. The cliffs are bold and their tops are covered with grass and heather; many sandy beaches lie at their feet.

Pointe de Morgat, a bold headland with a lighthouse on top (see photograph), hides the village and anchorage until it has been rounded. Two conspicuous above-water rocks at its foot can be passed closely, say within 50m. The breakwater of the new harbour lies just to the north of them, but there is a concrete obstruction in the intervening bay.

Approaching from the south east, the only outlying dangers are the group of rocks, Les Verrès and La Pierre Profonde, which lie about 2 miles ESE of Pointe de Morgat. They are not marked, but they can be seen in daylight as they are respectively 12m and 7m high. There is a wreck 200m NE of Les Verrès, and Le Taureau 600m N of La Pierre Profonde and 1,000m W of Les Verrès dries. Approaching Morgat from this direction, leave La Pierre Profonde at least 200m to starboard.

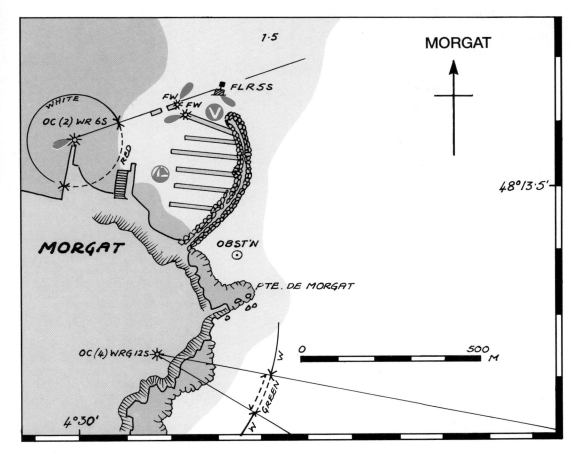

MLWS 1.4m; MLWN 2.9m; −0010 Brest, Index 4, MTL 4.3m
Based on French Chart No. 5186 with corrections (No. 6099 supersedes). Depths in metres; right hand
margin in cables

By night

The dangers south of Cap de la Chèvre can be cleared by keeping in one of the two white
sectors of Pointe du Millier light (**2**) until the Pointe de Morgat light (**3**) turns from red to
white. Then steer in the white sector of the Pointe de Morgat light. On close approach
keep clear of the coast with a course of not less than 035°, crossing the green sector of
Pointe de Morgat light. Keep a lookout for unlit mooring buoys. The light on the old
harbour breakwater (**5**) will open red, seen over the new breakwater; when it turns from
red to white, alter course to leave to port the harbour entrance buoy (**4**). There is a fixed
white light on the outer end of the visitors' pontoon/wave-breaker. Leave this close to
port on entry to avoid one or more floating wave-breakers to starboard, marked by
another fixed white light.

Morgat breakwater bearing 310°. Pointe de Morgat lighthouse far left. The conspicuous building is on the esplanade behind the harbour

Mooring
The yacht harbour has pontoons and mooring buoys; anchoring is not permitted in the area enclosed by the breakwater and floating concrete wave-breakers. Entrance is in the gap between the wave-breakers, marked by red and green paint (fixed white lights at night). Visitors secure to the S side of the long wave-breaker. There are 50 pontoon visitors' berths for yachts under 12m and mooring buoys are available.

Facilities
Water and electricity are on pontoons, with fuel berth, showers and ice onshore.

A drying slip, travel-lift, 6-tonne crane, large haul-out area, engineers and sailmakers are available.

There is $\frac{1}{4}$ mile walk to the shops on the beach. There is a launderette in Crozon, the nearest large town ($1\frac{1}{2}$ miles), and good bathing beaches are nearby.

In calm weather a dinghy trip to the caves (Les Grandes Grottes de Morgat) is great fun. They lie along the cliff below the lighthouse.

Morgat marina, looking NE

10 Douarnenez

Charts: English BA 798, 2643. Imray C36.
   French SHOM 6099. ECM Navicarte 542.
High water: −0010 Brest, Index 4, MTL 4.2m.
   MHWS 7.0m; MLWS 1.4m; MHWN 5.5m; MLWN 2.9m.
Tidal streams: Tidal streams inside the Baie de Douarnenez are very weak.
Depths: In Rosmeur the depths vary, but there is a considerable area with 3m to 5.5m. In the Rade du Guet the depths shoal from 4m to 0.4m. In the marina at Tréboul the dredged depth is 1.5m. Port Rhu dries 3m.
Lights:
   1. Ile Tristan; Oc(3)WR 12s, 35m, 13–10M. Grey tower, white band, black top.
   2. Tréboul breakwater head; Q G, 7m, 6M. White column, green top. Fishing harbour.
   3. N mole head; Iso G 4s, 9m, 6M. White and green pylon.
   4. S mole, N head; Oc(2)R 6s, 6m, 6M. White and red pylon.
   5. Elbow, Rosmeur mole head; Oc G 4s, 6m, 6M. White pylon, green top.

Douarnenez is an important fishing harbour situated in the SE corner of the bay of the same name. It is off the beaten track of yachts bound south or north, as it lies 17M to the east of Pointe du Raz, but the detour is worth while. The town and harbour are interesting, and the town provides all facilities and the harbour protection in all weathers.

Douarnenez from the NW. The entrance to the Rivière de Pouldavid is below the right hand spire. The lighthouse appears above the trees to the left on Ile Tristan and the fishing harbour wall is further left in the picture

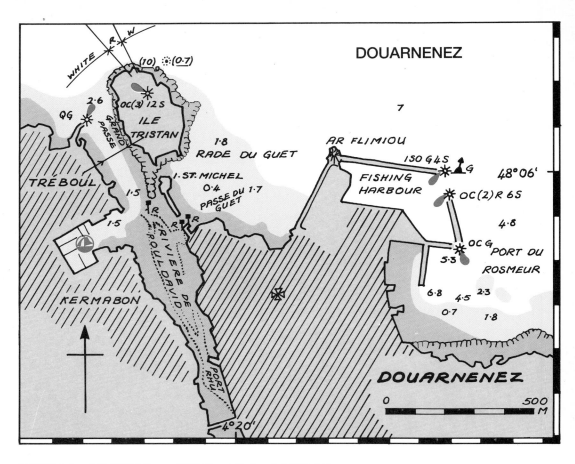

MLWS 1.4m; MLWN 2.9m; −0010 Brest, Index 4, MTL 4.2m
Based on French Chart No. 6128 with corrections (No. 6099 supersedes). Depths in metres; right hand margin in cables

Approach

The only considerations in the approach are Basse Veur, with 4.7m over it and Basse Neuve with 1.8m. Except near LW or when a sea is running these can be ignored. To clear them keep Pointe du Millier lighthouse (5 miles W of Douarnenez) open of Pointe de la Jument (3 miles W) until Ploaré church, at the back of the town, comes open to the left of Douarnenez church and Ile Tristan lighthouse; the two churches and lighthouse are almost in one line. The town is easy to locate from seaward, with Ile Tristan in the foreground, the two churches, and the harbour mole to the eastward.

By night
Navigate on Ile Tristan light (**1**) until the lights on the moles are picked up, then steer round them to the anchorage. Ile Tristan light has a red sector covering Basse Veur and Basse Neuve.

Anchorage and mooring

There are several anchorages or harbours at Douarnenez. As the vessel approaches the first to be seen is the Rivière de Pouldavid on the west side between the land and Ile Tristan. The river has been dredged to 3m and there is a yacht harbour, dredged to 1.5m, at Tréboul on the west side, with quays at Port Rhu, farther up on the east side. Next there is the Rade du Guet, an anchorage not much used, in the bay between the east side of Ile Tristan and the main fishing harbour. To the SE of the fishing harbour is the Port de Rosmeur. The following descriptions start with Port de Rosmeur and work back westwards.

Port de Rosmeur

This lies to the east of the town; it is protected by land on the W and S and by the breakwater on the N. Though open to the E, the land there is only 2 or 3km away. The north-western half of the harbour is for fishing boats and there are many yacht moorings and fish rafts in the remainder of the bay. It may be possible to borrow a mooring. If not, anchor in around 5m outside the moorings. There is good holding in mud. Inshore the depths vary rather irregularly and once the 3m line is crossed they shoal quickly in places.

Fishing harbour

Yachts may not use this harbour.

Rade du Guet

This lies between Ile Tristan and the mole leading to Roche d'Ermitage (Ar Flimmou). It is sheltered except from winds from NW to NE, to which it is completely exposed. In offshore winds it is a good anchorage with a convenient dinghy landing at the slip in Passe du Guet. It is quieter than Port de Rosmeur. The depths decrease steadily towards the SW from 3m. Go in as far as draught and tide permit to get as much shelter as possible. There are a number of visitors' moorings in the bay. The Passe du Guet, leading from the anchorage into the river, dries 3.5m, the best water being on the southern side near the beacons marking the slip.

The Port de Rosmeur, looking NE from the quay

The Rivière de Pouldavid, looking seaward over Port Rhu at LW on a tide rather greater than mean tide (Index 11). The channel to Tréboul has now been dredged

Rivière de Pouldavid
This is entered through the Grande Passe, west of Ile Tristan. There are rocks close under the island shore, and the best water is nearer the breakwater head on the west side. The river is dredged to 3m and is crossed by power lines with a clearance of 25m above the highest tides. The river can also be entered through the Passe du Guet (dries 3.5m). There are two trots of mooring buoys on the starboard side in the channel. Visitors may moor, bow and stern, here if a place is vacant.

Tréboul
Turn to starboard after passing the trots of moorings and a slipway. The visitors' pontoon is in the entrance on the starboard side. Visit the Bureau du Port on the quay to obtain a berth, or mooring.

Port Rhu
This is the commercial port. There is a short spur into the river above which are the quays. The bottom dries 3m (mud and sand) for the most part, but 3.5m near the root of the spur. There is no charge for mooring here.

Facilities
At Tréboul water and electricity are on the pontoons, fuel berth, two cranes (6 tonne), showers, toilets, launderette, shops. There is a shipyard in the fishing port, marine engineers, repairs.
  At Rosmeur there is a water tap near the dinghy slip and restaurants near the quays.
  Douarnenez has all the usual facilities of a moderate-sized town.
  The nearest railway station and airport are at Quimper.

11 Ile de Sein

Charts: English BA 798, 2351, 2643, 2645. Imray C36, C37.
French SHOM 6609 P, 7067 P. Navicarte 541.

High water: −0010 Brest, Index 3, MTL 3.8m.
MHWS 6.4m; MLWS 1.2m; MHWN 5.0m; MLWN 2.6m.

Tidal streams: Between Ile de Sein and Tévennec the NW stream begins +0535 Brest, SE stream begins −0045 Brest, spring rates 3 knots. To the north of Nerroth the flood begins NNW at −0600 Brest, turning steadily to W by HW Brest. The ebb begins at +0200, running S.

Depths: The approach is deep until Nerroth is reached; thence the channel has 0.8m. In the anchorage there is 1.8m.

Lights:

1. Ile de Sein, main light; Fl(4)W 25s, 49m, 29M. White tower, black top.
   Radio beacon; call SN, 303.4 kHz, 1/6 min, begins H+2 min.
2. Men Brial; Oc(2)WRG 6s, 16m, 12–19–7M. Green and white tower.
3. Cornoc an Abraden by (stbd); Iso G 4s, 7m, 3M. Whistle.
4. Tévennec; Q WR, 28m, 9–6M. White square tower and dwelling.
5. Le Chat; Fl(2)WRG 6s, 27m, 9–6–6M. Cardinal S tower.

Entering Men Brial. The leading line for the North Channel has been left in order to leave the green beacon to starboard. The white house with the vertical black stripe, which is the rear mark for the leading line, is just to the right of the sunlit pier head

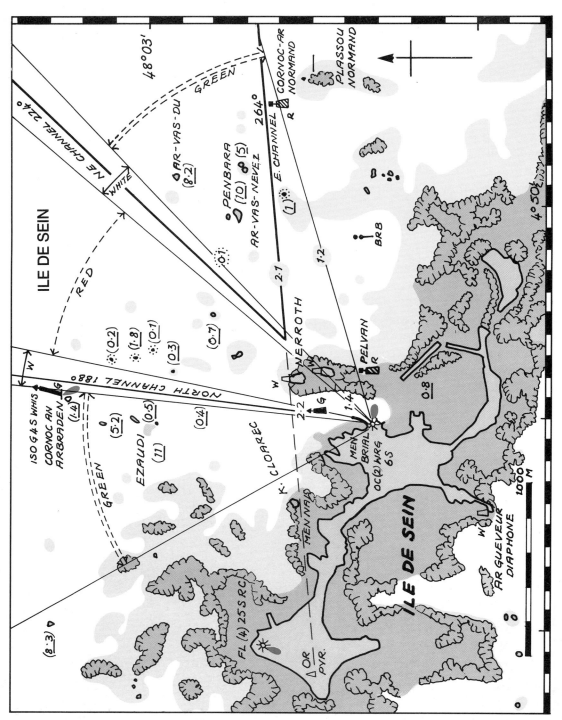

MLWS 1.2m; MLWN 2.6m; −0010 Brest, Index 3, MTL 3.8m
Based on French Chart No. 5252 with corrections (No. 6609 supersedes). Depths in metres; right hand margin in cables

On even the largest scale British chart, no. 798, the Ile de Sein appears to be so surrounded by reefs and rocks that it looks unapproachable, especially when associated in one's mind with the fierce tides of the Raz. But, except in bad visibility or heavy weather, navigation in the area with a chart on a sufficiently large scale is not difficult because:

(1) The plateau is compact on the NE and E sides and the fringes are indicated by the whistle buoy on the N, the above water rock Ar Vas Du to the NNE, the Cornoc ar Vas Nevez tower to the E and Le Chat tower to the ESE. There are no dangers if a vessel is over $\frac{1}{2}$ mile seaward of these visible marks.

(2) The tidal streams on the Sein side of the Raz are not so strong as they are on the E side.

(3) The entrance channels are clearly marked. However, when visiting the island for the first time, it is best to wait for settled weather, with clear visibility and neap tides.

The Ile de Sein is sufficiently detached from the busy world to remain largely unspoilt. Its inhabitants exist largely by catering for tourists, from fishing and by farming small plots of soil won from hard rock, which is always so near the surface that it is difficult even to find depth for burying the dead. The entire male population left the island during the war to join the Free French forces in Britain. It is said that when Colonel de Gaulle, as he then was, reviewed the troops he said 'Where is this Ile de Sein? It seems to be half France.'

The local fishing boats are mostly small, but the harbour is a base for larger vessels from Audierne and Douarnenez, which fish by day and anchor at Sein sufficiently early in the evening to patronize the numerous bars. When the fishing fleet is in the harbour is crowded, but there is still room for a few yachts.

Ile de Sein. Men Brial from the entrance to the N channel. Cornoc an Arbraden buoy (stbd) far right, with wave breaking on rock. Church left of centre, Men Brial lighthouse further left

The anchorage looking NE, showing the inner lifeboat jetty and the white pyramid on the S end of Nerroth. *Provident*, of the Island Cruising Club, is scrubbing on the beach; she needs her legs and previous reconnaissance for rocks

Though there is considerable tripper traffic with the mainland, the island is a strange, out-of-the-way place which is worth visiting if only to see the curious rock formations, but it also has a practical use, as the harbour is convenient if you are late on the tide, especially when bound south. The facilities are quite good and the anchorage is secure in southerly and westerly winds. It is exposed to the N and NE; if there is a threat of winds from this quarter it is best to leave the Ile de Sein to visit another time, for if the winds are moderate there will be a swell in the harbour, and if they are strong it may be dangerous to remain.

Approach

Nerroth is the key to pilotage in the Ile de Sein. Situated in the approach to the harbour, it looks like a small island: in fact it is composed of three very large rocks; only at low water does it form a continuous island, with a finger of rocks extending from its southern end to the eastern breakwater. There are two white masonry beacons, at its northern and southern ends, which are important leading marks.

North channel

This is the principal channel and the easiest for a stranger. The channel is deep until abreast of Nerroth, after which the depth is 1.4m to the jetties.

Having given a wide berth to all beacons and visible rocks (not less than ½ mile if approaching from the Raz), approach the Cornoc an Arbraden pillar whistle buoy (stbd) from the northward. Bring Men Brial lighthouse into transit, at 188°, with the third house from the left by the quay; this house is painted white with a black vertical stripe which should be kept just open to the left of the lighthouse if the latter tends to hide it. This transit leaves both the buoy and the rock which it marks very close to starboard. It is advised, therefore, to borrow say 50m to port until the rock is passed as the tides set very strongly across the channel. Thence follow the alignment; there are drying rocks on either side, but no dangers for 50m on either side of the line. When Nerroth is abeam, if the tide is high, Pelvan concrete beacon (port, R) will come into transit with the E end of the eastern breakwater, bearing 155° (at LW the breakwater is obscured). Follow this transit (or steer 155° for Pelvan) leaving Guernic concrete beacon (stbd) to starboard. When Guernic is well abaft the beam borrow a little to starboard of the transit, and when Men Brial lighthouse bears 220° the shoal is passed and course can be altered to SW for the anchorage.

By night
There must be enough light to make out Nerroth and Guernic concrete beacon on near approach. As it may not be easy to find the best water, it is desirable also that the tide should be high enough to allow some margin, preferably above half tide.

Enter in the white sector of Men Brial light (**2**), bearing from 187° to 190°, leaving Cornoc an Arbraden buoy (**3**) to starboard. When Nerroth is abeam alter course to 160°, and enter the red sector of Men Brial, leaving Guernic tower 60m to starboard. When the other white sector of Men Brial is entered it is safe to steer for the anchorage.

North east channel
This channel carries 3.6m until it joins the north channel by Nerroth; thence depths are as for the north channel.

Make a position 300m NW of Ar Vas Du, a rock 8.2m high (above datum). Here the white masonry beacon south of Nerroth will be in transit with Men Brial lighthouse bearing 224°; follow this transit. When the white masonry beacon at the north end of Nerroth bears 265° turn to starboard, and leaving the northern white beacon 100m to port, join the north channel.

By night
There is a white sector of Men Brial light (**2**) covering this channel, but sufficient light is needed for the deviation round Nerroth and into harbour.

East channel
This channel carries 2.3m until it joins the north channel by Nerroth; thence depths are as for the north channel.

The channel is entered 100m N of Cornoc ar Vas Nevez tower (R). When coming up through the Raz be careful to avoid the shoals E and N of Le Chat tower (card S) and Plassou Normand to the SE of Cornoc ar Vas Nevez tower. These shoals will be avoided if the tower is kept bearing less than 290°. The leading marks for this channel are the white masonry beacon on the north end of Nerroth in transit, at 264°, with a pyramid with fluorescent orange top, 300m S of the Ile de Sein main lighthouse. Also on the transit is Karek Cloarec, a rock which is never covered, and behind it and just south of the transit is Men Nai, a promontory rising to 18m above datum. If the pyramid cannot be identified either of the above could be used instead, and they will in any case serve to confirm the identification. The marks must be held very closely, as Ar Vas Nevez, drying 5m, is close to the north of the transit, while shortly after there is a rock drying 1m close to the south.

On close approach to Nerroth, bear to starboard and round it to join the north channel, leaving the white masonry beacon 100m to port.

Near high water it is possible to make a short cut east of Nerroth by steering to leave Pelvan concrete beacon (port) close to port, then steering for 200m towards the southern quay to avoid rocks to starboard before rounding into the anchorage. This passage is a *severe* one which cannot be recommended to those who do not know the area.

Anchorage

The anchorage is immediately off the lifeboat slip, near the Men Brial lighthouse and SE of it. Off the slip there is 1.8m, and 1m further to the SE. Near and south of the quays the whole harbour dries out. The fishing fleet enters the harbour in the evening, and is often there by day. Its position indicates the best water. The round red buoys belong to the fishermen and do not leave much room to anchor between them and the slip; it may be necessary to anchor to the east of them. Permission can sometimes be obtained to use one.

The anchorage is sheltered from S to NW, and from E below half tide. Swell enters if the wind goes into the north and the anchorage would be dangerous in strong winds from any northerly direction. It is also exposed to the east when the rocks are covered. Yachts should not remain in the anchorage if fresh northerly or easterly winds are expected. The bottom is a layer of mud over rock. The stream in the anchorage is weak.

Yachts that can take the ground can anchor in the bay south of the slips and can find 1.5m at LW neaps. The bottom is sand with some stony patches and much Jap Weed.

Facilities

There are several small shops and restaurants, and ship and engine repairs can be arranged; chandlery is at the fishermen's cooperative shop. Water is scarce and yachts should bring enough with them.

The village has a considerable population; the houses are clustered together in a small area, providing shelter from the winds in narrow alleyways. Bread comes on the first launches from the mainland.

12 Raz de Sein (passage notes)

Tidal streams:

Southgoing, ebb stream

Position	begins Brest	direction	spring rate, knots
Off Pointe du Van	−0130	SW	1½
Between Sein and Tévennec	−0045	SE	2¾
Off La Vieille	−0045	SSE	5½
In centre of Raz	−0030	SW	5½
In southern part of Raz	−0045	SE	5½

There is a north going eddy between La Vieille and a position near La Plate

Northgoing, flood stream

Position	begins Brest	direction	spring rate, knots
In southern part of Raz	+0535	NW	6½
In centre of Raz	+0550	NE	6½
Off La Vieille	+0535	NNW	6½
Between Sein and Tévennec	+0535	NW	2¾
Off Pointe du Van	+0605	NE	2¾

There is a southgoing eddy for ½ mile north of La Vieille. In the inshore Passe du Trouziard the streams are much stronger and in the approaches to the pass they do not run true with the channel. They turn earlier, the S stream beginning about −0120 Brest; the time the N stream begins is not known, probably about +0445 Brest.

Lights:
1. Tévennec; Q WR, 28m, 9-6M. White square tower and dwelling.
   Also Dir Iso W 4s, 24m, 12M.
2. La Vieille; Oc(2+1)WRG 12s, 33m, 17-13M. Grey square tower, black top.
3. La Plate; VQ(9)W 10s, 19m, 8M. Cardinal W tower.
4. Le Chat; Fl(2)WRG 6s, 27m, 9-6M. Cardinal S tower.
5. Men Brial; Oc(2)WRG 6s, 16m, 12-9-7M. White tower, green top.
6. Ile de Sein Main light; Fl(4)W 25s, 49m, 29M. White tower, black top.
   Radio beacon, call SN, 303.4 kHz, 1/6 min, begins +2 min.

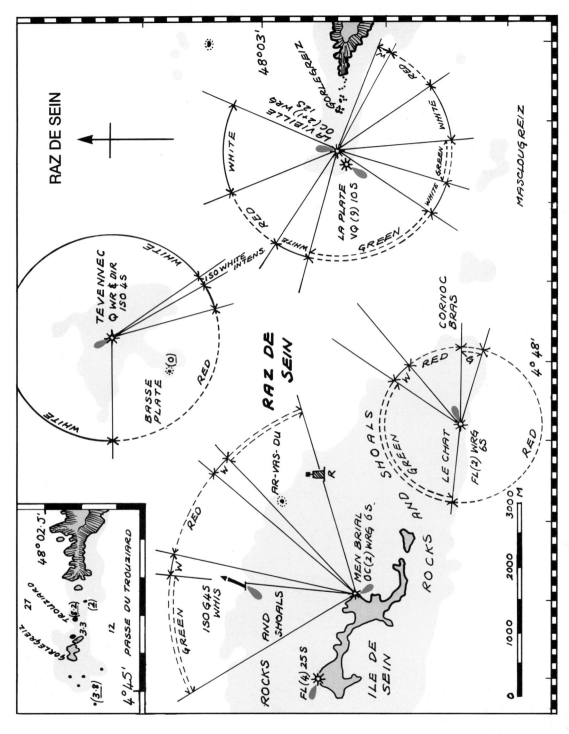

RAZ DE SEIN

Based on French Chart No. 5252 with corrections (No. 6609 supersedes). Depths in metres; right hand margin in cables

66

Passe de Trouziard, bearing 040° at LW. The yacht has been swept too far to the W; on this approach there is an outlier showing off Gorlégreiz. (See p. 70)

The Raz de Sein is the area between the Pointe du Raz on the mainland and the Ile de Sein. The scene viewed from the Pointe du Raz during gales, with the wind against a spring tide, is so impressive that it forms an inspiration to artists and photographers. Taken under reasonable conditions, however, the passage through the Raz presents no great difficulties and is a smoother passage than out at sea. It is largely a matter of timing. A yacht leaving the Four channel on the last of the fair tide can usually cross the Iroise, where the tides are less rapid and set nearly across the course, during the foul tide, so as to arrive at the Raz at the correct time, when the tide is just starting to turn fair.

The channel between La Plate tower and the rocks on the Ile de Sein is 2 miles wide. In the northern approach lies the island of Tévennec, surrounded by rocks; to the SW of Tévennec a rock, Ar Vaz, narrows the western passage to $1\frac{1}{2}$ miles.

Approach and passage
The Raz de Sein is rough, especially in the overfalls off La Vieille, even in moderate winds if they are contrary to the stream, as may occur with a fair tide if sailing south against a SW wind. When wind and tide are together the passage is smoother than outside. In light weather, at neap tides and in the absence of swell, the passage can be taken at any time by vessels having auxiliary power. The seas caused by the irregular bottom knock the way off a boat very quickly. Except when wind and tide are together, slack water for the passage is always to be preferred. The Raz is temperamental and the seas there vary considerably, but in strong winds contrary to the tide the overfalls are dangerous.

Tévennec, the small island and lighthouse in the northern approach to the Raz de Sein, bearing about SW

La Vieille lighthouse centre, with La Plate (card E) tower bearing 080°. Behind them is the Baie des Trépasses, with the Pointe du Van extreme left and the Pointe du Raz to the right

Pointe du Raz from the S. To the left is La Vieille lighthouse, with La Plate (card E) tower far left

From the north
Steer for La Vieille lighthouse, bearing 180°, about midway between Pointe du Van and Tévennec. When ½ mile off La Vieille, bear to starboard to pass west of La Plate tower (card W), allowing for any tidal set. There are overfalls west of La Vieille and La Plate.

After passing La Plate the sea soon begins to moderate, but in rough weather the Masclougreiz, 9m, and Cornoc Bras, 3.6m, must be avoided as the seas break heavily over them. If proceeding seawards the Pointe du Van in transit, at 041°, with Gorlégreiz, the large rock between Pointe du Raz and La Vieille, leads between the shoals. If bound for Penmarc'h, steer with Tévennec bearing 324° astern open to the left of La Plate.

By night
Steer for La Vieille light (2) at 180° in the white sector. When Le Chat (4) turns from green to white, steer in that white sector until the directional isophase light on Tévennec (1) opens; then steer about 150° in that sector. Bound seaward steer out in the first white sector of La Vieille, about 205°; bound for Penmarc'h, continue in the directional sector of Tévennec until clear. When Le Chat turns from green to red, bearing 108°, the vessel is clear of the southern dangers.

From the north west
The approach is between Tévennec and Ile de Sein. There is the Ar Vaz ½ mile SW of Tévennec to be avoided; keep Coumoudoc islet open to the right of Gorlégreiz, bearing 118°. The dangers off Ile de Sein are fairly well defined by the whistle buoy, Ar Vas Du rock, which never covers and a R tower. Follow these dangers on the Ile de Sein side, leaving them ½ mile to starboard, and Le Chat tower (card S) ¾ mile to starboard. Or steer for La Vieille in transit with the southern limit of the cliffs SE of the Pointe du Raz, bearing 112°. When ½ mile off La Vieille alter course to round La Plate as before.

The ebb stream SW of Tévennec is weaker than in the Raz, and the race itself appears weaker on the Ile de Sein side, though there is no official confirmation of this. In W or SW winds most of the passage is under the lee of the Ile de Sein plateau, and not so rough as east of Tévennec; care must be taken not to get set onto Cornoc Bras.

By night
Steer for Men Brial light (5) on Ile de Sein, in the white sector (186° to 192°). When La Vieille (2) turns from red to white, steer in this white sector until the directional isophase light on Tévennec (1) opens; thence proceed as described for the northern channel.

From the south
In good visibility keep Tévennec open to west of La Plate on a bearing of 327°. When ½ mile from La Plate, bear to port, avoiding overfalls.

If heading north, round the tower about ½ mile distant to steer 020° until, with due attention to tide, Jaune du Raz (BRB) isolated danger buoy is abeam to starboard.

At spring tides, counter the set of the flood stream towards the Tévennec dangers by holding La Vieille tower on a bearing of 180° when clear north of La Plate. If going west of

Tévennec steer handsomely to port to make good a course of 295° from La Plate until the NE-going stream is entered.

The south coast of Pointe du Raz is steep to so that, with visibility of ½ mile and otherwise favourable conditions, it is possible to steer to sight the cliffs well to the east of the point and follow the coast west, keeping half a mile off until La Plate tower has been identified.

By night

Passage at slack water is preferred. Keep in the directional isophase sector of Tévennec light (**1**) until, with Tévennec bearing 330°, La Plate (**3**) bears 110°. A course of 020° will then lead northwards clear of the Raz, while a course of 295° leads north west between Tévennec and Ile de Sein.

Passe du Trouziard

This passage is *severe*, see page 16. It can only be navigated by those with experience of these waters, in calm weather, at slack water, with good visibility and with reliable auxiliary power.

Identify Gorlégriez, which is the largest rock off the Pointe du Raz. At high water it appears as two large slightly separated rocks, and Trouziard is the small rock midway between them and the shore. The passage lies between Gorlégriez and Trouziard and is deep and clean, except for a 0.5m outlier to the north of the eastern end of Gorlégriez. Approach on a N or SSW course, allowing for any cross set of the tide in the approach, and go through the centre of the channel. Soon after slack water, even at neaps, the tide runs so hard that the yacht goes out of control and any sea makes the passage highly dangerous. Note that the tide turns early in the pass (see page 65).

Anchorage

There is a good fair-weather anchorage in the Baie des Trépassés, sheltered between NE and SE, in which to wait for the tide. The bay is sandy and shelving, so anchor in the most suitable depth; the best position is in the centre, facing the valley.

13 Audierne

Charts: English BA 2351, 2645, 3640. Imray C37.
      French SHOM 7147 P. ECM Navicarte 541, 543.
High water: −0030 Brest, Index 1, MTL 3.1m.
  MHWS 5.3m; MLWS 0.9m; MHWN 4.1m; MLWN 2.1m.
Tidal streams: In the approach the NW stream begins at −0515 Brest, the SE at +0025 Brest.
  Streams in the approach are weak, but strong in the harbour itself.
Depths: The approach is deep until ESE of Ste Evette mole, where there is a depth of 2.2m. The
  anchorage (with moorings) at Ste Evette has depths of from 1.0m to 3.0m. The entrance
  channel is dredged to 0.5m above LAT but is subject to silting. Yachts may lie afloat at the
  pontoons in 1m at MLWS and 2m at MLWN (1988).
Lights:
1. Pointe de Lervily; Fl (2+1) WR 12s, 20m, 14-11M. White round tower, red top.
2. Kergadec; FR, 43m, and Dir 006°Q WRG, 43m, 11M. White tower, red lantern.
3. Jetée de Ste Evette Head; Oc (2) R 6s, 2m, 7M. Red lantern.
4. Jetée de Raoulic Head; Oc (2+1) WG 12s, 11m, 14, 9M.
   (Front light of Passe de l'Est ldg lts 331°.) White tower.
   (Rear light of Passe de l'Est; Kergadec FR.)
5. Coz Fornic. Groyne; Oc R 4s, 6m, grey mast.
6. Vieux Môle. Groyne; Iso R 4s, 7m, mast.
7. Pors Poulhan. E side of entrance Q R, 14m, 9M. White square tower, red top.

The port of Audierne, like all French fishing centres, is interesting and the harbour is picturesque. The outside anchorage at Ste Evette, while well protected except from the E and SE, is bleak and only suitable for a short stay when on passage. The entrance channel has been dredged and pontoons have been established in the inner harbour to cater for between 25 and 35 visitors.

Approach and entrance
At the mouth of the Goyen river, Audierne is situated in the NE corner of the bay of the same name and the white slate-roofed houses will be seen from a distance clustered on the hillsides, with another group above the village of Pors Poulhan, 4 miles to the SE.

   The entrance to the harbour can be dangerous in strong onshore winds and swell, but the Ste Evette anchorage is protected by the land and a breakwater except from the E and SE.

Approach from the west and south
There are no dangers until the vessel approaches within 1 mile of Pointe Raoulic, on which stands the harbour jetty. The channel, ½ mile wide, lies between Le Sillon and

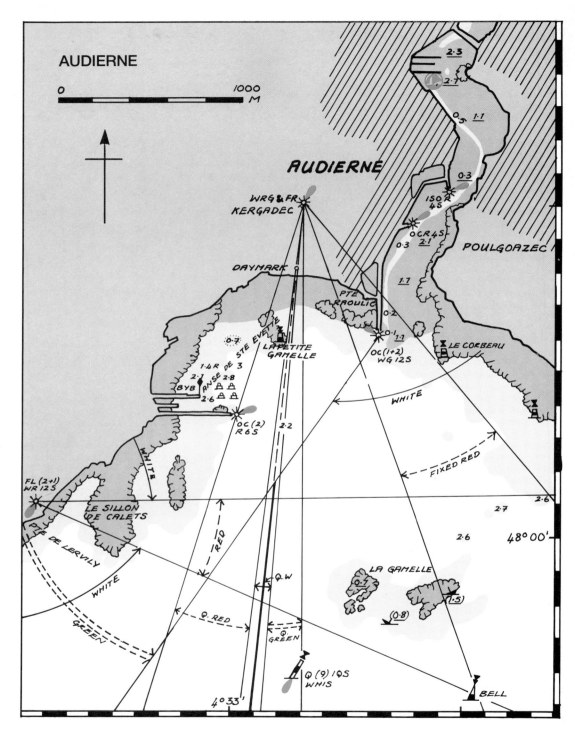

AUDIERNE

0   1000
                 M

MLWS 0.9m; MLWN 2.1m; −0030 Brest, Index 1, MTL 3.1m
Based on French Chart No. 5937 with corrections (No. 7147 supersedes). Depths in metres; right hand margin in cables

Audierne breakwater, right, bearing 030°. Kergadec lighthouse on skyline, left, in line with disused lighthouse on shore, bearing 006°

adjacent rocks on the west side and a group of rocks named La Gamelle, which only dry at springs, on the east side. If there is a swell the seas break on La Gamelle. There is a whistle buoy (card W) $\frac{1}{4}$ mile SW and a bell buoy (card S) $\frac{1}{4}$ mile SE of La Gamelle.

The approach may be made with the two lighthouses, one disused, to the west of Pointe Raoulic in transit, bearing 006°. The rear lighthouse, Kergadec, is on the skyline, but the old front lighthouse, Trescadec, is on the foreshore in a gap between some houses and is not easy to locate. A good initial landmark is the microwave telephone-link mast a few degrees to the right of Kergadec.

This line leaves the whistle buoy (card W) about 200m to starboard and passes over a 2.2m patch E of the Ste Evette mole. If bound for the anchorage, steer for the mole head when it bears NW and round it, but not very closely. If making for the inner harbour, leave the transit of the lighthouses and steer for the end of the Raoulic jetty when it bears 034° and is in transit with the rather small steeple of Poulgoazec church, which may be detected, situated on a grassy knoll on the eastern side of the river.

By night
Enter the narrow white sector of Kergadec quick flashing light (**2**) on (006°). When the light on the Ste Evette mole head (**3**) bears NW alter course for the Ste Evette anchorage. If proceeding to the inner harbour, alter course for the head of the Raoulic jetty when the light on it (**4**) turns from white to green, bearing 034°.

South eastern approach
There is no difficulty in the south eastern approach as the channel between La Gamelle

Audierne entrance at LW

Audierne yacht pontoons (1988), looking upstream from the fish quay. The pontoons are being extended to accommodate more visitors

on the west and the land on the east is wide and carries a least depth of 2.5m on the leading line. However, Audierne is not easy to locate when approaching from the south and it is best to follow the coast 4 miles or so offshore after rounding the Pointe de Penmarc'h.

Three conspicuous, equally spaced landmarks on the skyline indicate the harbour entrance from a distance of 3 or 4 miles. To the west is a church spire, in the centre over the Kergadec lighthouse a water tower and to the east a tall microwave telephone-link mast. Identify Kergadec light tower (white with a red lantern) and keep it on a bearing of 325° leaving La Gamelle well to port.

By night
Approach with Raoulic light (**4**) and Kergadec (FR) light (**2**) in line on 331°. Pointe de Lervily light (**1**) has a red sector covering La Gamelle. When this light turns from red to white the way is open to steer for the Ste Evette anchorage.

The outer anchorage
The Ste Evette anchorage ½ mile SW of the harbour is good. It is sheltered from W and N by the land and from the S by the mole, though some swell enters if there is S in the wind

and this may be considerable if the wind is strong. The depths are 2.5–3.1m north of the end of the mole, decreasing steadily towards the shore. There are tightly packed moorings in the anchorage, with a charge collected for their use. There may be room to anchor east of them, with less shelter from the south. The holding ground is not very good and there are a few rocky patches. It is best to tuck in behind the mole as far as depths allow, so as to get out of the swell. The northern of the two slips, used by the ferries, extends a long way; the end is marked by an inconspicuous (card E) beacon. A small tower (card S) marks a rock, called La Petite Gamelle, in the northern part of the anchorage; west and north of this the bay is shallow.

Land at the ferry slip or, above half tide, at the little pier in the NW corner of the bay. There is a restaurant facing the bay at Trescadec and a small store at Kergadec, but most of the shops are in the town over a mile away. It is also possible to land at Raoulic jetty and leave the dinghy in a pond near its root, but this pond dries out towards low water.

The harbour
Much of the harbour or river mouth dries out at low water and there is a bank, which dries, outside the entrance nearly 1 cable to the SE of Raoulic jetty head. The channel is dredged to 0.5m above LAT but shifts and is subject to silting so that it is best to enter within 1½ hours of high water. As a general rule, keep close to the jetty as far as the bend in the wall some 2 cables from the entrance. Thence the channel passes near the ends, marked by lit, red beacons, of the two spurs, Coz Fornic and Vieux Mole, projecting from the west side, after which it crosses over to run along the quay at Poulgoazec. Finally the channel swings back to the west bank along the Audierne quays and ends at the yacht pontoons.

Strangers are not advised to attempt this channel on a dark night.

Facilities
Audierne is a substantial town with a pleasant atmosphere which does attract tourists. The harbourmaster and his wife are most helpful and the mayor is keen for yachtsmen to enjoy their stay.

There is water and electricity on the pontoons. There is also a shipyard, and repairs can be undertaken.

The fishermen's fuelling berth is being adapted to serve yachts.

Municipal showers and a 'Rallye Supermarché' a short walk upstream past the bridge. Shops, banks, restaurants and hotels in the town are close to the pontoons. There is a bus service to Douarnenez and Quimper.

14 Saint Guénolé

Charts: English BA 2351, 2645. Imray C37.

      French SHOM 7147 P, 6645 P. ECM Navicarte 543.

High water: −0020 Brest, Index 0, MTL 2.8m.

  MHWS 5.0m; MLWS 0.6m; MHWN 3.8m; MLWN 1.8m.

Tidal streams: For streams in the offing see under Penmarc'h, page 80. In the harbour the streams are weak, except in the final approach channel.

Depths: In the approach channel and anchorage 2m.

Lights:

1. Eckmühl; Fl W 5s, 60m, 24M. Grey eight-sided tower. Siren 1min.
   Radio beacon, call ÜH(..--/....), 289.6 kHz 50M, 1/6.
2. Menhir; Oc(2)WG 6s, 19m, 8, 5M. White tower, black band.
3. Basse Gouac'h buoy (stbd); Fl(3)G, 12s, whis.
4. Passe de Groumilli ldg lts 123°.
   Front FG 9m, 9M. Rear FG 13m, 9M. Fluorescent orange-red spheres on white columns with black bands.
5. Intermediate ldg lts 051.5°; front Q G, 5m, 1M.
   Rear F Vi, 12m, 1M. Platforms on green and white metal columns.
6. Final ldg lts 026.5°; front sync Q R, 8m, 4M. Red mast.
   Rear sync Q R, 12m, 4M. Mast, red and white bands.
7. Scoëdec; Fl G 2.5s, 6m, 3M, Green tower.

Telephoto of Pointe de Penmarc'h from a position N of Basse Gouac'h buoy (stbd). To the left of Eckmühl lighthouse are the leading marks for the entrance of the St Guénolé channel. Scoëdec tower (stbd) is between them, bearing 128°

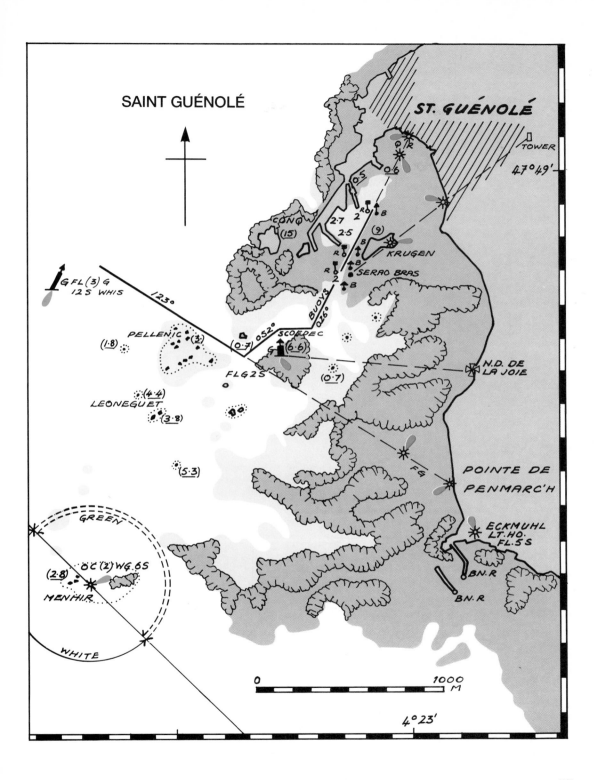

SAINT GUÉNOLÉ

ST. GUÉNOLÉ

TOWER

47° 49'

CONQ
(15)

Q R

0·6

0·5

R O   B

2·7   2

2·5   (9)

B

R O

KRUGEN

B

SERAO BRAS

2   B

B

G FL (3) G
12 S WHIS

123°

BUOYS   026°

052°

SCOEDEC
(6·6)

PELLENIC   (3)

(1·8)

(0·7)

G

N.D. DE
LA JOIE

FLG2S

(0·7)

(4·4)

LEONEGUET

(3·8)

F4

(5·3)

POINTE DE
PENMARC'H

ECKMUHL
LT. HO.
FL. 5 S

GREEN

OC (2) WG.6S

BN. R

(2·8)

MENHIR

BN. R

WHITE

0   1000
M

4° 23'

The small town of St Guénolé, situated about 1 mile north of Pointe de Penmarc'h, cannot be mistaken. It has a long and interesting history. Before the war the harbour, open to the westward, was untenable in bad weather sweeping in from the Atlantic. Then a sea wall was built, enclosing this entry, and a channel blasted through the rocks to the south, the quays extended and the harbour dredged. Although the entrance is exposed and dangerous in bad weather, the harbour now offers good shelter in all winds. A considerable fishing fleet is based here, but there is no local yachting activity. Yachts are not welcome, but entry is described for interest.

No attempt should be made to enter the harbour except in settled weather, with no swell; a first entry should be made with the tide more than half up, in daylight; a night entry should not be attempted unless the channel is well known. There is very little room for error in following the channel.

Approach

From the north
Bring Eckmühl lighthouse on a bearing of 145° and make good this bearing until Menhir tower (card W), lying about 1 mile W of Penmarc'h, bears 175°. Alter course to make good this bearing, 175°, which leads clear of all the inshore dangers and about ¾ mile westward of St Guénolé sea wall. When Basse Gouac'h whistle buoy (stbd) is 300m ahead the leading marks for the Passe de Groumilli will come in transit, bearing 123°. They are masonry towers with BW horizontal bands, with large fluorescent red spheres as topmarks. They will be seen to the left of Eckmühl lighthouse.

From the south
Give the Menhir tower (card W) a berth of 800m to starboard. When it bears 090° steer 020° for the whistle buoy (stbd). Pass the buoy on either hand and hold the same course for 300m, when the marks for the Passe de Groumilli will come into transit (see above) bearing 123°.

Entrance

Enter with the BW towers with red sphere topmarks in transit, bearing 123°. This leaves the Pellenic rocks, which dry, close to starboard; Scoëdec tower (stbd G) will be seen on the port bow. After ½ mile, before Scoëdec tower is reached, the church of Notre Dame de la Joie, on the coast ½ mile north of Penmarc'h, comes into transit with Scoëdec tower, bearing 096°. At about the same time a rock 9.6m high, seen between the outer two of three concrete beacons (stbd), comes in transit with a church tower on the east side of St Guénolé, bearing 052°. This rock, named Searo Bras, rises like a leaning tooth out of the sea at high water, and out of a flat expanse of rock at mid-tide. The tower is square with a very squat steeple and does not come into view until shortly before the alignment is reached. This transit is also marked by lights on WG metal columns.

Steer 052° on this transit; when Scoëdec bears 180°, borrow to starboard, steering about E magnetic, until the channel through the rocks opens bearing 026°. The channel,

The leading marks for the second line, bearing 052°, are indicated; the rock is conspicuous, the church only just shows through the houses. No. 1 concrete beacon on the right

said to be dredged to 2m, is defined by two pairs of small R and G buoys and by nos 3 and 5 green concrete beacons to starboard and nos 2 and 4 red concrete beacons to port. The alignment is marked by two concrete poles near the town, carrying the leading lights, but these are not easy to pick up by day; they are a little way to the right of a large square white building.

Steer on this alignment, 026°, until no. 4 port hand beacon is well abaft the beam, then steer round the end of the mole into the pool.

By night
Only those who are already familiar with the harbour should attempt a night entry. Some, but not all, of the transits are lit.

Anchorage and facilities
The pool is dredged to 2.5m. Anchor out of the way of the fishing boats, probably near the lifeboat house, but the bottom is foul and a tripping line should be used. The bottom is rock, covered with muddy sand.

All shops, shipyard, several hotels, buses to Quimper, museum of prehistoric megalithic culture about 1 mile distant are available. Water could probably be obtained from the fish market on the quay. There is no fuel nearby.

The final leading line: the poles carrying the lights are indicated, but they are not easily seen. The tide runs strongly through this channel, especially when the rocks at the side are uncovered. The anchorage is to the left inside

15 Pointe de Penmarc'h (passage notes)

Lights:
1. Eckmühl; Fl W 5s, 60m, 24M. Grey eight-sided tower, siren 1 min.
2. Menhir; Oc(2)WG 6s, 19m, 8–5M. White tower, black band.

The Pointe de Penmarc'h is a low headland, in contrast with the very high octagonal lighthouse of Eckmühl on it, which is 60m high. There are reefs of rocks extending in all directions from the headland, with numerous towers on them. In bad weather the whole scene is grim, but the point need not be closely approached except when on passage north of the Iles de Glénan. When rounding Pointe de Penmarc'h progress often seems slow with Eckmühl lighthouse in sight for a long time, as the course follows an arc over 1 mile offshore.

Navigationally the principal consideration is the tidal stream. This does not compare in strength with that in the Four channel or the Raz de Sein, as the spring rates are only $1\frac{1}{2}$ to 2 knots, except perhaps in the vicinity of the Menhir tower.

Some 4 miles south of Penmarc'h the streams are rotary clockwise: N at −0325 Brest, E at −0020 Brest, S at +0240 Brest, WSW at +0600 Brest.

The tidal stream divides at the Pointe de Penmarc'h, the flood setting northerly towards Audierne and easterly towards the Iles de Glénan; the ebb sets in the opposite direction, the streams meeting off the Menhir tower, where there are overfalls in rough weather. North of Penmarc'h the NNW stream begins at about −0540 Brest, the SSE at about +0025 Brest, spring rates 2 knots. South of Les Etocs the E and NE stream begins about −0600 Brest, the W and WSW at about HW Brest, spring rates $1\frac{1}{2}$ knots. The streams on the coast eastward of Penmarc'h are much affected by wind.

There is a radiobeacon at Eckmühl lighthouse: call ÜH 289.6 kHz 50M. First in sequence of four beacons (**1** Eckmühl, **2** St Nazaire, **3** Pointe de St Mathieu, **4** Pointe de Combrit) 1/6 min, begins H+0 min.

Pointe de Penmarc'h; Eckmühl lighthouse and Menhir beacon, bearing 090°

16 Le Guilvinec

Charts: English BA 2351, 2645, 3640. Imray C37.
  French SHOM 7146 P, 6646 P. ECM Navicarte 543.
High water: −0020 Brest, Index 0, MTL 2.8m.
  MHWS 5.0m; MLWS 0.6m; MHWN 3.8m; MLWN 2.8m.
Tidal streams: Outside, the E stream begins about −0610 Brest, the W at HW Brest, spring
  rates 1.5 knots, but much affected by winds. There is negligible stream in the harbour.
Depths: On the main leading line the least depth is 2.8m, but more water can be found. In the SE
  approach the least depth is 0.2m. The harbour is dredged to 3m to the inner end of the fish
  quays and in the area of the visiting yacht mooring buoys.
Lights:
  1. Basse Nevez (card N buoy); V Q 7m, 8M.
  2. Spineg (S card buoy); Fl (6Q+1L) 15s, 7m, 5M, whistle.
  3. Lost Moan; Fl(3)WRG 12s, 7m, 9–6–6M. White tower, red top.
  4. Locarec; Iso WRG 4s, 11m, 10–7M, W beacon tower on rock.
  5. Three leading lights, 053° Sync Q W;
       Front; on stbd mole spur, 13m, 10M, white pylon.
       Middle; 210m from front, Q WG, 17m, 14–11M,
         orange/red sphere on red and white pylon.
       Rear; 1100m from front, Dir Q W 31m, 15M,
         orange/red sphere on red and white pylon, in front of white gable end of building.
  6. Capelan (lat stbd buoy); Fl(2)G, 6s.
  7. N mole spur head; Fl R 4s, 11m, 9M, white tower, red top.
  8. N breakwater head; Fl(2)R 6s, 4m, 5M, red structure.
  9. S mole head; Fl G 4s, 5m, 7M, round white hut, green top.
  10. S mole spur; Fl(2)G 6s, 4m, 5M, green structure.

Situated some 4 miles east of Penmarc'h, Le Guilvinec (officially Guilvinec, but always
called Le Guilvinec) is an important centre for fishing vessels of all kinds, and has
processing factories. The town is not a tourist centre and derives its living entirely from
the fishing industry. It has the attractions of a busy working town and there are a number
of shops. Provided that care is taken to avoid the outlying rocks, the approach is
straightforward and the harbour is sheltered. There is only limited room for yachts,
which are tolerated rather than encouraged. Visitors are limited to a one night stay and
there is no local yachting activity.

Approach
The landscape east of Penmarc'h is dotted with white houses with grey slate roofs so that

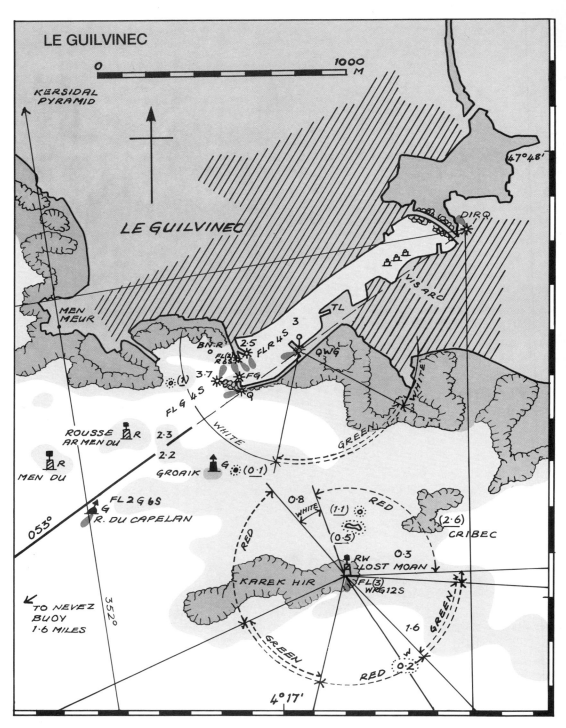

LE GUILVINEC

0   1000
M

KERSIDAL
PYRAMID

LE GUILVINEC

47°48′

DIRO

VIS ARC

MEN
MEUR

ST.L

BN·R
FL(2)
R.65S

2.5

FL.R.4.S 3

Q.W.G

WHITE

3.7 FG

Q

FL G 4.S

GREEN

ROUSSE
AR MEN DU

R

2.3

WHITE

2.2

MEN DU

R

GROAIK

G

(0·1)

0.8

RED

WHITE

(1·1)

(2·6)

FL2 G 6S

G

(0·5)

CRIBEC

R. DU CAPELAN

RED

0.3

053°

RW
LOST MOAN

0.3

352°

KAREK HIR

FL(3)
W.R.G.12.S

TO NEVEZ
BUOY
1·6 MILES

GREEN

1.6

GREEN

W

RED

0·2

4°17′

MLWS 0.6m; MLWN 1.8m; −0020 Brest, Index 0, MTL 2.8m
Based on French Chart No. 5284 with corrections (No. 7146 supersedes). Depths in metres; right hand
margin in cables

82

Le Guilvinec, approaching from S. Conspicuous grey house left of centre with white painted rock further left. Capelan buoy (stbd) to the left of chimney, right

Le Guilvinec tends to be inconspicuous among them. It may be located by a somewhat thicker cluster of houses and the fishmarket, which is a long white building with a higher part at the west end, rather like a ship with the bridge aft. Also to be seen are the lighthouse, with a red top on the north mole, a conspicuous blue trawler travel lift and the fluorescent orange/red sphere topmarks of the leading line.

Visitors' buoys at the top of Le Guilvinec harbour

Main western approach

From westward give Les Etocs, a prominent group of above-water and drying rocks, a good berth. Thence make a position 100m to the NW of Nevez pillar buoy (card N). This buoy lies 700m SE of Raguen tower (card S) which is itself on the SE side of Les Etocs. From eastward make for the Basse Spineg whistle buoy (card S), and either leave it close to starboard and make for the Nevez buoy, or when the north mole lighthouse is identified, make for it, bearing not less than 020°, the lighthouse seen just to the right of the fishmarket.

From the position 100m NW of Nevez buoy the leading marks should be in transit, bearing 053°. They are: two enormous fluorescent orange-red spheres on orange/white columns. It is safe to steer in with the conspicuous lighthouse with a red top, on the north mole, bearing between 020° and 050°, until the buoys and beacons near the entrance are approached. On these bearings the north mole lighthouse will be approximately in transit with the eastern edge of the fishmarket.

The leading line crosses the Basse aux Herbes with a depth of 1.8m. Near low water, especially in rough weather, it may therefore be necessary to borrow 150m to starboard while the *old* Penmarc'h light tower is in line with Locarec tower, bearing 292°; at night, in the red sector of Locarec light (4). After Basse aux Herbes is passed, return to the leading line, leaving:

Men Du concrete beacon (port), 200m to port,
Capelan conical buoy (stbd) close to starboard,
Rousse ar Men Du concrete beacon (port), 120m to port
Groaïk tower (stbd), 200m to starboard.

South eastern approach

At sufficient rise of tide a shorter approach from the east may be followed; this can most easily be treated as drying 1.1m, but with care a depth of 0.2m can be carried through.

First make a point 200m E of Les Putains tower (Ar Guisty) (card S). Here Lost Moan tower (card E) should be in transit with the low round white building with a green top, on the outer, southern mole head, bearing 327°. Steer on this transit, nothing to westward, until Lost Moan is approached; then alter course to leave Lost Moan 200m to port. Thence steer for the mole head, leaving Groaïk tower (stbd) 200m to port. If the tide is so low as to make it necessary to avoid the rocks north of Lost Moan, steer sharply to port as soon as Lost Moan is abeam, passing 100m north of it. Note that the *striking mark* for the first rock is Rousse ar Men Du concrete beacon (port) in transit with Groaïk tower (stbd), bearing 295°, so that Groaïk tower must be kept on a bearing of 300°, well open to the right of Rousse ar Men Du, until Lost Moan tower is in transit with Les Putains (Ar Guisty) tower astern, bearing 150°. Then steer 330° on this stern transit until Groaïk tower is abaft the beam, when alter course to enter harbour.

Southern approach

This is the easiest daylight route with ample water provided the leading marks can be identified. Make a position midway between Les Putains (Ar Guisty) tower and Spineg buoy (card S), 600m to the SW of Les Fourches rocks which never cover; then identify the Men Meur white painted rock at the W end of the Guilvinec waterfront buildings which transits a slender pyramid with large diamond topmark a mile to rear on bearing 352°. Follow this transit for 1¾ miles to the Capelan buoy (stbd), which is left to starboard to continue as on the western approach.

By night
Entry by the main channel is straightforward. Entry may also be made by the south eastern channel, at sufficient rise of tide, if there is enough light to judge distance off Lost Moan tower at 200m. Enter in the white sector of Lost Moan tower (**3**) between 317° and 327°, round the tower leaving it about 200m to port and continue in the white sector between 140° and 160° astern, until it is necessary to alter to round the southern mole head.

Entrance and anchorage
Steer to leave the head of the outer southern mole to starboard and then the northern mole head and spur to port. The northern mole head has a white rectangle with red border on the end, the ends of the spurs being marked by flashing red and green lights.

   Le Guilvinec is an active fishing port and visitors must not get in the way. Yachts must not enter or leave between 1600 and 1830 hrs and can only secure to a quay or a fishing boat in an emergency. On the starboard spur is a notice for visiting yachts. They must proceed to the upper end of the harbour and secure bow and stern to a pair of metal mooring buoys. There are three buoys and, by rafting, six visiting yachts may be accommodated. Their stay may not exceed one night and a listening watch on channel 12 is required.

Facilities
The main part of town is on N side of harbour. Market day is Tuesday; there are excellent supermarkets, and showers at municipal baths near the western pontoon on Thursdays, Fridays, Saturdays, and Sunday mornings.

Le Guilvinec entrance, having passed Capelan buoy (stbd). The orange-red spheres of the leading marks are to the right of the blue travel lift

17 Loctudy

Charts: English BA 2645, 2351, 2352, 3641. Imray C37.
      French SHOM 6649 P, 7146 P. ECM Navicarte 543.
High water: −0020 Brest, Index 0, MTL 2.8m.
    MHWS 4.9m; MLWS 0.6m; MHWN 3.8m; MLWN 1.8m.
Tidal streams: In the offing the NE stream begins about −0610 Brest and the SW at HW Brest,
    spring rates 1.5 knots. In the harbour the spring rates are: flood 3 knots, ebb 3.5 knots.
Depths: The least water in the approach is 0.9m. Off Loctudy there is 3m. Off Ile Tudy 1.0m or
    more may be found and there is a deep pool with 5m on the opposite side of the channel just
    upstream of Ile Tudy jetty, with depths of 2m or more above and below it.
Lights:
1. Pointe de Langoz (Loctudy); Fl(4) WRG 12s, 12m, 15-11M. White tower, red top.
2. Basse Bilien (card E buoy); VQ(3) 5s, 4m, 5M. Whistle.
3. Karek-Saoz; Q R, 3m, 1M. Red truncated tower.
4. Les Perdrix; Fl WRG 4s, 15m, 11-8M. BW chequered tower.
5. Le Blas; Fl(3)G 12s, 5m, 1M. Green pylon on pedestal.

Geographically Loctudy and Ile Tudy, on the peninsula facing Loctudy across the river entrance, lie between Le Guilvinec and Bénodet. Likewise, in character they stand midway between the wholly fishing port of Le Guilvinec and the holiday and yachting resort of Bénodet. At Loctudy and Ile Tudy, fishing and sailing flourish together. The estuary of the Rivière de Pont-l'Abbé is now full of moorings and the walls of a marina which is under construction at Port Tudy were complete in August 1988. The approach is sheltered in westerly winds and the harbour is secure.

Les Perdrix tower at the entrance to Loctudy, bearing 294°. Two red dinghy sails below the right hand house and another to the left of the tower

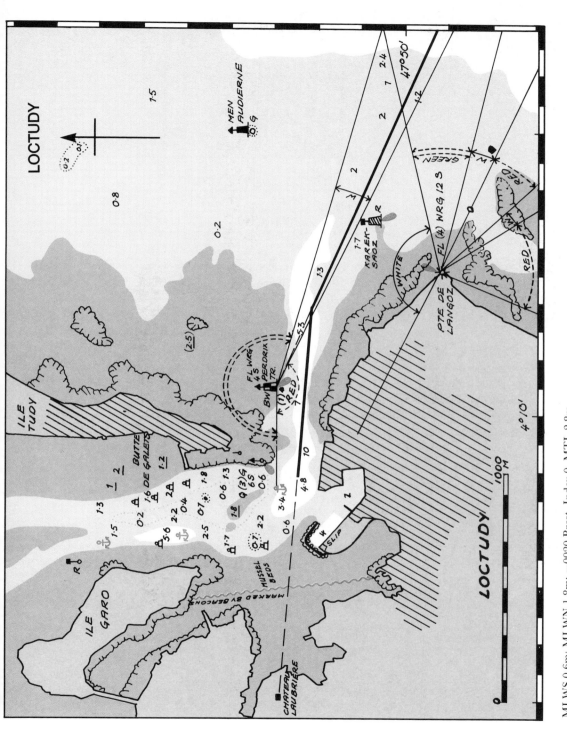

MLWS 0.6m; MLWN 1.8m; −0020 Brest, Index 0, MTL 2.8m
Based on French Government Chart of 1980 with later corrections and with Admiralty modifications.
Depths in metres; right hand margin in cables

87

Loctudy, looking upstream and across to Ile Tudy from new harbour wall

Approach

From the west the outside approach is the same as for Bénodet (see page 92), turning to port shortly after passing the Basse du Chenal buoy (card E). Many will prefer to coast along the shore, which is considerably shorter. Except near low water it is sufficient, after clearing Les Etocs near Pointe de Penmarc'h, to leave not less than 500m to port Les Fourches (never covers), Les Putains (Ar Guisty) tower (card S), Reissant (a small round rock which never covers), Les Bleds tower (card S), Men Du tower (card E), Karek Hir tower (card E), Men Bret tower (card E) and Karek Saoz tower (R). This course has a least depth of drying 0.1m. Near low water it will be necessary to stand further offshore, using the chart and the outer buoys. Topmarks and paint were lost in the October gale of 1987 from Les Putains (or Ar Guisty) tower, Reissant beacon column and Les Bleds tower. They may not be restored for some time.

From the E and SE the distant approach is the same as for Bénodet (see page 94) as far as Ile Aux Moutons, then steer more to the NW, leaving to port Les Poulains tower (card N) and Men Diou tower (card E). Half a mile NW of Men Diou is a rock with 2m over it. If necessary this can be left to the SW by keeping Ile Aux Moutons lighthouse midway between Les Poulains beacon and Men Diou tower. Thence leave ½ mile to port the buoys on Roche Malvic (card W), Basse du Chenal (card E) and Basse Bilien (card E).

By night

Follow the direction for Bénodet (see pages 93 and 94) until the white sector of Les Perdrix (**4**) is entered. Then alter course to keep in this sector until within 400m of the lighthouse. There are no navigational lights in the river except for Le Blas (**5**), and it will be necessary to rely on the shore lights. A first entry should be made in adequate daylight.

Entrance

Bring the Perdrix tower (BW cheq) to bear 294°. On this bearing it will be just open to the left of the promontory of Ile Tudy and midway between two large houses on the shore (see photograph). This lead crosses the bar in a depth of 1m; the sea breaks here when there is a heavy swell or in rough conditions, especially on the ebb. Karek Saoz beacon (port) should be given a good berth; there are said to be isolated rocks near it as a result of blowing up a wreck.

Loctudy, Fish Quay and new harbour walls

When Les Perdrix tower is about 300m distant alter course to port and steer 274° for the northern corner of the marina wall or, if it is not obscured by the marina, the Château Laubière, a conspicuous three-storey house with symmetrical lower wings on each side, and a level roof-line between chimneys each end.

If proceeding northward to the Ile Tudy anchorage, turn to starboard after passing the Banc Blas beacon (stbd), leaving the middle ground, which dries 1.8m, to port. Steer towards a position some 30m off the end of the jetty at Ile Tudy. 100m N of the jetty head is the Butte des Galets, a shingle patch on which it is easy to ground when it is covered near high water. Between 1800 and 1900 hours, entry is only permitted under power, sailing being prohibited.

Anchorage

The areas out of the fairways north west of the fish quay and marina are now fully occupied by moorings. Only one or two corners are left for anchoring and if space is found further north it will entail a long dinghy journey against a fast tide. A number of white buoys are reserved for visitors and an excellent and continuous ferry service is provided from 0700 till 2000 hours.

After half tide, there is water for a draught of 1.3m to go 3 miles up river to Pont L'Abbé, but the river is not fully marked and there is limited room to dry out against the quays.

Facilities

This was the situation in 1988 and facilities will improve on completion of the marina: at Loctudy there are all shops, restaurants and hotels, shipyard and marine engineers. Water is by hose at the quay. The harbour is very lively when the fishing fleet is in, especially if dinghy racing is taking place as well.

At Ile Tudy there are also shops and hotels, but it is rather less sophisticated. There is a water tap at the root of the jetty. From both sides of the river there are buses to Quimper.

18 Bénodet and Odet river

Charts: English BA 2645, 2352, 3641. Imray C38.

French SHOM 7146 P, 6679 P, 6649 P. ECM Navicarte 543.

High water: −0020 Brest, Index 0, MTL 2.9m.

MHWS 5.0m; MLWS 0.6m; MHWN 3.75m; MLWN 1.75m.

Tidal streams: In the centre of the bay the streams are rotary clockwise running N at +0600 Brest, NE at −0330 Brest, SE at −0015 Brest and WNW at +0245 Brest, spring rate at about 1 knot. In the river the flood begins at about −0540 Brest and the ebb at HW Brest, spring rates 2.75 knots.

Depths: The approach, entrance and the river for several miles upstream are deep. The upper reaches of the river dry.

Lights:

Buoys to SW

1. Cap Caval (card W); VQ(9) 15s. Whis.
2. Karek Greis (card E); Q(3)10s. Whis.
3. Basse Boulanger (card S); VQ(6)+L.Fl 10s.
4. Bilien (card E); VQ(3)5s.

Lighthouses:

5. Menhir; Oc(2)WG 6s, 19m, 8-5M. White tower, black band.
6. Pointe de Langoz; Fl(4)WRG 12s, 12m, 15-11M. White tower, red top.
7. Pointe de Combrit; Oc(3+1)WR 12s, 19m, 12-9M. White square tower, grey corners. Radio Beacon; call CT, 289.6kHz, 20M. 4th in Seq. 1/6.
8. Pyramide (Bénodet main light); Oc(2+1)W 12s, 48m, 11M. White tower, green top.
9. Ile aux Moutons; Oc(2)WRG 6s, 18m, 15–11M. White tower and building.
10. Leading lights 346°;

    Front, Pointe du Coq; Dir Oc(2+1)G 12s, 11m, 17M. White tower, vertical green stripe.

    Rear, Pyramide; Oc(2+1)12s, 48m, 11M. White tower, green top.
11. Trévignon; Oc(3+1)WRG 12s, 11m, 14-11-11M. White square tower, green top.

Buoys to SE:

12. Grands Porceaux (card N); VQ W.
13. Basse Jaune (card E); Q(3)W 10s.

Beacon

14. Pointe de Toulgoët; Fl R 2s, 2m, 2M. Red mast.

General

The port of Bénodet at the mouth of the river Odet, situated some 25km to the eastward of Penmarc'h, is one of the principal yachting centres in the north of the Bay of Biscay. With pontoons and numerous buoys on both sides of the river, it has good moorings and

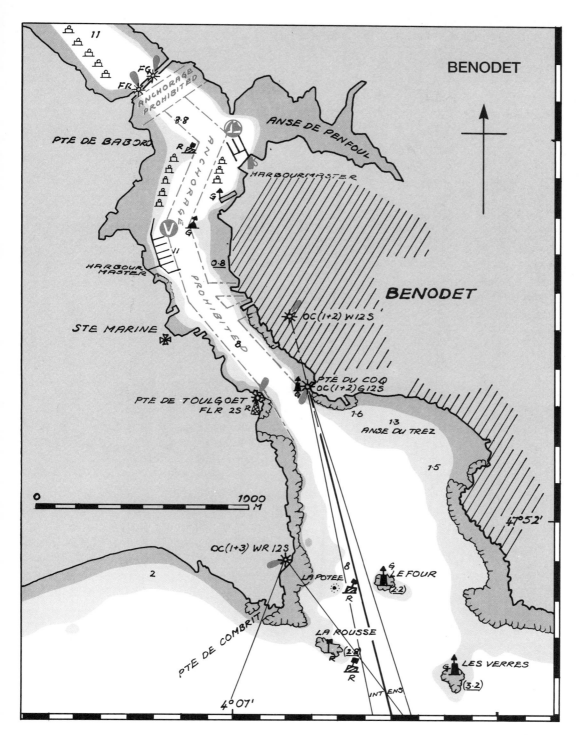

BENODET

PTE DE BABORO

ANSE DE PENFOUL

HARBOURMASTER

ANCHORAGE PROHIBITED

FR

FG

3·8

R

G

V

G

VI

0·8

HARBOUR MASTER

STE MARINE

PTE DE TOULGOET
FLR 2S R

PROHIBITED

ANCHORAGE

BENODET

OC(1+2) W 12S

PTE DU COQ
OC(1+2) G 12S

G

1·6   1·3
ANSE DU TREZ

1·5

47°52'

11

OC(1+3) WR 12S

2

LA POTEE
R

8   G LE FOUR
G   (2·2)

LA ROUSSE
R   (2·8)
R

G LES VERRES
G   (3·2)

PTE DE COMBRIT

INT ENS

4°07'

0   1000 M

MLWS 0.6m; MLWN 1.9m; −0020 Brest, Index 0, MTL 2.8m
Based on French Chart No. 5301 with corrections (Nos. 6649 supersedes). Depths in metres; right hand
margin in cables

Looking upstream from Ste Evette slipway. Yacht pontoons in left background

facilities and is a natural port of call for British yachts. The little town itself is a yachting and holiday resort, where a yachtsman can get most of the things he needs. The only disadvantage is that it is extremely crowded in midsummer.

The Anse de Bénodet is a fine wide bay, some 5 miles across with sandy shores, sheltered from the N and W. The port of Loctudy lies on the west side and to the east lies the Baie de La Forêt, partially sheltered from the west, with marinas at Port de la Forêt and Concarneau. To the south there are the Glénan Islands only 12 miles away. The Odet river, which is completely sheltered, is navigable near HW nearly up to the cathedral city of Quimper; unless the yachtsman is in a hurry to sail south, he has plenty of local sailing to interest him. The whole bay is a centre of intense local sailing activity, with less popular waters to the west and to the south east. Communications with England are good for crew changes.

Approach

From the west
After rounding Menhir tower off Penmarc'h at a distance of $\frac{1}{2}$ mile, make good 135° until Cap Caval W card buoy is abeam to port. Then make good 120° to leave Spinec S card buoy to port. If Ile aux Moutons light (white tower 18m and house) can be identified on a bearing of 083° hold it on this bearing, or make good a course of 083° for 8 miles when

Bénodet and Odet bridge from Joël de Kerros' boatyard

Roustolou E card buoy should be seen ¾ mile abeam to port. At this point Bénodet main lighthouse (white tower 48m with green lantern) will come into transit with Pointe de Combrit light tower (white square tower, grey corners), bearing 000°. Alter course and steer on this transit leaving Roustolou buoy to port and passing between Basse du Chenal E card buoy (to port) and Basse Malvic W card buoy (to starboard). The passage between these last two buoys leads clear of dangers and into deep water should identification of the transit marks at a distance prove difficult. Within a mile of Pointe du Combrit alter course to starboard for the entrance.

In good weather a course can be followed closer to the shore, leaving Spinec buoy close to port, Les Putains (Ar Guisty) beacon well to port, and Karek Gris, Basse Boulanger and Billien buoys close to port.

By night
After rounding Menhir tower (**5**), steer 135° leaving Cap Caval buoy (**1**) to port and keeping in the white sector of Menhir light (**5**). When Ile aux Moutons light (**9**) turns from red to white on a bearing of 081°, follow this edge until Bénodet main light (**8**) comes into transit with Pointe de Combrit (**7**) on a bearing of 000°. Follow this transit, watching the Pointe de Langoz light (**6**); it will change from red to white to red to white to green to white. When it finally changes from green to white bearing 257° the way is clear to turn to starboard to bring the Bénodet leading lights (**10**) in line on 346° and enter the river. Many lights other than those described will be seen.

93

From the south east
Leave Basse Jaune whistle buoy (card E) to port and make good a course of NW, leaving Les Pourceaux about 1.5 miles to port. This rocky area is marked by a beacon tower (card E) on its SE side and a buoy (card N) on its NW side. Continuing the same course, leave Ile aux Moutons 1.5 miles to port, Les Poulains tower (card N) to port, La Voleuse buoy (card S) to starboard and Men Diou tower (card E) to port. The leading lighthouses of Bénodet should then be seen and course altered to bring them in transit on 346°, leaving Le Taro tower (card W) to starboard.

By night
Before the Basse Jaune buoy (**13**) is abeam to port get into the white sector of Ile aux Moutons light (**9**) and in or just south of the intense sector on a bearing of 285°. Continue in this sector until *either* the intense sector of the Concarneau rear leading light, Q.W, is entered *or* Pointe de Langoz light (**6**) is seen and Trévignon light (**11**) has turned from white to green bearing more than 051°. When one or other of these occur steer to starboard and enter the white sector of Pointe de Langoz light, bearing 295°. Steer in the white sector of Pointe de Langoz light until Pointe de Combrit light (**7**) opens white bearing 325°. Then steer for this light, crossing the green sector of Pointe de Langoz light and bring the Bénodet leading lights (**10**) in transit on 346°. Many lights other than those described will be seen.

Entrance
Bring the leading lighthouses in transit on 346°. The tower of the main light is conspicuous, but the front light, Le Coq, has been painted in green and white vertical stripes which tend to conceal it. It will be seen some way to the left of the conspicuous letters YCO on the grassy bank in front of the yacht club. This alignment leaves 2 buoys and one beacon (all port hand) to port and two starboard hand beacon towers to starboard. When within 400m of Le Coq, bear to port and steer up the middle of the river between a port hand and a starboard hand beacon tower. (See photograph p. 96.)

By night
Entrance is straightforward but the river is congested with moorings, and anchoring is prohibited in the channel until well beyond the bridge. The leading lights (**10**) lead clear of all unlit buoys and beacons. When within 400m of Le Coq (**10**), bear to port to pass half way between Le Coq and Pointe du Toulgoët light tower, Fl R 2s (**14**). Fixed red and green lights will be seen on the bridge and the shore lights may give some guidance. Those on the quays are left on all night.

Anchorage and mooring
There is good anchorage during offshore winds in the Anse du Trez on the starboard side of the entrance, especially if one arrives in the dark. There is some hazard here from sailboard and *optimist* dinghy schools, but it becomes peaceful at night. West of the Pointe de Combrit, the bay, with a long sandy beach, makes a pleasant lunch-time stop.

There are moorings, some of them marked '*Visiteurs*', on both sides of the river up to and a short distance beyond the bridge. Anchoring is prohibited in this area. There are marina pontoons on the port side above Ste Marine and on the starboard side at the entrance to the Anse de Penfoul. Approach the visitors' berths in both marinas against the stream and with caution. A strong current sets across the pontoons during both flood and ebb. For west bank moorings apply to Ste Marine marina and for east bank moorings apply at the Port de Plaisance in the Anse de Penfoul.

It is possible at tide time to secure to the quay to do any business in the town and then go up the river where there is room to anchor.

Facilities

All the facilities of a sophisticated yachting centre with restaurants and hotels on both sides of the river. Food shops are of moderate standard.

There is water and electricity on both marina pontoons with a fuel pontoon at Anse de Penfoul. Showers and toilets are available in both marinas.

On Anse de Penfoul quay there are groceries at the café, a launderette, chandlery and engineers.

There are yacht builders on both sides of the river and an excellent wooden-boat builder (Joel de Kerros, Ste Marine Combrit, 29120 Pont l'Alle, phone 98 56 35 05).

Communications

There are buses to Quimper from Bénodet and Sainte Marine.

A secret anchorage in the Odet river

River Odet

The river Odet is a famous beauty spot with steep tree-covered banks, and ferries ply regularly from Bénodet to Quimper on the tide. There is no difficulty in sailing up the first 5 miles in depths of more than 2m. The deep water is in the middle and the only obstruction is a rock on the sharp turn to starboard which is marked by a green conical buoy.

Odet river entrance. The front leading mark, Pointe du Coq lighthouse, is just left of the Bénodet lighthouse. La Potée buoy (port) is to port and Le Four concrete beacon (stbd) is to starboard. (See p. 94)

Above Lanros the river is shallow, but well marked by beacons as far as the port of Corniguel; above that the river dries and the beacons are farther apart. A bridge prevents masted yachts from reaching Quimper, but yachts that can take the ground may anchor or borrow a mooring below the bridge and visit Quimper by dinghy, while motor yachts can carry a depth of drying 1.5m up to the first quays on the port hand in Quimper. The bottom here is hard and uneven for drying out.

There are no facilities on the way up the river, but everything can be got at Quimper, a large city, famous for its pottery, with an attractive cathedral with nave and chancel out of line.

In using the river, especially when anchoring, it is important to remember that occasionally large ships go up to Corniguel and need all the room available. They must be given absolute right of way.

When looking for a place to anchor one wants to find a bight clear of the worst of the tide and where the mud has settled; in the river much of the bottom is rock. Among

96

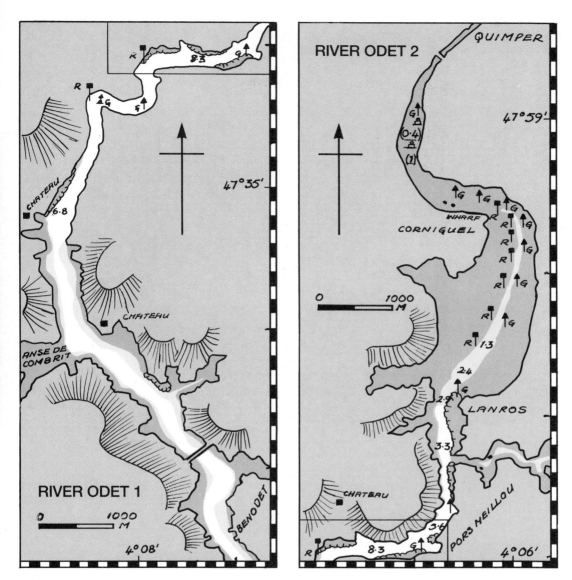

RIVER ODET 1

RIVER ODET 2

QUIMPER

CORNIGUEL

LANROS

PORS NEILLOU

CHATEAU

ANSE DE COMBRIT

BENODET

47°35'

47°59'

4°08'

4°06'

MLWS 0.7m; MLWN 1.8m; −0020 Brest, Index 0, MTL 2.9m
Based on French Chart No. 5368 with corrections (No. 6679 supersedes). Depths in metres; right hand margin in cables

several such places the Anse de Combrit and the bay opposite Lanros may be mentioned. There is a beautiful anchorage just below Lanros in the inlet on the eastern side, but care must be taken to avoid a rock on the south side of the entrance where it opens out. Keep close to the north side of the channel. In this pool a large area has 1m depth and 2m can be found in which to swing on short scope. At the end of the first pool, there is a rock with 1m or less, on the inside of the sharp turn to the N and mud on the S side.

Charts: English BA 2645, 2352, 3640. Imray C38.

   French SHOM 7146 P, 6648 P, 6647 P. ECM Navicarte 543, 243.

High water: −0020 Brest, Index 0, MTL 2.9m.

   MHWS 5.0m; MLWS 0.8m; MHWN 3.9m; MLWN 1.8m.

Tidal streams: Near the islands the streams are rotary clockwise, setting N, 1 knot at +0330 Brest; ENE, 2 knots at −0230 Brest; S, 1 knot at HW Brest and WNW, 1 knot at +0330 Brest, spring rates in each case. Amongst the islands the streams run in the direction of the channels, the flood setting N and E and the ebb S and W, spring rates up to 2 knots.

Depths: There is enough water in the anchorages for most yachts at all tides. Above half tide there is enough water to sail freely in the channels and in the large pool between Penfret and St Nicolas, but near low water the pilotage becomes intricate and a number of the channels cannot be used.

Lights:

1. Ile aux Moutons; Oc(2)WRG 6s, 18m, 15-11-11M. White square tower and dwelling. Auxiliary light; Dir Oc(2)W 6s, 17m, 24M. Sync with main light.
2. Penfret; Fl R 5s, 36m, 21M. White square tower, red top. Auxiliary light; Dir Q W 34m, 12M, on same structure.
3. Ile Cigogne; Q(2)RG 5s, 5m, 2M. Red tripod. Shown 1 May to 1 October.

Buoys: There are several lit buoys surrounding the islands but these are not listed as it is inadvisable to enter the area at night.

Situated about 12 miles south of Bénodet and 10 miles from Concarneau, this archipelago is an intricate mixture of islands, rocks and shoals. It is the home of the Centre Nautique de Glénans (CNG), which is almost certainly the largest sailing school in Europe. Founded by Philippe Viannay, it gives to young people systematic training at all levels from basic seamanship to cruising and ocean racing. The main base of the CNG is on Ile

Penfret lighthouse, left, with Ile de Guiautec beacon, right, bearing 205°

GLÉNAN POOL

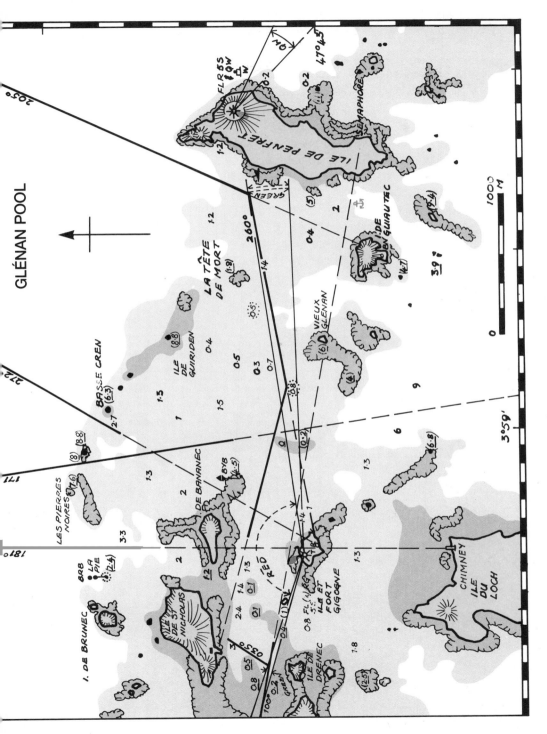

MLWS 0.8m; MLWN 1.8m; −0020 Brest, Index 0, M'T'L 2.9m
Based on French Chart No. 5285 with corrections (No. 6648 supersedes). Depths in metres; right hand margin in cables

99

Cigogne with camps on the other Glénan islands, but there are centres in other parts of France and the rest of Europe including one in Eire.

The fleets of CNG boats are in evidence everywhere among the islands. The CNG is very hospitable to visitors, but the latter should be careful not to impose on this hospitality as the *moniteurs* have a very full programme.

The Ile de St Nicolas, where some of the more popular anchorages are, has a small café which can on occasions supply bread, and the shellfish tanks of a famous restaurant, and rent out holiday cottages.

The islands should be visited only in good weather as all the anchorages are somewhat exposed, at least at high water. They form a fascinating area to explore and practise one's pilotage, spending a week or more happily knob-dodging. It is hoped that the plans in this book will suffice for a quick visit, using the main channels, but for any exploration large-scale charts are essential. ECM Navicarte 243 is comprehensive, SHOM 6648 covers all the islands although called Iles de Glénan partie Sud, while SHOM 6647, Iles de Glénan partie Nord only covers Ile aux Moutons and Les Pourceaux. BA 3640, covering Audierne, Guilvinec, Lesconil and Glénan, may also be consulted. A vessel should be fully provisioned before going to the islands as there are no shops.

Approach

The main islands are easily distinguished by the conspicuous lighthouse on Ile de Penfret, the largest and most easterly of the group; a stone fort having a tall concrete tower, the top of which is painted black on the SE side, on Ile Cigogne; a disused factory chimney on Ile du Loc'h; some houses on the SE side of Ile de Drenec; the summer cottages on Ile de St Nicolas and the shellfish tanks with adjacent house on the south side of the same island which can provide a useful mark if they are not hidden behind the yachts in a crowded summer anchorage. A number of islets stretch out to the west of Ile de St Nicolas and the western edge of the archipelago is marked by Les Bruniers tower (card W). The southern and south eastern sides are guarded by buoys (see BA 2352 or Imray C38).

Entrance

The entrances are described on the basis that one is aiming for La Chambre, the most

Les Pierres Noires. Three yachts are coming out through the second northern entrance near HW. Penfret lighthouse is to the right of the right hand sail, bearing 115°

La Pie and the pool N of Ile de Bananec. Arrows indicate the leading marks for the third northern entrance

popular and therefore the most crowded summer anchorage. Once inside the pool between Penfret and Bananec, the various alternative anchorages are easily reached.

The CNG people recommend the Chenal des Bluiniers western entrance and frequently use a north-west channel which leaves Castel Bihan rocks close to starboard. Yachts from Bénodet and Concarneau use the northern entrances and the feeling by all is that southern channels should not be used. For a stranger, the easiest entrance is that from the north-east. Once inside, the necessary landmarks can be more easily identified and exit can be made by another channel which can then be used for a subsequent entry.

When manoeuvring in the pool La Tête de Mort (dries 1.8m) is a well-known hazard to be avoided, also a shallow patch (drying 0.2m) 700m E of Cigogne.

North-eastern entrance

This channel carries a least depth of 1m, but passes close to shoals of 0.7m and should be treated as carrying that depth. Leave the northern end of Le Penfret 300m to port and steer 205° on the stone beacon on Ile de Guiatec. When Ile Cigogne concrete tower bears 260° alter course to make good the bearing, which also holds Penfret lighthouse dead astern. If the E cardinal beacon SE of Bananec can be located, alter course for it when it bears 290° and so avoid the shallow patch to the east of Cigogne. Alternatively alter onto 285° when the semaphore building at the southern end of Penfret is on a reciprocal bearing of 105°. Hold 285° which should lead into La Chambre with the shellfish tanks right ahead behind the moored yachts. Using either course, leave the east cardinal beacon SE of Bananec to starboard to enter the buoyed channel of La Chambre.

Northern entrances

All three entrances should be regarded as carrying 1m although with careful pilotage through the pool, using a large-scale chart, more water can be found. In the approach care must be taken to avoid Les Pourceaux rocks, marked on their SE side by a tower (card E).

The three entrances are taken in order from east to west; the easiest for a stranger is La Pie, the third. The vital clues to the first two entrances are four rocks which are never covered: Basse Cren (dries 6.4m) in the E, then two adjacent rocks of Les Pierres Noires (drying 8.5m and 7.9m) and finally in the W a single Pierre Noire (dries 7.5m) which has others to the SW which dry soon after HW. All these rocks stand on compact rocky bases

St Nicholas pier, looking SE towards Fort Cicogne

and must be distinguished from Ile de Guiriden to the SE; this has a considerable sandy expanse, which covers near HW, leaving only the rocky head (dries 8.8m).

The first entrance leaves Basse Cren (dries 6.4m) 50m to 100m to port steering on Fort Cigogne tower, bearing 212°. Once Basse Cren is fairly passed the vessel can bear to port as convenient.

The second entrance leaves the two adjacent heads of Les Pierres Noires (drying 8.5m and 7.9m) 20m to 60m to port. Steer on Ile de Brilimec, bearing 171°, which leads fairly into the pool. As a check Cigogne tower bears 200° in the entrance. This is a popular entrance for local yachts but should not be used for a first visit as Ile de Brilimec and Les Pierres Noires must be positively identified by close observation.

For the third entrance, La Pie, bring the chimney on Ile du Loc'h just open to the right hand side of the Cigogne tower, bearing 181°. Steer so until inside Les Pierres Noires and La Pie Beacon (BRB with 2 balls topmark but do not leave it to port) is abeam to starboard. Near low water the chimney dips behind the fort and one must then steer to leave La Pie beacon 100m to starboard. Except near high water there is no problem about knowing when Les Pierres Noires are passed as a rock which dries 5m marks their SW extremity. However, this rock covers at HW springs. When La Pie beacon is in transit with the N side of Ile de Brunec, bearing about 280°, steer to port into the pool, unless heading for the anchorage north of Ile de Bananec, in which case steer straight on.

Western entrance
The Chenal des Bluiniers carries a least depth of 0.5m drying, but it is safer to regard it as

drying 0.8m. If this gives insufficient margin, it is better not to use this entrance, but to skirt the north edge of the rocks and enter by La Pie. Visibility of 3 miles is needed except towards high water.

Make a position 200m S of Les Bluiniers tower (card W); if coming from the NW round this tower at not less than 200m distance. From this point steer E for Le Broc'h tower (card N), keeping at least 100m S of of a line joining all the dangers that show to the north and keeping Penfret lighthouse open to the north of Le Broc'h tower, bearing about 090°. Approaching Le Broc'h tower leave it 100m to starboard and bring the semaphore, near the southern point of Ile de Penfret, open to the left of Fort Cigogne by the width of the fort (not the tower), bearing 100°. Steer so until the eastern part of Ile de Drenec is abeam to starboard; this island is in two clearly defined parts separated by a sandy strip which covers at HW. Thence steer 035° on the summer cottages to the east of the shellfish tanks to enter La Chambre. Near HW the detailed directions above can be disregarded; having passed Le Broc'h tower it is only necessary to sail 100m N of Ile de Drenec and then make straight for La Chambre or the pool as required.

Notes on entry by night and by the south-eastern entrance are not included in this edition as it is felt that both operations should only be attempted after a thorough knowledge of the area has been acquired.

Anchorages

East of Ile de Penfret
This anchorage is in the sandy bay south of the hill on which the lighthouse stands. Approach with the middle of the bay bearing 270°. This leaves a rock drying 0.5m 200m to starboard and another, with 0.0m over it at LAT, 100m to port. This latter rock lies 150m N of an islet, Castel Raët, which dries 11m and is joined to Penfret by a ridge of rocks. There is a large metal mooring buoy on the N side of the bay, but it is preferable to anchor, on soundings, closer to the beach in sand, taking care to avoid patches of weed. The anchorage is well protected from the west but should not be used if there is any chance of a *vent solaire* during the night.

South of the islet is another bay with a slip and containing CNG moorings. This bay is unsuitable for anchoring.

South-west of Ile de Penfret
There is a good anchorage in 2.5m outside the CNG moorings between the island and Ile de Guéotec. The tide runs fairly hard here, but the islands give a good deal of shelter, even from the W and it is well sheltered from the east. This anchorage should normally be approached from the north; from the south the pilotage is intricate and requires the large-scale chart. At high water take care to avoid the rock drying 5m, 150m off the shore opposite the CNG boatsheds.

East of Ile Cigogne
Anchor in 1m to 1.4m, north of the rocky ledge running SE from Cigogne.

ILES DE GLÉNAN

MLWS 0.8m; MLWN 1.8m; −0020 Brest, Index 0, MTL 2.9m
Based on French Chart No. 5368 with corrections (No. 6648 supersedes). Depths in metres; right hand

East Penfret anchorage

La Chambre

This anchorage south of Ile de St Nicolas is the most popular one for visitors. The depths are up to 3m; although the best spots are occupied by moorings there is normally no difficulty in finding room to anchor. Do not anchor in the channel used by the launches and marked by small port and starboard buoys.

Avoid a rocky shoal which extends 350m SE from Ile de Bananec, the end marked by an E cardinal beacon. The bottom is also rocky for about 100m out along the south shores of St Nicolas and Bananec. Between the two islands however is sand. At low water they are joined by a sandy ridge, on either side of which bays are formed, drying 1m, which make excellent anchorages for yachts that can take the ground.

Coming from the pool, make for a position 100m S of the E cardinal beacon SE of Ile de Bananec. If La Chambre is full of yachts, follow the marked channel in until a suitable anchorage is found. If the shellfish tank is not obscured, keep it on 285° until Bananec is passed and then bear a little to port if wishing to proceed further into La Chambre. At low water depths of less than 1m may be encountered in La Chambre. The water is clear and it is necessary to look for a sandy patch on which to anchor as there is much weed.

North of Ile de Bananec

There is a popular anchorage in the bay NW of Bananec and E of St Nicolas. The depth shoals from 2m; choose a spot according to tide and draught. There is a clean, sandy bottom. The anchorage is exposed to the N and E at high water and is not recommended except in calm conditions by the CNG.

Charts: English 2645, 2352, 3641. Imray C38.

French SHOM 7146 P, 6650 P. ECM Navicarte 543.

High water: −0015 Brest, Index 0, MTL 2.8m.

MHWS 4.9m; MLWS 0.6m; MHWN 3.8m; MLWN 1.8m.

Tidal streams: Are weak in the bay.

Depths: The channel in la Forêt river is dredged to 1.2m or more.

Lights:

1. Cap Coz, shelter mole head; Fl(2)R 6s, 5m, 6M. Red lantern on grey post, white hut.
2. Kerleven shelter mole head; Fl G 4s, 8m, 6M. Green lantern on grey mast, white hut.
3. Marina mole head; Iso G 4s, 5m, 5M. Green lantern on grey mast.

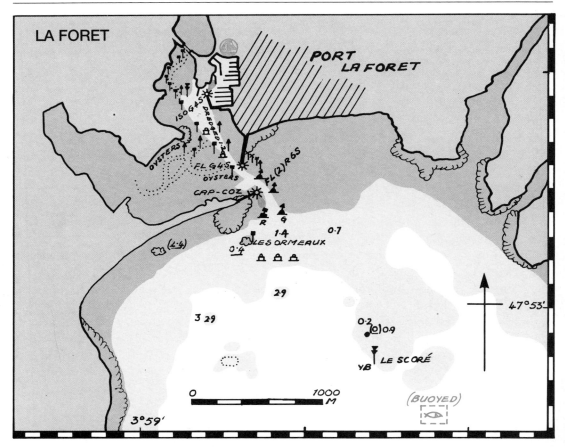

MLWS 0.6m; MLWN 1.8m; −0015 Brest, Index 0, MTL 2.8m
Based on French Chart No. 5359 with corrections (No. 6650 supersedes). Depths in metres; right hand margin in cables

Port La Forêt entrance, passing Kerleven breakwater head

Baie de la Forêt lies just to the NW of Concarneau. It is rectangular in shape, with shoals on each side of the entrance. It thus affords anchorage in most weather, even in SW winds. The shelter is sufficient for many local boats to lie on permanent moorings in the summer off Beg Meil. The E and NE sides of the bay are foul. The marina in the estuary at the head of the bay is part of a planned holiday village complex which has been slow to develop. The pontoons in the marina suffered damage during the storm of October 1987 and have since been repositioned.

Approach and entrance
The entrance to the estuary lies to starboard of the wooded promontory of Cap Coz. Pass between the loose boulder breakwaters of Cap Coz to port and Kerleven to starboard. The channel is well marked with lateral buoys and beacons. The moorings near the top of the estuary are reserved for fishermen, but there are a number of moorings for yachts up to 25m length on the port hand opposite the marina entrance in 2.5m. Turn sharply to starboard to round the marina breakwater head, marked by a named, green and white column and pole.

By night
Cap Coz (**1**) and Kerleven (**2**) lights in line on 334° clears Le Scoré and a night entry is possible if there is enough light to see the unlit channel buoys and beacons.

Mooring
There is room in the marina for several hundred yachts on pontoons with 2.5m to 3m below datum. Secure to the visitors' pontoon and obtain a berth from the port captain.

Facilities
Water and electricity are on the pontoons. There is a fuel berth, travel lift, slipway and haul-out area. Engine and yacht repairs can be undertaken. There are showers and toilets, groceries, a café and chandlery in the marina.

It is 1 mile to the town of La Forêt Fouesnant. There are fairly frequent buses from the port to Quimper and Concarneau, so the marina provides a good stopping point for a crew change.

Charts: English BA 2352, 2645, 3641. Imray C38.

French SHOM 7146 P, 6560 P. ECM Navicarte 543.

Highwater: −0015 Brest, Index 0, MTL 2.8m.

MHWS 4.9m; MLWS 0.67m; MHWN 3.8m, MLWN 1.8m.

Tidal streams: The streams in the harbour run about 2 knots at springs.

Depths: The entrance is deep as far as La Médée tower, where there is a 2m shoal. The Avant Port marina has 1m to 2m but beware of rocks along the fuel berth wall which should only be approached near HW. The Anse de Kersos shoals steadily from 3m.

Lights:

1. Le Cochon; Fl(3)WRG 12s, 5m, 9–6M. Green beacon tower.
2. Basse du Chenal; Q R, 6m, 6M. Red beacon tower.
3. Men Fall by (stbd); Fl G 4s.
4. Leading lights 028.5°;
   Front: La Croix; Oc(3)12s, 14m, 13M. Red and white tower.
   Rear: Beuzec; Dir Q W, 87m, 23M. Belfry.
5. Lanriec; Q G, 13m, 7M. Black window in white gable, name in green.
6. La Médée; Fl R 2.5s, 6m, 4M. Red beacon tower.
7. Passage de Lanriec; Oc(2)WR 6s. Red tower below wall of La Ville Close.

Concarneau is an important fishing port with some commercial traffic and at present the inner harbour is wholly devoted to these activities. The Avant Port, on the other hand, is wholly devoted to yachting, of which the port is a busy centre. During the storm of October 1987 pontoons and yachts were literally rolled up against the walls of the Ville Close. In August 1988 half the pontoons had been replaced and moorings were available in the remaining space.

The town is large and contains all resources; the Ville Close is picturesque, but very commercialized for the tourist. Though rather off the route to the south it is a place of character, at one time the main port for the sailing *thoniers* whose graveyard is the Blavet river. Concarneau is worth a visit and is a good place for re-victualling.

Approach and entrance

Whatever the direction of approach the buildings on the hill rising up at the back of the town are unmistakable. Steer for a position about half a mile W of the tree covered promontory Pointe de Cabellou.

The official leading line is Beuzec belfry, on the ridge a mile inland, in transit with La Croix lighthouse, on the sea front, bearing 028.5°. The belfry is not conspicuous and La Croix is undetectable in front of a new apartment block. Le Cochon green beacon tower is more easily identified and it is sufficient to leave it 150m to starboard and a red buoy and

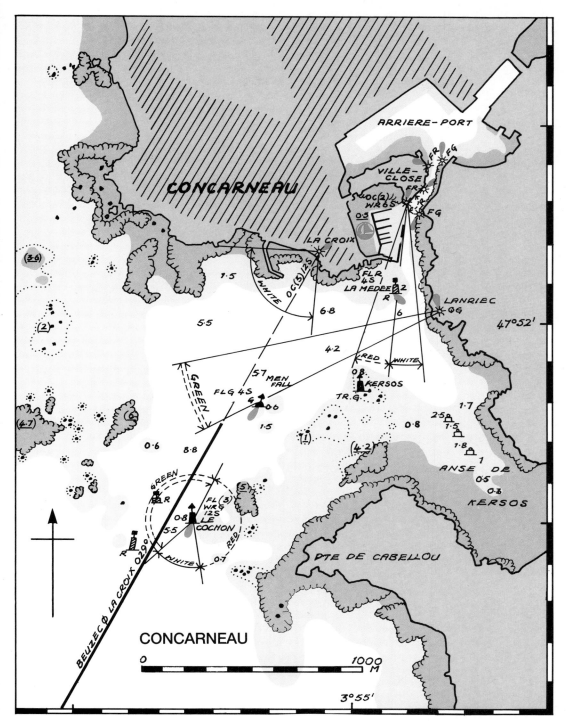

CONCARNEAU

Concarneau approach. The yachts ahead have turned to round the Men Fall buoy (stbd) to steer for the Lanriec mark. La Croix lighthouse is directly below the head of *Capelan*'s jib. It can be located from a distance as it is in front of the large A-framed, grey-roofed apartment block with white balconies. Beuzec belfry can be seen on the skyline behind the apartment block

red tower to port. Continue on this course for 600m to leave Men Fall (G) buoy to starboard. Round the buoy and steer 065° while attempting to identify the next mark, 'Maison Feu de Lanriec'. This is the end gable of a white house, among many white houses, with what appears to be a black window in the upper half. Binoculars may reveal the name in green under the window, or the mark can be identified for future reference on leaving Concarneau.

The channel is wide and, leaving Kersos G beacon tower 200m to starboard, it is sufficient to steer to leave La Médée R beacon tower to port to enter the Avant Port. A floating wavebreaker is connected to the head of the harbour wall and visitors can secure along the inner side before visiting the harbour office to arrange for a berth.

By night

Approach in the white sector of Le Cochon (**1**) and bring Beuzec and La Croix lights (**4**) in transit on 028.5° or thereabouts. Hold this course past Le Cochon and Men Fall buoy (**3**). As Men Fall buoy is passed, Lanriec Q G light (**5**) will open. Steer about 070° in this sector until the Passage de Lanriec light (**7**) on the Ville Close opens red and then turns white. When it turns from red to white steer about 000° in the white sector, leaving La Médée (**6**) to port. There should be sufficient light to see to round the floating wave breaker and secure to the inside or raft to another yacht. The channel to the inner

110

Concarneau, approaching Men Fall buoy (stbd). Lanriec Light is the black spot near the top of the white end-gable of a house to the right of the sail

harbour, past the Ville Close is marked by four lights, two fixed green to starboard and two fixed red to port.

Mooring

The charge for staying on the wavebreaker is half that for a pontoon berth, but there is no water or electricity and there is disturbance from the wash of passing vessels. The outside of the wavebreaker is used by ferries. If moving to a pontoon near the wall, beware at low water of the shallow rocky patch by the fuel berth.

A pontoon for large deep draught yachts may be installed on the north side of the Ville Close in 1989 and there are some rather crowded double-ended moorings in this area. However, the inner harbour is fairly noisy, dirty, rather unattractive and the quays are reserved for the fishing fleet.

There may be no places available in this popular harbour during the busy season. If so the Anse de Kersos offers shelter from the N through E to SW, but is exposed to the W and NW. To anchor, go in clear of the moorings as far as draught and tide will permit. There are no facilities and it is a long and exposed journey in the dinghy back to Concarneau.

Should the wind be westerly, Beg Meil is not far off and will provide shelter, or a berth can be found at Port La Forêt.

Facilities

There are showers, toilets and an excellent launderette in the Capitainerie, and water and

111

electricity on the pontoons. Two good sailmakers and chandlers are near the Avant Port, with fuel berth and slipways. There are workshops round the inner harbour where all kinds of repairs can be undertaken.

All the facilities of a large town are available: shops of all kinds, banks, hotels and every type of restaurant. A large supermarket is behind the fishmarket N of the inner harbour. Ice can be obtained from the fishmarket. Bonded stores, available to yachts proceeding directly to a foreign port, are best obtained using the dinghy from Fourniership, which is to be found in a street behind the eastern quay of the inner harbour.

There is a delightful beach a couple of kilometres NW of the port. The Musée de Pêche in the Ville Close is interesting. The annual Fête de Pêche des Filets Bleus is held on the second last Sunday of August: a cheerful, noisy festival of Breton costume, dancing, music and wrestling, with an illuminated procession of boats.

22 Pointe de Trévignon (passage notes)

The early part of the flood stream divides at this headland, one branch turning NW towards Concarneau and the Baie de la Forêt, the other turning E, flowing past Ile Verte and along the land. The latter part of the flood stream flows S and E round the point. This pattern is reversed on the ebb. Between the Pointe de Trévignon and Ile de Groix the stream is weak.

There is a wide passage between Ile Verte and Ile de Raguenès, although rocks extend $\frac{1}{4}$ mile off each island. East of La Pointe de Raguenès is a sandy beach off which there are a number of summer yacht moorings. The island gives some protection from westerly winds and a pleasant overnight anchorage can be found in about 4m outside the moorings.

Pointe de Trévignon, with its conspicuous semaphore station (disused), bearing roughly 020°

23 Aven and Bélon rivers, Port Manec'h

Charts: English BA 2352, 2645. Imray C38.
French SHOM 7031 P. ECM Navicarte 544.
High water: −0020 Brest, Index 0, MTL 2.8m.
MHWS 4.9m; MLWS 0.6m; MHWN 3.8m; MLWN 1.8m.
Tidal streams: The flood runs to the E and the ebb to the W at rates which are uncertain but not
very great. The streams in the rivers are stronger.
Depths: The approach from the SSW and S is deep, but coming from the SE inside Les Verrés
there is a shoal having 2.6m over it. The bars into both rivers vary a little but should be treated
as drying 1m.
Light: Pointe de Beg-ar-Vechen; Oc(4)WRG 12s, 11m, 14–11–11M. White tower, red lantern.

Both rivers are very pretty and offer good anchorage or mooring. Both offer good
restaurants, but not much in the way of shops except at Port Manec'h and Pont Aven; the
Bélon is famous for its oysters. Both have shallow bars, but whereas that of the Bélon is
impassable in bad weather, the Aven bar is sheltered and rarely breaks. It is perhaps for
this reason that the Aven is much more visited than the Bélon; given reasonable weather,
the Bélon is more attractive than the Aven.

Port Manec'h harbour slipway

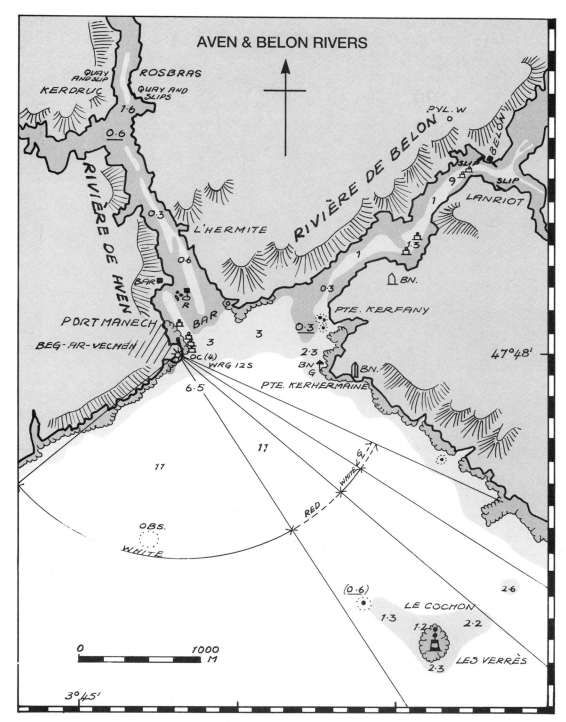

AVEN & BELON RIVERS

KERDRUC
QUAY AND SLIP
ROSBRAS
QUAY AND SLIPS
1·6
0·6

RIVIÈRE DE BELON
PYL. W

RIVIÈRE DE AVEN
BELON
SLIP
9
SLIP
LANRIOT
1
1·3

0·3
L'HERMITE

0·6
BAR
R
BN.

0·3
PTE. KERFANY
PORT MANECH
BAR
BAR
BEG-AR-VECHEN
OC (4)
WRG 12S
3
3
0·3
2·3
BN.
G
BN.
47°48'

PTE. KERHERMAINE

6·5

11
WHITE Ǫ
17
17
RED

OBS.
WHITE

(0·6)
2·6

LE COCHON
1·3
1·2
2·2

LES VERRÈS
2·3

0   1000
                    M

3°45'

MLWS 0.6m; MLWN 1.8m; −0020 Brest, Index 0, MTL 2.8m
Based on French Chart No. 5479, enlarged, with corrections (No. 7031 supersedes). Depths in metre
right hand margin in cables

115

Approach and entrance

The entrance is easy to locate by the Beg-ar-Vechen lighthouse at Port Manec'h on the west side of the entrance. On the east side there is a large white masonry beacon with a black vertical stripe on Pointe Kerhermain and a beacon (stbd) off the tip of the point.

Approach can be made from any direction having regard to the following dangers. To the W Les Cochons de Rousbicout lie a $\frac{1}{4}$ mile off a small inlet, dry 0.3m and are unmarked. To the SE Les Verrés dry 2.6m and are marked by a BRB tower, missing its topmark (1988). An outlier, Le Cochon, lies $\frac{1}{2}$ mile NW of the tower and dries 0.6m. There is a clear passage between Les Verrés and the land carrying a depth of 2.6m. Enter as convenient between Port Manec'h and the stbd beacon off Pointe de Kerhermain, giving them a berth of 100m.

By night
The white sectors of Port Manec'h (Beg-ar-Vechen) light (Oc(4)WRG 12s) lead in. The red sector covers Les Verrés and the green sector the rocks along the coast to the SE. Having made the entrance, a stranger should anchor or pick up a mooring off Port Manec'h and wait for daylight.

Port Manec'h

On the point below the lighthouse is a white building with a grey roof. The short Port Manec'h breakwater, marked at its head by a red rectangle with a white border, runs upstream from the point. Behind it is a small quay and slipway. East of the breakwater are a number of white visitors' mooring buoys with 2.5m or more for deep draught vessels. Upstream of them are a number of red mooring buoys. These provide double-ended moorings with heavy chain but are in shallower water and are only convenient for boats of less than 10m length. There is a charge for using the moorings. A shallow inlet runs west of the drying rocks marked by a red beacon at the Aven bar and shoals towards a sandy bathing beach. This provides a convenient anchorage, clear of the bathers, for shallow draught vessels that can take the ground. There is a pleasant café/bar west of the beach.

Port Manec'h from the SE

Land at the quay or on the beach. There is water on the quay and shops, restaurants, a hotel and a Logie de France in the village. There is no post office or bank and the nearest garage is nearly 3 miles away.

Aven river

The river in general is shallow and the position of the bar, which can dry 1m, changes periodically; in 1988 it was abreast of the red beacon (see chart, page 115). There are pools up as far as Kerdruc and Rosbras but these tend to be occupied by moorings for local boats. It is a pleasant river to explore near high water. A shallow draught vessel may proceed beyond Rosbras but must be prepared to take the ground.

Enter on a rising tide when the rocks marked by the red beacon are covered and one can expect 1.8m over the bar. Leave the beacon comfortably to port and proceed up the centre of the river. Half a mile up there is an inlet called Port l'Hermite on the eastern side. Here the river deepens for a little and 2m or more may be found. Moorings indicate the best places.

Farther up the river shoals to dry 0.6m and there is a large drying creek branching off to the west with a chateau at its mouth. Beyond the river narrows with the quays and slips of Kerdruc on the west bank and Rosbras on the east. Between them is a long, deep pool with mooring trots on either side in up to 3m at LWS. It is possible to dry out alongside the quays in mud at Kerdruc and shingle and mud at Rosbras or to borrow a vacant mooring. The river runs at up to three knots and it is essential to moor bow and stern.

Rosbras can offer a water tap on the upper slip, toilets and a bar/crêperie at a short walk. Kerdruc has a bar with food by the quay.

Above the quays the river widens and shoals. A channel marked sporadically by perches leads a further 2 miles to Pont Aven and is navigable by shallow draught vessels or a dinghy and outboard although there is much weed. There is a quay drying 2–3m against which a yacht may berth. The town has shops and restaurants and is a famous haunt of artists.

If the curves of the channel have been memorized, it is possible to return down river at night, armed with a good spotlight and making use of the cat's-eye reflectors attached to the perches. They should be in the shape of a square on one side and a circle on the other but this must be confirmed during the journey up river.

Bélon river

Make a position about 100m W of the beacon (stbd) off Pointe de Kerhermain; that is, about 200m W of the point itself. Thence steer about 010° for the next headland, Pointe Kerfany, on the east side of the mouth. This course, passing over three small rocks awash at datum, leaves the bar, drying about 0.3m, to port and a bay with a popular bathing beach to starboard.

On arrival off Pointe Kerfany keep close to it, as the shore is clean except for rocks immediately edging it. Thence steer towards the NW side of the river, leaving a concrete fish-tank to starboard and heading well W of the hut on the shore shown in the

Rosbras on the Aven river near LW

Looking upstream to Bélon on the Bélon river

Bélon river entrance. The white beacon with vertical black stripe is on the Pointe Kerhermain. Behind the sail is a sandy cove, and the river entrance is far left

photograph. This leads up a channel with about 0.3m, but it is narrow, so that it is not easy to find the best water. As the tide rises there is much more latitude.

Having reached the NW side of the river steer back towards the headland forming the SW side of a large bay. Steer to leave the headland fairly close to starboard and follow round well into the bay, leaving to port the inner bar, which projects from the NW side of the river. There are stakes marking oyster beds on the bar, but there are similar stakes planted in the bay and on both sides of the river so that it is not easy to distinguish the channel. Once past the bar the channel leads straight up river, keeping rather to the E side. Half a mile on the river turns to starboard and on the port hand side of the curve in comparatively still, deep water (9m) are three large white metal mooring buoys for visitors, suitable for rafting.

Further on is a drying slip with a fish restaurant beside a quay. On the starboard bank is a long slip with the lower end marked by a green beacon and the upper end leading onto the curving quay of Lanroit where there is a restaurant but no shops. Here the river is wide with many fishing boat and yacht moorings but it soon shoals and above Lanroit, where it dries, there are extensive oyster beds and yachts should not proceed much beyond the visitors' moorings.

Near high water it is possible to cross the outer bar rather than enter by the channel; however, fresh winds from the S or SW quickly bring swell making the bar impassable and entry by the channel inadvisable.

Charts: English BA 2352, 2645. Imray C38.

French SHOM 7031 P. ECM Navicarte 544.

High water: −0020 Brest, Index 0, MTL 2.8m.

MHWS 4.9m; MLWS 0.6m; MHWN 3.8m; MLWN 1.8m.

Tidal streams: Outside the flood sets to the E, the ebb to the W, rates uncertain, but probably not exceeding 1.5 knots at springs. There is some stream in Merrien creek but little in Brigneau.

Depths: There is 1.7m just outside the entrance to Brigneau and 1m outside the entrance to Merrien. Brigneau dries 1–2m from the quay to the head of the harbour and 0.3m can be found at Merrien.

Lights:

1. Brigneau mole head; Oc(2)WRG 6s, 7m, 12–9–9M. White column, red top with name in white.
2. Merrien; Dir Q R, 26m, 7M, vis 004°–009°. White square tower, red top.

Brigneau

The port of Brigneau lies in a small inlet about 3 miles SE of Port Manec'h. In onshore weather the swell gets right in and it is untenable, but in fine weather it is an interesting and pretty place to visit. The quay dries out; in very fine weather one can stay afloat at the entrance, anchored or on a buoy.

Brigneau, the quay

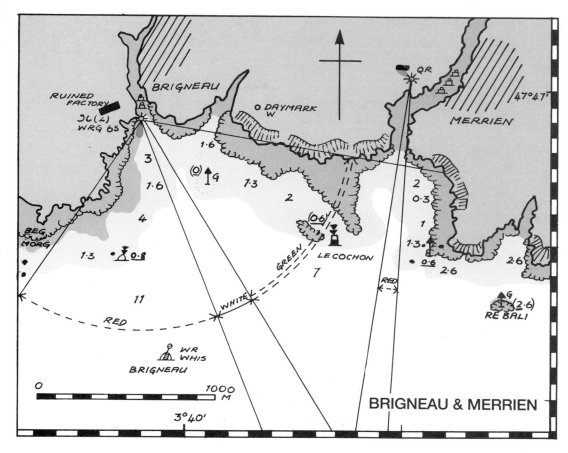

Map labels:

BRIGNEAU

RUINED FACTORY

JL(4) WRG 6S

O DAYMARK W

QR

MERRIEN

47°47'

3

1.6

(0) G

1.6

1.3

4

2

BEG MORG

1.3

0.8

GREEN

(0.6)

LE COCHON

2

0.3

1

1.3

0.6

2.6

2.6

11

WHITE

7

RED

RED

G (2.6)

RE BALI

RED

WR WHIS

BRIGNEAU

0   1000 M

3°40'

BRIGNEAU & MERRIEN

MLWS 0.6m; MLWN 1.8m; −0020 Brest, Index 0, MTL 2.8m
Based on French Chart No. 5479, enlarged, with corrections (No. 7031 supersedes). Depths in metres; right hand margin in cables

Drying visitors' moorings, Merrien, at HW

At the beginning of the twentieth century Brigneau was a busy sardine port. Now activity is divided between a sailing school and a small fishing fleet, with a 'Cooperative des Pêcheurs et de Plaisance'.

Approach and entrance

The point to the west of Brigneau falls away to the low rocky spit of Beg Morg with Les Cochons de Beg Morg (drying 0.3m) 400m off the point. Three-quarters of a mile due south of the entrance is an unlit RW landfall whistle buoy ('Brigneau'). From this point the port can be identified by the large ruined factory building on the west side, with the breakwater below. Steer due north for a point E of the breakwater, leaving to port a small south cardinal buoy, indicating the position of a S card beacon destroyed in October 1987 on a rock drying 0.6m. Leave 200m to starboard a green beacon on a rock awash at LWS and bear to port to enter the harbour, leaving the breakwater head, marked by a red rectangle with a white border, to port.

A leading line is provided on 335° using the Brigneau light structure as front marker and for rear marker, to the right of a white house with blue shutters, a white open tubular frame with a wire mesh rectangle at the top which is not conspicuous.

There are two trots of visitors' moorings on the E side of the harbour and one can either borrow a mooring or, if tide and draught permit, secure to the quay on the W side without interfering with the fishing boats. Shallow draught vessels can continue up harbour to the inner end of the quay and a wall, above which the construction of a wet basin is projected.

By night

Entrance can be effected without difficulty in calm weather by keeping in the white sector of the mole head light (**1**) on 335° until close to and then bearing to starboard to claim a mooring with the aid of a spotlight, or anchoring outside in 8m to starboard of the line, having passed the starboard beacon and with due attention to fishing buoys.

Brigneau. The factory ruin left of the entrance makes a good landmark

Facilities

There are water taps and electric points along the quay. Fuel is available (0700–1200 and 1300–2000) in the summer. (telephone 98 71 02 21). There is a village shop and cafés.

Merrien

Particularly for bilge-keelers, or yachts equipped with legs, Merrien is a delightful place to visit. In calm conditions deep draught vessels may anchor in 3m or more or secure to a large white metal buoy in the bay outside. Inside the entrance is a wide pool with a flat sandy bottom which should be taken to dry 0.3m. Above the pool the river narrows and turns to starboard, leading to the village on the E bank and a trot of visitors' moorings where shallow draught vessels can expect to lie afloat on most tides and in complete shelter.

Approach and entrance

The entrance is easy to identify from the west, ¾ mile E of Brigneau. From the east, the entrance will open after passing a headland topped by some holiday houses, white with grey roofs, 1¾ miles W of Doëlan.

The chart on page 121 shows the dangers; to the W a spit of rocks terminating in the ubiquitous Cochon whose cardinal S beacon was destroyed and is replaced by a small conical buoy with a card S topmark. To the E rocks extend for 100m out along the side of the headland, marked by a green starboard beacon somewhat inshore of their SW tip. 500m further E is an isolated rock, Roche Bali, marked (1988) by a rusty pole, without its green conical topmark, lying 300m off a small creek.

Port de Merrien. The leading light tower is directly over the deep water mooring buoy with house gable behind, bearing 005°. The pool behind the buoy has a flat sandy bottom, drying 0.3m. A turn to starboard at the head of the pool leads to Merrien quay and the drying moorings

From a position due south of the entrance to the river the white light tower will be seen at the head of the pool, backed by a large grey-roofed house with a gable on the E end. Keep the light tower on a bearing of 005° to enter the river or to anchor or moor outside.

At night

Entry to the pool is possible, though not advisable, keeping strictly in the narrow red sector of the light (**2**) on 005°. Should the light disappear it will be hard to make the correct course alteration to bring it back.

Anchorage

For a short visit, with enough water, the pool inside the mouth is inviting, with a sandy bottom. Keep at least 50m offshore in the outer half as the sides are rocky. There are steps leading down on the starboard side of the entrance to a flat stone jetty, submerged at high water and marked by a green beacon. After the sharp turn to starboard there is another landing place on the port side, marked by a red beacon and the visitors' buoys and Merrien quay and slipways are on the starboard side of the channel. Do not proceed beyond the quay as the river is full of oyster beds.

Facilities

Water and electricity are available on the quay. Fuel is available 0700–1200 and 1300–2000 in the summer. There is a restaurant up the hill, and shops at some distance inland.

25 Doëlan

Charts: English BA 2352, 2645. Imray C38.
       French SHOM 7031 P. ECM Navicarte 544.
High water: −0200 Brest, Index 0, MTL 2.8m.
  MHWS 4.9m; MLWS 0.6m; MHWN 3.8m; MLWN 1.8m.
Tidal streams: Outside, the flood sets to the east, the ebb to the west, rates uncertain but probably not exceeding 1 knot at springs. There is little stream in the harbour.
Depths: There is 3m just inside the breakwater where the fishing boats lie. Inside this the harbour shoals rapidly and the quays dry 0.7–1.5m.
Lights:
  1. Leading lights on 014°:
      Front: Oc(2+1)WG 12s, 20m, 13-10M. White tower, green band and lantern.
      Rear: Q R, 27m, 9M. White tower, red band and lantern.

The port of Doëlan, though larger than the other small ports on this coast, is still very small. It supports a small but active fishing fleet and there are a number of yachts which take the ground at the back of the harbour, in shelter provided by a bend in the creek. The outer harbour is exposed to the S and entry should not be attempted except in settled offshore weather. It is a pretty little place and quite a resort of artists.

Doëlan. The port hand breakwater head is between the two tall leading lighthouses. The front lighthouse is white with a green band and top, the rear is white with red band and top (leading line 014°)

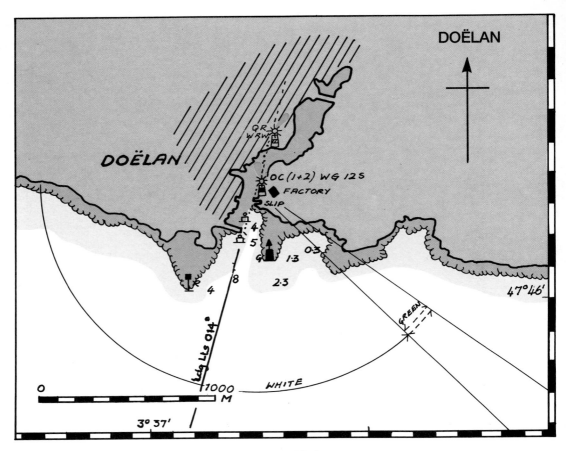

DOÈLAN

MLWS 0.6m; MLWN 1.8m; −0020 Brest, Index 0, MTL 2.8m
Based on French Chart No. 5479, enlarged, with corrections (No. 7031 supersedes). Depths in metres;
right hand margin in cables

Approach and entrance

The port is easily recognized by the conspicuous factory buildings with a slender chimney
on the east side of the entrance and the two lighthouses that provide the leading line.
Enter with the lighthouses in line bearing 014°. The transit leaves a small red conical
buoy (replacing the beacon destroyed in October 1987) to port and a green beacon tower
to starboard.

By night

Approach and enter with the leading lights (1, 2) in line on 014°. Coming from the
direction of Lorient, a vessel can avoid the rocks SE of Le Pouldu (Le Grand et le Petit
Cochon!) by keeping out of the green sector of the front light (**1**) which covers them.

Mooring

There is no room to anchor and lie afloat as the entrance is taken up with heavy double

126

Doëlan, looking up the inner, drying, harbour

ended moorings to enable the fishing vessels to ride out rough weather. The fishermen are friendly to visitors and it may be possible to borrow one of these moorings or to raft with other visitors to a large white metal buoy or 'Tonne à Flot' with a rail round its edge. There is one of these just outside and one inside the breakwater on the W side of the entrance. For a yacht that can take the ground it should be possible to borrow a mooring up harbour.

Alternatively one can dry out at one of the quays. Near the entrance to the harbour there is a landing slip on each side; these were marked by starboard and port beacons, of which the port hand one, situated a few metres inside the end of the slip, was destroyed and presented a hazard in 1988. The quays lie inshore of these slips. Local advice should be obtained before drying out. The quay on the port hand is not suitable as the bottom slopes outwards. The first two quays on the starboard hand should, however, be suitable, the bottom drying about 1.5m.

Facilities
Water and electricity are available on the quays. There are bars and restaurants on both sides and provisions may be obtained from two bars on the W bank where there is a good chandler S of the Hotel Café Du Port. The nearest shops are at Clohars Carnoet 1½ miles inland.

Charts: English BA 2352, 2645. Imray C38.
　　　　　French SHOM 7031 P. ECM Navicarte 544.
High water: −0200 Brest, Index 0, MTL 2.8m.
　　MHWS 4.9m; MLWS 0.6m; MHWN 3.8m; MLWN 1.8m.
Tidal streams: Outside the flood sets to the E, the ebb to the west; the streams are weak. The
　　streams in the river are fierce, up to 6 knots springs.
Depths: The bottom is sandy and both the position and depth of the channel are liable to change.
　　Without prior exploration it should be regarded as drying 2m, but there is more water when it
　　can be found and there is a deep pool above Le Pouldu.
Lights: There are none. Keep well off at night.

Le Pouldu, at the mouth of the Laita or de Quimperlé river, has a character quite different from its neighbouring ports. If we can liken the Aven to a miniature Salcombe and Doëlan to a miniature Dartmouth, here we have a miniature Teignmouth. It has a much more open valley, shifting sands and searing tides, and because of these it is much less frequented by cruising yachts.

A visit is only practicable in fine settled weather as the bar breaks heavily when the wind is onshore and, once inside, a change of wind can make departure impossible for several days. Exploration is an interesting exercise in a bilge-keeler but can be disturbing in a deep draught vessel and should only be undertaken at mean tides as there is scarcely

Le Pouldu, looking downstream from the anchorage

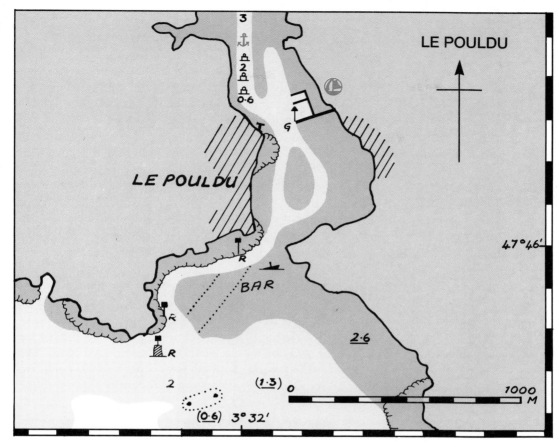

MLWS 0.6m; MLWN 1.8m; −0020 Brest, Index 0, MTL 2.8m
Based on French Chart No. 5479, enlarged, with corrections (No. 7031 supersedes). Depths in metres;
right hand margin in cables

enough water at neaps and the tides are uncomfortably strong at springs. At low water
the anchorage outside is a deep peaty colour, justifying the name Le Pouldu (the Black
Anchorage).

Approach

The entrance is not difficult to make out from a reasonable distance; 1 mile to the west is a
group of grey roofed holiday cottages behind a sandy beach. The land then rises with low
cliffs and a rocky cove, the eastern headland of which forms the western side of the
entrance to the river. The town of Le Pouldu lies behind the cove. The eastern side of the
entrance is low and sandy.

Approaching from the south east, leave Le Grand Cochon S cardinal beacon (topmark
missing, 1988) well to starboard and, keeping a mile off shore, follow a long curving sandy
beach, broken by rocky outcrops, to the cliffy headland, on the top of which is a white
house with a round tower, the former Fenoux pilot's station.

The final approach is made with the headland bearing 010° to avoid rocks drying 0.6m and a shoal drying 1.3m 400m to the SSE.

Entrance

Without previous reconnaisance near LW or local advice, entry should only be attempted in calm conditions shortly before HW. Under these conditions the flood stream will not dictate the course followed, but there may be no indication where the channel lies. It can only be misleading to give precise directions as the channel shifts frequently and unpredictably. In general a sandy spit runs out from the east side of the entrance as shown on the chart on page 129.

The main channel follows the west bank and is marked by the red beacon tower at the entrance followed by a port hand beacon pole and, after curving to starboard, a second port hand beacon pole near the end of a small rocky spit. In 1988 this was the channel, the beacons needed repainting and a group of fishing boats was anchored close upstream of the first beacon pole in apparently still water. However, the strong tides tend to cut through the spit, so that the channel may follow the dotted line shown on the chart, and a steep-sided sandy island may build up which can on occasions come close to blocking the under-cliff channel.

Leave the second beacon pole 40m to port and keep this distance off to avoid a rocky shelf. The river opens out with a wide shallow bay to starboard and the protecting breakwater of a marina suitable for small yachts will be seen ahead on the east bank. The best water is more likely to be found by following the west bank until the next point is reached, with two hotels and a small jetty. Thence one can cross to enter the marina or

Le Pouldu entrance. Approach the red tower from the SW, round it to leave the beacon pole, which has lost all its red paint (1988), fairly close to port

continue up river to find deep water (2m or more) for anchoring along the west bank above some mooring buoys and just downstream of a shallow creek. The holding appears to be good in spite of the stream and some weed. There is a drying sandbank in the middle of the river and there are many small craft moorings on the eastern side and in the bay downstream.

The river is navigable at HW up to Quimperlé but a bridge with 10m clearance 2 miles from the entrance prevents the passage of masted vessels.

Facilities

The pontoon on the west bank is for fishermen, but a dinghy landing is permitted and there are two hotels close by with Le Pouldu and its shops 1 mile down the road. On the east bank by the marina are restaurants catering for a camping site and a large supermarket is situated a few minutes' walk round the bay towards the entrance.

Showers are available at hotel on west bank, and water is probably available from the hotels and restaurants.

Charts: English BA 2352, 2646. Imray C38.

       French SHOM 7031 P. ECM Navicarte 544.

High water: −0020 Brest, Index 0, MTL 2.8m.

     MHWS 5.0m; MLWS 0.6m; MHWN 3.9m; MLWN 1.7m.

Tidal streams: Off the harbour the flood runs to the E and the ebb to the W, spring rates $1\frac{3}{4}$ knots. There is no stream in the harbour.

Depths: 3m abreast the breakwater, shoaling steadily towards the shore.

Lights: There are no lights to assist entry at night.

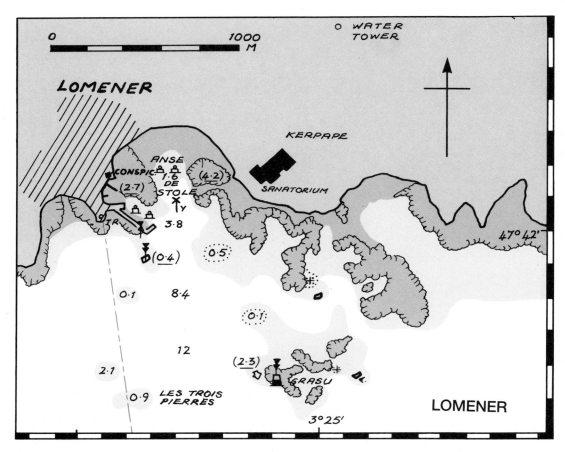

MLWS 0.6m; MLWN 1.7m; −0020 Brest, Index 0, MTL 2.8m
Based on French Chart No. 5912 with corrections (No. 7031 supersedes). Depths in metres; right hand margin in cables. Anchoring prohibited W of line

Lomener, from the end of the mole. The prominent building helps identification

The port of Lomener, with the adjacent Anse de Stole, is a small harbour on the north side of the channel between Ile de Groix and the mainland. It is exposed to the S and would be uncomfortable in fresh winds, and dangerous in gales, from the S. However, a considerable fleet of fishing vessels and yachts lie on moorings, both in the harbour and in the Anse de Stole, so the shelter must be sufficient for normal summer conditions.

It is sheltered from the N and in fine settled weather, when the *vent solaire* is in evidence, it provides good shelter for a night's stop when on passage; better indeed than Port Tudy opposite, where the excitement begins in the early hours of the morning when the wind freshens from the NE.

Approach and entrance

The harbour is not difficult to identify. It lies about half way along the coast forming the northern side of the channel north of Ile de Groix, with a very prominent block of flats behind the breakwater (see photo). The approach is between the rocks round the Grasu S cardinal beacon tower and the shoal of Les Trois Pierres (0.9m) if the tide makes the latter relevant. Steer for the block of flats on a bearing of 335°. A S cardinal beacon marks a rock (drying 0.4m) 200m SSE of the breakwater head and a W cardinal beacon marks Roliou just S of the breakwater head. Make the final approach with the right-hand end of the breakwater in line with the flats.

The chart on page 132 shows the drying, rocky spurs on both sides of the bay and the yellow beacon surrounded by a circle of small yellow buoys in the centre of the harbour where the fishermen store their fish-tanks. Anchor where space and soundings permit, or borrow a mooring by arrangement, making sure that there is room to swing. The beaches behind the breakwater and in the Anse de Stole are excellent for drying out. There is a landing slip on the spur inside the harbour. Avoid the breakwater wall as there are vicious rocks at its foot.

Facilities

Water and electricity on the quay. All the ordinary shops of a small seaside resort. Shellfish can be bought from the fishermen on the quay. There is no post office.

28 Lorient, with Kernével, Port Louis, the Blavet river and Locmalo

Charts: English BA 2352, 2646, 304. Imray C38.

French SHOM 7031 P, 6470 if available. ECM Navicarte 544.

High water: −0020 Brest, Index 0, MTL 2.8m.

MHWS 5.0m; MLWS 0.6m; MHWN 3.9m; MLWN 1.7m.

Tidal streams: Outside, between the Ile de Groix and the shore, the flood sets E and SE, the ebb W and NW, spring rates $1\frac{3}{4}$ knots. The main flood and ebb into and out of the harbour run through the Passe du Sud, spring rate $1\frac{1}{2}$ knots. In the Passe de l'Ouest there is a slack for two hours, starting at HW, the spring rates of the flood and ebb are 1 knot. The strongest streams occur in the narrows off the citadel of Port Louis, where the spring rate is $3\frac{1}{2}$ knots; on extreme tides the ebb may reach $4\frac{1}{2}$ knots if the rivers are in flood. The stream in the narrows sets to the W on to La Jument and Le Pot during the last of the flood and the whole of the ebb. Once through the narrows the streams are weaker, spring rates everywhere less than 2 knots. Generally the streams flow in the direction of the channels, but just to the north of the narrows the stream is rotary anticlockwise, the main strength being NE $1\frac{1}{2}$ knots 4 to 3 hours before HW and SSW 1 knot 4 to 5 hours after HW.

Depths: The main channels are deep. Enough water can be found in all the usual anchorages, except Locmalo, for yachts of normal draught. In the Blavet 3.5m or more can be found at half tide up to Hennebont. The Baie de Locmalo has 3m just inside the entrance, but as little as 0.6m off the pier at Locmalo.

Lights:

Passe de l'Ouest:

1. Leading lights 057°;

Front, Les Soeurs; Dir Q W, ?m, 13M. Tower, RW horizontal bands.

Rear, Port Louis; Dir Q W, ?m, 18M. Rectangle, RW horizontal bands.

2. Les Trois Pierres; Q RG, 11m, 6M. Tower, BW horizontal bands.

Passe de la Sud:

3. Bastresse Sud buoy (stbd); Q G, Bell.

4. Les Errants buoy (port); Fl(2)R 6s.

5. Leading lights 008.5°;

Front, Halles du Port de Pêche; Sync Q R. White rectangle, fluorescent red vertical stripe.

Rear, La Perrière; Sync Q R. Fluorescent red rectangle, white vertical stripe.

Port:

6. La Citadelle; Oc G 4s, 6m, 5M. Green tower.

7. La Petite Jument; Oc R 4s, 5m, 6M. Red tower.

8. Ile Saint-Michel, leading lights, 016.5°.

Front; Dir Oc(3)G 12s, 8m, 16M. White tower, green top.

Rear; Sync Dir Oc(3)G 12s, 14m, 16M. White tower, green top.

9. Leading lights on submarine base, 350°.
    Kéroman, front; Dir Oc(2)R 6s, 25m, 17M. RW horizontal bands.
    Kéroman, rear; Sync Dir Oc(2)R 6s, 31m, 17M. RW horizontal bands.
    Radio beacon, 47° 45.7'N, 03° 26.4'W, call LOR, 294.2 kHz, 80M contin.

The city of Lorient is a combination of naval base, fishing harbour, commercial port and yachting centre. The naval base is in the north of the harbour, but to the south of the city the submarine pens remain as a reminder of the Second World War. Bombing devastated the city during the war, but it is now rebuilt and is a thriving place. It is the principal fishing port in Brittany; the fishing vessels, ranging in size up to the largest deep-sea stern trawlers, have the exclusive use of the Port de Pêche at the south end of the city, to the east of the submarine pens. Further to the north, at Kergroise, are the quays used by commercial vessels.

Port Louis, situated near the harbour entrance on the east side, also has a fishing fleet. It is named after Louis XIII, and the fortifications were created by Richelieu.

The principal yachting centres are: the new marina at Kernével, opened May 1988, near the entrance on the west side, Port Louis opposite and the Port de Commerce in the centre of the city. Pontoons have been and are being installed at several sites on the east side of the harbour and a visitor will have no difficulty in finding a berth, or borrowing a mooring.

The Port de Commerce in the centre of the city was the operational base of the French East India Company and it is from this that the city takes its name. There is still a very limited commercial activity here – the ferries for Port Louis and the Ile de Groix start here and sand dredgers unload at the quays – but much of it is is now devoted to yachting. Near the entrance there are pontoons and moorings for a considerable number of locally based boats and the wet dock has been restored as a yacht harbour. It is reserved primarily for visiting yachts, for which it offers a convenient berth in the heart of the city.

Lorient, looking up harbour from the Citadel narrows. Le Cochon (RGR) tower is on the left, with the Submarine Pens to the right of it. Ile St Michel far right; the silo over the left hand end of the island is conspicuous from seaward (see p. 139)

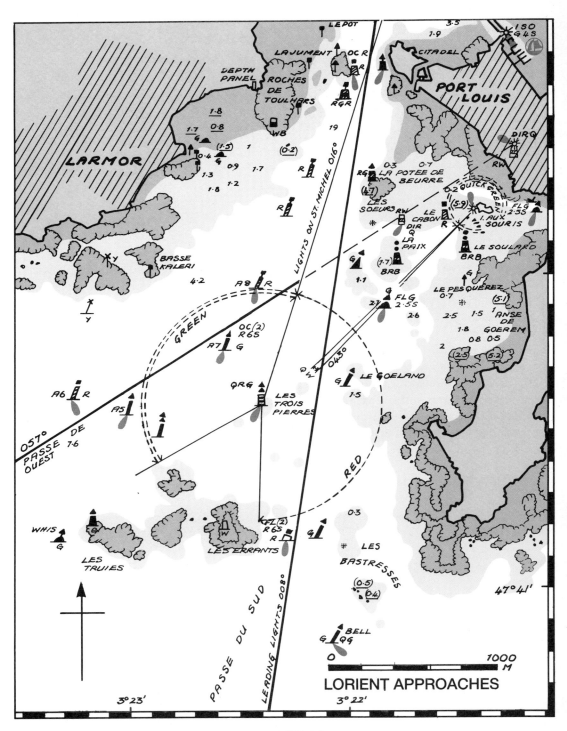

MLWS 0.6m; MLWN 1.7m; −0020 Brest, Index 0, MTL 2.8m
Based on French Chart No. 6470 with corrections (No. 7031 supersedes). Depths in metres; right hand
margin in cables

Approaching Lorient yacht harbour in the old Port de Commerce. The buoy (port) to the right of the picture must be left to port on turning in. (See p. 141)

Lorient is a good place for changing crew as communications are good and there is plenty to explore if one has a day in hand.

It is possible to go up the river Blavet to Hennebont, whence with a draught not exceeding 0.8m one can enter the Brittany canal system. After going up the Blavet to Pontivy one climbs over the hills and down to Redon, whence one can reach St Malo, Nantes or the sea via the Vilaine.

Approach

The approaches to Lorient are partly sheltered by the Ile de Groix, some 4 miles to the SW. They are well marked and the huge white grain silo in the commercial port is conspicuous. There are two channels: the Passe du Sud and the Passe de l'Ouest. For a first visit, not all the leading marks are easy to identify and the front marker on the roof of the Port de Pêche wharf building can be obscured by a large trawler. The numerous buoys and beacons make navigation by day easy, though the plethora of lights can confuse at night.

Changes were made in 1988 to the channels, buoys and leading marks. A small craft channel was established W of the main channel past the Citadel for access to the large marina opened at Kernével. At night use the main channel and beware of 'Le Pot' unlit port hand buoy. This was actually illuminated by searchlight by a kindly lookout on the Citadel for a disorientated British yachtsman in June 1988!

The larger ships using the port have little room to manoeuvre in the channels and all yachts should get out of their way in good time. Ships above a certain size carry a sphere by day (a red light at night) at the yard arm or masthead and these have absolute right of way over all other vessels. Sailing vessels must not hinder powered vessels of over 20m overall length.

Passe du Sud

The approach to this channel lies NE of the E end of Ile de Groix and ½ mile W of Pointe de Gavres on the mainland. In good visibility, a group of some six tower blocks and a water tower are conspicuous to the W of the entrance and the tall white grain silo is conspicuous to the E.

Lorient approach channel, looking east into the Baie de Locmalo entrance (centre). The leading marks for the Passe de l'Ouest were changed in 1988. They are now the red tower with white band on Les Soeurs rocks and a red and white panel onshore (to the left of Les Soeurs tower). Leading line 057°. (See p. 137)

Steer for the Citadel on 010° until the leading marks are made out, or the yacht's position is confirmed by the channel buoys. The first buoy is Les Bastresses S (lat stbd, Q Fl G, bell). To port will be seen Les Errants beacon tower (white with black square topmark) with a statue beside it and further up channel the conspicuous beacon tower Les Trois Pierres with BW horizontal bands. This is also left to port, after passing between Les Bastresses N (lat stbd by) and Les Errants (lat port by). The main channel, the Passe de l'Ouest, is then joined and is well marked to the Citadel.

The day leading marks bearing 008.5° are on and behind the Fish Market Hall at the S end of Lorient; the front mark is a rectangular white board with a fluorescent red vertical stripe and the rear mark a fluorescent red board with a white vertical stripe. If these are not obscured by a trawler, they will lead up the channel and through the narrows.

Traffic signals, on the simplified system, are made for large ships only, from the signal station on the Citadel of Port Louis. No yacht should enter the narrows when one of these signals is shown.

By night

The leading lights on 008.5° ((**5**) sync dir Q R) have an intensified sector extending out beyond both sides of the channel. Do not assume that, if you are in the intensified sector, you are in the channel as some of the buoys are unlit. The transit should be maintained through the narrows where La Citadelle ((**6**) Oc G 4s) and La Jument ((**7**) Oc R 4s) mark the port and starboard sides. The line passes close to Les Errants buoy (port) ((**4**) Fl(2)R 6s) and to Le Pot (lat port by, unlit). For movement by night in the harbour see below.

Passe de l'Ouest

This channel is entered ¾ mile S of the conspicuous Grasu tower (card S). New leading marks have been established. The outer mark is a tower on 'les Soeurs' rocks, red top, white centre and red base. The rear marker has horizontal bands of fluorescent red (top), white, red, white (base). These are in transit on a bearing of 057° true and lateral buoys have been established to mark the new channel which is slightly north of the original line. Hold this transit until Les Trois Pierres beacon tower (BW horizontal bands) is abaft the beam to starboard. The narrows will then open and when the two white towers with green tops on the west side of Ile St Michel come into line bearing 016°, you may then: (1) turn onto this transit to lead through the narrows, (2) carry on and enter by the 008° transit of the Passe du Sud; or (3) enter the *Chenal Secondaire* on the west side of the narrows.

By night

The intensified sector of the leading lights ((**1**) sync dir Q.W) on 057° covers the channel and all the new lateral buoys are lit. While following up this transit, identify other relevant lights, particularly Les Trois Pierres ((**2**) Q G on this bearing) to starboard as the turn to port is made when it is abaft the beam. Look for La Citadelle ((**6**) Oc G 4s) and La Petite Jument ((**7**) Oc R 4s) marking the narrows and when the leading lights ((**5**) sync dir Q R) behind them are in line bearing 008.5°, turn onto this transit to pass through.

Chenal Secondaire

This channel is unlit and passes over Le Cochon (dries 1m) but is convenient, given sufficient water, when making for Kernével marina when the narrows are congested. Illuminated depth indicator panels are situated on shore at each end of the channel as an experiment; 1m must be subtracted from the reading to allow for Le Cochon.

A spar buoy (RGR, preferred channel to stbd) marks the entrance to the channel. Leaving this buoy to starboard, the channel is seen to be marked by red and green beacons up to Le Cochon beacon tower (RGR) to be left to starboard, after which the main channel is re-entered.

Proceeding up the harbour

Passing through the narrows by the main channel, when Le Cochon beacon tower is abeam, the submarine pens will be seen with two sets of leading lights on the roof. The green pair are for deep draught vessels and the red pair are for general use. At night the green lights are switched on only at the pilot's request.

By day

Steer 349° with the RW marks in transit.

By night

Ignoring the Oc(3)G 12s leading lights on Ile St Michel (**8**) the Port de Pêche transit (**5**) leads over the Banc du Turc, SW of Ile St Michel. After passing La Citadelle, turn to port when the submarine base lights ((**9**) sync dir Oc(2)R 6s) are in transit on 350°.

The entrance to Kernével marina is ½ mile NNE of the Citadelle on the W side of the harbour.

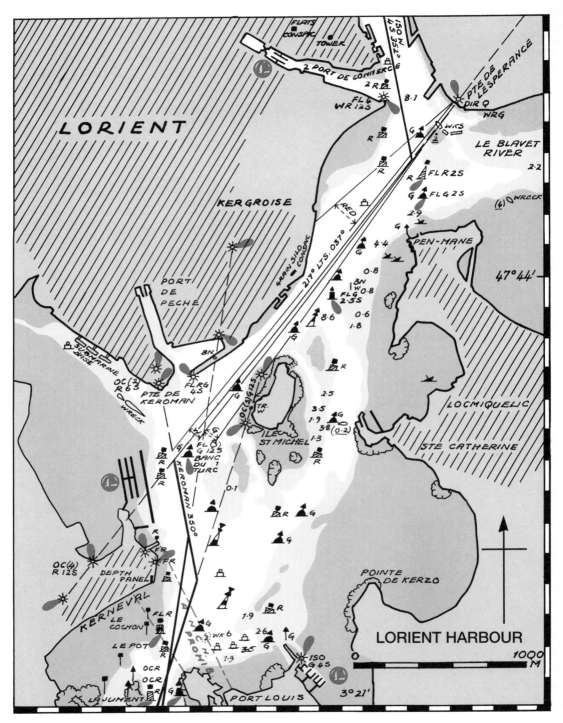

MLWS 0.6m; MLWN 1.7m; −0020 Brest, Index 0, MTL 2.8m
Based on French Chart No. 6470 with corrections (No. 7031 supersedes). Depths in metres; right hand
margin in cables

Continuing up harbour
By day
Follow the buoyed channel, leaving Ile St Michel to starboard, the fishing port quay and the grain silo to port and turn to port to enter the Port de Commerce or to starboard to enter the Blavet river.

By night
The white sector of the Dir Q WRG light on Pointe de l'Espérance leads past Ile St Michel on 037°, passing rather close to unlit channel buoys. For the Port de Commerce, when the Iso WRG 4s light on the Port Militaire bridge turns from red to white, steer for it on 352°. Identify the light (Fl(4) 12s) on the S side of the Port de Commerce entrance and turn in, avoiding an unlit port-hand buoy.

The entrance to the Blavet channel is marked by lateral buoys (Fl G 4s and Fl R 4s). Entry at night is not advised without previous experience of the river in daylight.

Port de Plaisance Kernével
This marina was opened in June 1988 with 400 pontoon berths, half with 3m and the rest with 2m depth.

Entrance
A line of floating wave-breakers secured to piles protects the marina which can be entered by day or night from the south by leaving a red beacon (Fl R 1.2s) to port. The pile at the S end of the wave-breaker with a yellow top and a light (Fl Y 2.5s) is left to starboard on entry.

Facilities
Fuel berth, slipway for hauling out. Showers and toilets in the Capitainerie, which is a large late nineteenth century mansion. There are a few shops and restaurants within walking distance in Kernével. Two large supermarkets are situated about 1 mile NW round the bay and there is a frequent bus service to Lorient, where chandlers, workshops and engineers can be found. The marina staff are most helpful.

Port Louis
There are a large number of moorings in the shoaling bay to the east of the Citadel and it is usually possible to find one vacant in sufficient water. If anchoring, avoid the eastern side of the bay where there are rocks and wrecks drying 3m and a ruined slipway.

East of the ruined slipway is a pier. A green beacon at its head marks the starboard side of a channel leading into some pontoons in the Anse Driasker where it may be possible to find a vacant berth with 2m. Keep in the channel close to the pier as there are obstructions in the bay. When visited in July 1988 a number of new pontoon berths were observed in bays on the east bank up to the mouth of the Blavet, but the facilities ashore were not investigated. Port Louis itself is a sleepy eighteenth-century town with all ordinary facilities and a recommended Hôtel du Commerce.

Port de Commerce

The wet dock is a fully pontooned yacht harbour in pleasant surroundings, as the roads are well set back. As entry past the bridge and sill is only possible for 1 hour either side of HW springs and less at neaps, it may be more convenient, for a short stay, to use one of the waiting pontoon berths just outside the dock. It will also be cheaper as there is a charge for opening the bridge. Report to the Bureau du Port on arrival.

The pontoons on the S side of the Avant Port are for local boats and just past them is the Ile de Groix ferry berth. The Avant Port is dredged to 3m with 2.5m at the waiting pontoons and 2.3m in the wet basin.

Facilities

Everything is at hand for the wet dock and the waiting pontoons.

Available are: water and electricity on the pontoons; fuel berth; showers and toilets in the office building; shops, banks, main post office, chandlery; shipyards and sailmakers, slipway, crane or travel lift in the Avant Port. Bonded stores are available from one of the ships chandlers in the Port de Pêche.

Hennebont on the Blavet river. *Capelan* is secured to the pontoon, where a six-hour stay is permitted. Visitors' moorings are just downstream

Communications
The rail and bus services for Lorient are good and there are flights to Paris from Quimper.

Le Blavet river
The channel is buoyed or beaconed up to the road bridge (headroom 28m) $2\frac{1}{2}$ miles from the river mouth, with extensive mudbanks on the south side. The depth under the bridge at LW neaps was 5m. Above the bridge the river narrows and winds a further 4 miles to Hennebont, passing under a second road and a rail bridge with plenty of clearance. The depth was found to be never less than 3.5m on a rising tide arriving at Hennebont at HW−3 or half tide. The river is a sad graveyard for sailing tunnymen but is otherwise attractive with plenty of bird-life. There are many possible anchorages on the way up to Hennebont, where there is a short-stay pontoon and visitors' moorings.

Hennebont is a very pleasant market town with good rail connections. Fuel can be obtained from a garage close to the bridge on the port bank. There is a water tap in the toilets close to the pontoon.

Locmalo
A pleasant anchorage, if sufficient depth can be found to stay afloat at low water, out of the tide, in the bay south of Port Louis.

Entry can only be made at sufficient rise of tide. There are two approaches, for both of which a large-scale chart, BA 304, or SHOM 6470 is essential. The first is to approach north of La Potée de Buerre (eight-sided green tower), with the north side of Ile aux Souris bearing 112°, in transit with the end of the ferry slip on the south side of the entrance to the Baie de Locmalo. This transit leads in between the rocks. On approaching Ile aux Souris and the detached above-water rock on its western side alter course to leave Ile aux Souris to starboard and steer on the north side of the channel to pass between the red and green towers. The channel curves NE towards the jetty at Locmalo and an anchorage may be found in depths from 0.6m to 2.3m.

For the second approach, from the SW, pass between the two BRB towers, leaving La Paix to port and Le Soulard to starboard. Then steer midway between Le Cabon Red tower (to port) and the detached rock to the west of Ile aux Souris (to stbd), to join the channel already described.

29 Ile de Groix

Charts: English 2352, 2646. Imray C38.
       French SHOM 7031 P. ECM Navicarte 544.

High water: −0020 Brest, Index 0, MTL 2.8m.
   MHWS 5.0m; MLWS 0.6m; MHWN 3.9m; MLWN 1.7m.

Tidal streams: Between the Ile de Groix and the mainland the flood runs to the E, the ebb to the W, spring rates $1\frac{3}{4}$ knots. Off Pointe de la Croix, at the eastern end, the flood runs to the S, the ebb to the N, spring rates 1 knot. To the SE of Les Chats, the southern point, the streams are rotary clockwise, the greatest rates being ESE $1\frac{1}{4}$ knots at −0130 Brest and SW 2 knots at +0300 Brest.

Depths: At Port Tudy 2m on the moorings, the inner harbour dries, 2–3m in the wet basin. At Loc Maria 0.5m in the anchorage, the jetty dries.

Lights:
1. Pen Men; Fl(4)W 25s, 59m, 29M. White square tower, black top.
   Radio beacon, call GX, 301.1kHz, 10M contin.
2. Pointe des Chats; Fl R 5s, 16m, 19M. White square tower and dwelling, red lantern.
3. Pointe de la Croix; Oc WR 4s, 16m, 12–9M. White pedestal, red lantern.

Port Tudy
4. East mole head; Fl(2)R 6s, 11m, 6M. White round tower, red top.
5. North mole head; Iso G 4s, 12m, 6M. White round tower, green top.

The Ile de Groix is a fairly high island, edged for the most part by cliffs, but falling away to the low Pointe des Chats in the south east. It is about 4 miles long by $1\frac{1}{2}$ miles wide. Although the coast is rocky it is reasonably clear of outlying dangers for about 3 miles eastward from Pen Men, the western extremity, on both north and south coasts. The

Port Lay, the harbour entrance

Pointe de la Croix (the NE corner of Ile de Groix). The sands are conspicuous, and extend a long way seaward at low water. The lighthouse is indicated, bearing about 330°

eastern end of the island, on the other hand, is foul; E of Port Tudy rocks extend 600m offshore, off Pointe de la Croix the sandy shoals extend 300m seaward and there are several dangerous wrecks further out, and S of Pointe des Chats the rocks extend 1 mile.

The main harbour, and the only secure one, is Port Tudy, half way along the northern shore. It was formerly one of the principal tunny fishing ports, since it was easy to make and leave under sail, but with the advent of the marine engine the tunnymen have gone to the more convenient mainland ports. Some inshore fishing activity remains and the port is a very popular staging point for English and French yachts on passage along the coast.

Some ½ mile west of it is Port Lay, a small harbour protected by a breakwater. In addition to fishing boats a sailing school operates here, but the harbour dries out beyond the pierheads and the swell gets in when the wind is from the north. Although a suitable objective for a day sail, it is not a harbour at which to spend the night and is not treated in detail here. Yachts should not anchor off it, as it is in a prohibited anchorage zone, but there are a number of moorings laid by the sailing school, which could be used for a short time by arrangement.

On the south side of the island there is the pretty little harbour of Loc Maria, which is well worth a visit under the right conditions, but is dangerous if the wind comes in from the south.

Port Tudy

This is the only safe harbour in Ile de Groix. It is a very good one except in northerly and especially north-easterly winds, when the swell penetrates the outer basin between the pierheads. If the *vent solaire* is in evidence this happens in the early hours of the morning and, as yachts lie in tiers on the moorings, and very few French yachts use springs when so doing, a noisy and enjoyable party is had by all.

Port Tudy entrance bearing 235°. Look out for the ferry entering or leaving and keep well clear

Approach and entrance

The harbour is easily identified and the approach from the W and N is straightforward; there are some naval mooring buoys off Port Lay but no other dangers. From the E and SE care must be taken to avoid the dangers off the coast, which extend in places outside the line of buoys and beacons. A safe course is with the harbour lighthouses in transit bearing 217°. This leaves close to starboard a buoy (unlit, card E) ½ mile off the entrance; the buoy marks a wreck with 9m over it. The transit then leaves 200m to port a rock with 0.6m over it with other dangers marked by a red beacon closer inshore.

When close to the entrance bear to port and enter midway between the breakwater heads, steering in parallel to the northern breakwater; there are rocks at the base of the head of the eastern breakwater. If the ferry to the mainland is manoeuvring to enter or leave, stand off as it needs all the available room.

By night

The buoys in the approaches are unlit. The light (Fl(2) R 6s) on the eastern breakwater (**4**) is obscured over the dangers to the east of the harbour, so it is safe to steer in with this light showing and just open to the left of the light (Iso G 4s) on the north breakwater (**6**). It is obscured by the latter when in transit.

Anchorage and mooring

In the outer harbour yachts moor between the large white mooring buoys, ensuring that there is room for the ferry to manoeuvre. The harbour will be very crowded in the season, particularly weekends. Use long warps and persuade your neighbours to use springs, making sure that spreaders will not foul when the swell gets up. There is a small charge for mooring. The landing slip is reserved for ferries, there is no room to anchor and the

146

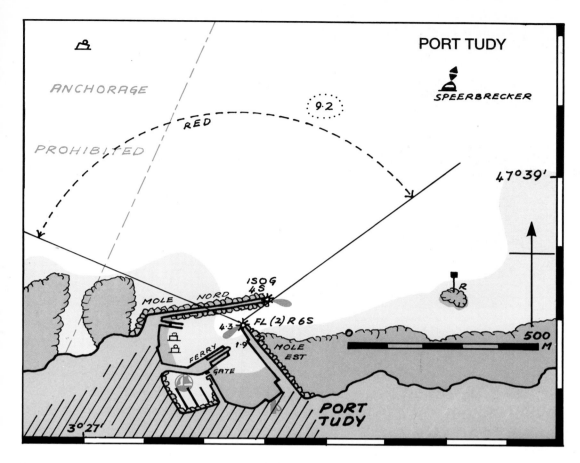

MLWS 0.6m; MLWN 1.7m; −0020 Brest, Index 0, MTL 2.8m
Based on French Chart No. 5912 with corrections (No. 7031 supersedes). Depths in metres; right hand margin in cables

bottom is said to be foul.

The inner harbour shoals inwards but shallow draught yachts may stay afloat at neaps moored bow and stern between rows of orange buoys where the bottom is about chart datum.

A wet dock has been formed from half of the inner harbour by installing a retaining wall and gates with a swing footbridge. Entry is possible between 0600 and 2200 some 2 hours either side of local HW. While waiting for the gates to open it is possible to secure to the inner landing slip, but beware of a stone shelf protruding below the top end of the slip near the gates. This will probably be submerged when coming alongside.

Visitors will be directed to a berth in from 2m to 3m. There is water and electricity on the pontoons and toilets and showers are available. Charges are average in the wet dock.

Port Tudy, inner harbour. Yachts are waiting for the gate to open

Facilities

Fuel is available from the depôt at the SE corner of the inner harbour. It will have to be carried. There is a marine engineer with hauling-out slip. Some chandlery. There are café/bars and bread may be obtained near the harbour. A launderette is available on the quay. Up the hill in the town are all shops, a supermarket and hotel.

Bicycles may be hired to explore this pleasant island. There is a frequent ferry to Lorient (Port de Commerce), from where there are good communications to all parts.

Loc Maria

This charming unspoilt little harbour is situated on the south of Ile de Groix, $\frac{3}{4}$ mile west of Pointe des Chats. The approach is open to the Atlantic, but the harbour itself is well sheltered from the W through N to E. A jetty provides some protection from the S, though with moderate southerly winds some swell penetrates round the end, and the harbour would be dangerous in strong winds or swell from this quarter. The harbour is shallow; the bottom dries as far as the head of the jetty, but depths of 1m may be found behind it, where most yachts will be able to lie afloat except at springs.

Approach and entrance

The distant approach must be made from the chart. If coming from the east or south east it will be necessary to make a detour round Les Chats. The tidal streams are quite strong at springs, the ebb generally setting westerly and the flood easterly, but the directions vary from point to point.

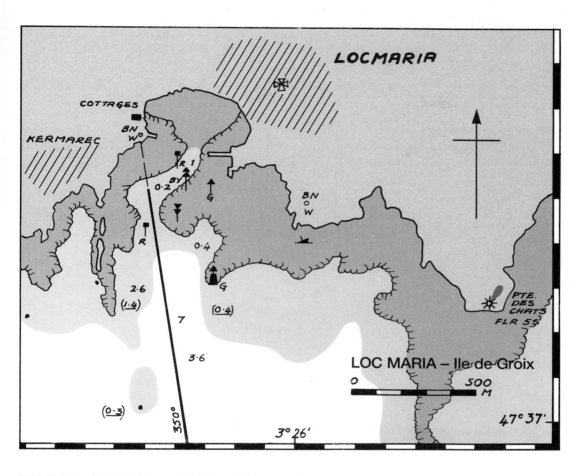

MLWS 0.6m; MLWN 1.7m; −0020 Brest, Index 0, MTL 2.8m
Based on French Chart No. 5479, enlarged, with corrections (No. 7031 supersedes). Depths in metres;
right hand margin in cables

Make a position 1 or 2 miles S of Loc Maria bay. On the eastern side will be seen the harbour and village, a green (stbd) beacon tower offshore and a white masonry beacon on the shore. On the western side is another smaller village. Between the two villages is a small group of houses on the NW side of the bay, with a small masonry beacon in front of them (see photograph).

Approach with the green beacon tower (stbd) bearing 005°, until the houses and beacon to the NW of the harbour have been identified. The lead for the channel, which carries about 0.2m, is the masonry beacon in transit with the centre window of the white cottage bearing about 350°. This cottage is the right-hand one of three and has a lean-to shed on its right hand side (see photograph); the windows have blue shutters.

Follow this transit until the vessel is about halfway between the two cardinal beacons to starboard, marking the middle ground; near low water, deeper water may be found by

Entering Loc Maria on the leading line of the small white masonry beacon with the house window, bearing 350°, just to the left of the white schooner at anchor in the only place suitable for a deep draught vessel

borrowing to the west when the outer port hand beacon comes abeam. Then bear to starboard for the pierhead keeping rather closer to the inner port hand beacon. There is a shallow channel to the east of the middle ground but it need not be used.

There are no lights and a night entry should not be attempted.

Anchorage

The harbour is choked with small boat moorings and there is no room to anchor and remain afloat. Vessels that can take the ground may anchor with a kedge astern after inspecting the bottom for rocky patches. Others may anchor outside the harbour with good holding just west of the leading line, with the outer middle ground beacon (S card) in transit with the green beacon tower, and the head of the jetty bearing about 060°. Soundings should be taken when coming to anchor, swinging and when leaving. The middle ground shoal extends westward beyond the beacons. Lying alongside the jetty is impossible owing to the lines on small boat moorings, but it may be used for landing.

Facilities

There are shops and a restaurant in the village. It is a pleasant $1\frac{1}{2}$ mile walk to Port Tudy. There are good bathing beaches.

Charts: English 2352, 2646. Imray C38.
       French SHOM 7032 P. ECM Navicarte 545.
High water: −0200 Brest, Index 0, MTL 2.8m.
    MHWS 5.0m; MLWS 0.6m; MHWN 3.9m; MLWN 1.7m.
Tidal streams: The tidal streams offshore do not exceed 1 knot and are much affected by wind. Streams in the river attain 4–5 knots at springs, but are somewhat weaker for 1½ hours after high and low water. The streams continue to run the same way for about 1 hour after high and low water. That is to say, a vessel arriving on the bar at high water will find that the tide is still flowing strongly into the river. On spring tides there is hardly any slack.
Depths: The bar varies greatly; it usually has about 0.5m but has been known to dry 4.5m. Once over the bar the river is deep except a section having 0.6m south west of the first water tower. Above the water tower 8m can be expected in the channel as far as the bridge.
Lights:
   1. Plateau des Brivideaux; Fl(2) 6s, 24m, 9M. BRB masonry tower, name on side, 10M SSW of entrance.
   2. West side of entrance; Oc(2)WRG 6s, 13m, 9–6M. Red metal framework tower.
   3. Epic de Plouhinec head; Fl R 2.5s, 1M. Red metal beacon.

The Etel river should not be approached by night, or in bad visibility, or on the ebb. First visits are not recommended in strong onshore winds, otherwise Etel is fun; there is no more delightful place, with its clean blue water and extensive sands.

Etel entrance, the semaphore and beacons (port)

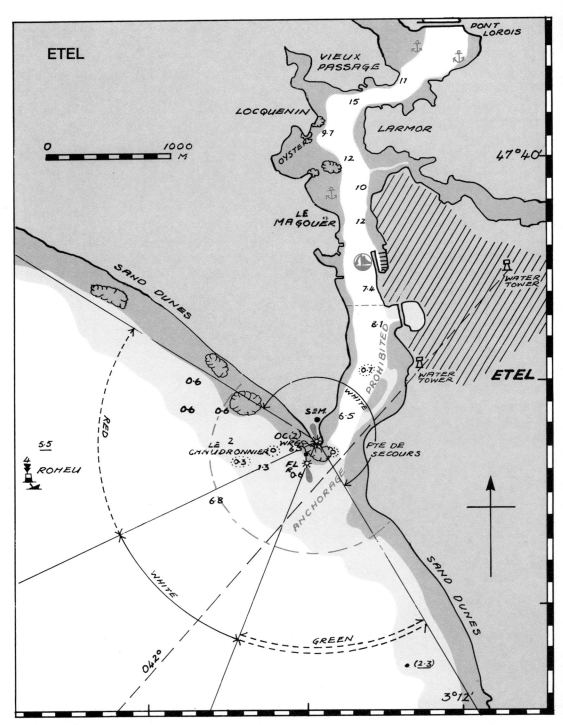

MLWS 0.6m; MLWN 1.7m; −0020 Brest, Index 0, MTL 2.8m
Based on French Chart No. 5560 with corrections (No. 7032 supersedes). Depths in metres; right hand
margin in cables

152

The entrance lies on the mainland halfway between Lorient and Quiberon, 8 miles due east of Groix. The aspect of the coast is low and sandy, but Etel can easily be recognized by its two water towers dominating the dunes. 3 miles to the NW of the town the church steeple of Poulhinec and two radio masts will be readily identified. To the S, the rounded hummock of Rohellan island will appear. A mile W of the actual entrance, the beacon tower (card S) on Roheu rocks, which are covered at HW, will be left to port. 1 mile S of the entrance, in the direction of Rohellan, will be seen the Poul-haut rocks.

Entrance

A convenient approach is with the water towers in transit, bearing 042°. While making the approach it is essential to contact the Fenoux (semaphore) station and to keep at least ½ mile off until contact has been established. In the past, this was achieved by hoisting an ensign to the masthead and directions for entry were signalled with the semaphore arms. For a vessel not equipped with VHF it is still possible to use the semaphore by telephoning 97 55 35 59 in advance and giving the operator an e.t.a.

The following signals are displayed from the semaphore mast:
1. Arrow horizontal: sea too rough – no entry for all vessels.
2. Black ball: no entry for undecked vessels under 8m length.
3. Red flag: not enough water or pilot not on duty.

With VHF, call 'semaphore d'Etel' on channel 16 or 'cross Etel' on 13 if there is no immediate reply. There is liable to be a somewhat confusing three-cornered conversation with these two, but once the pilot has taken over the instructions will be given in clear, simple French.

On leaving, after consulting the harbourmaster, keep a listening watch on the pilot's channel and he or she will call you as you approach the bar.

In 1988 the river was entered along a line from Roheu beacon tower to the red pole framework beacon on the end of a training wall, off the spit (Epic de Poulhinec) in front of the light-tower (see photograph). The stream is weak outside the bar, but may reach 6

Etel entrance. The conspicuous water towers are almost in transit on 040°. The outer port hand frame beacon is just right of the church tower and the semaphore building with grey roof is far left

Etel Fish Quay and yacht pontoons, looking up river

knots as the port hand beacon is passed. Leaving the beacon 100m to port, enter the river and continue up along the west side, where the best water may be found. Above the water tower soundings will increase.

By night
The entrance bar should not be attempted at night.

Anchorage and mooring

There is a small marina behind the fishing jetty with 12 places for visitors of less than 15m overall, with a least depth of 2.5m. Do not secure to the main jetty, which is reserved for the fishing fleet, and keep clear of the ferry berth on the innermost pontoon.

When anchoring it should be possible by sounding to get far enough in to be out of the main stream, except perhaps at springs. Keep clear of oyster beds and look out for mooring buoys that can run under in the current and only show at slack water. A good anchorage is just south of the conspicuous lifeboat house at the SW corner of the quays. One can anchor off Magöer, on the W bank, with a kedge to stop swinging into the shallows. Just above Etel the holding is good on both sides of the river but springs run at 6 knots and there are oyster beds in the shallows. There is a good anchorage just above Vieux Passage, but do not go far into the bay as the bottom is foul. Finally an anchorage, recommended by some, is just in to the northern side of the bay on the E bank below Pont Lorois. The southern part of this bay is foul.

154

Facilities

Water and electricity are on the pontoons, with a hose on the quay. Ice can be obtained from the fish hall and fuel from the quay (by unconfirmed report). Gas bottles can be filled at the camping store on the NE corner of the swimming and boating pool. Showers (free) and toilets (new 1988, traditional French style) are in the Capitainerie. The staff are helpful. Mooring charge fr46 for 10m (1988). There are shops, bars and good restaurants, excellent Shopi supermarket. Oysters and fish are sold in front of super-market. There is no launderette but dry cleaners will do the laundry; good unisex hairdresser. There is a large camping site on the dunes round the outer water tower and the town caters well for holidaymakers. Market day is Tuesday.

La Mer d'Etel

Above the bridge, Pont Lorois, said to have a clearance in the region of 9m, there is a wide expanse of water, the arms of which extend 5 miles inland. No official charts are available for the Mer d'Etel which, except for the currents (up to 10 knots under the bridge) and a larger tidal range, might be compared with Poole Harbour. There is 2m in the main channel for 3 miles up to La Pointe du Verdon. While no good for a seagoing yacht, it is an interesting place to explore in a dinghy with sufficient power to cope with the currents. There is an ancient Oratory at St Cado, which is a good place for a picnic, as are the many islands in this inland sea.

After passing under the bridge keep to port to round a green (stbd) beacon. Then cross over to leave the red beacon to port. The river up to this point is strewn with islets and submerged rocks over which strong eddies swirl. From there on up the stream should be weaker and exploration may commence.

Charts: English BA 2646, 2353. Imray C39.

   French SHOM 7032 P. ECM Navicarte 545.

High water: −0030 Brest springs, −0005 Brest neaps, Index 1, MTL 2.9m.

   MHWS 5.2m; MLWS 0.7; MHWN 3.9m; MLWN 1.9m.

Tidal streams: In the channel to the NE of Belle Ile the streams are rotary clockwise, except close to the shore. They set NW at low water, SE at high water, spring rates up to $1\frac{1}{2}$ knots at the north end, up to 1 knot in the middle and about $1\frac{1}{2}$ knots at the south end. The streams probably run harder close to the north and south points of the island. The streams in the harbours are weak.

Depths: The approaches to the harbours are deep. Le Palais has 3m at the usual moorings. Sauzon inner harbour dries, 1m or more should be found in the outer harbour. Port du Vieux Château (Ster Wenn) has about 1.5m.

Lights:

   1. Goulphar; Fl(2)W 10s, 87m, 24M. Grey tower, red lamp. Radio beacon discontinued 1989.
   2. Pointe des Poulains; Fl W 5s, 34m, 24M. White square tower and dwelling, red lamp.
   3. Pointe de Kerdonis; Fl(3)R 15s, 35m, 11M. White square tower and dwelling, red lamp.

Le Palais:

   4. South jetty; Oc(2)R 6s, 11m, 11M. White round tower, red lantern.
   5. North jetty; Fl(2+1)G 12s, 11m, 7M. White tower, green top.

Sauzon:

   6. West jetty; Q G, 9m, 5M. White tower, green top.
   7. NW jetty head; Fl G 4s, 8m, 8M. White tower, green top.
   8. SE jetty head; Fl R 4s, 8m, 8M. White tower, red top.

Belle Ile is the largest island off the south coast of Brittany, being about 10 miles long and up to 5 miles wide. The NE coast is fairly free of outlying dangers, except at its ends off Pointe des Poulains and Pointe de Kerdonis. This side of the island is sheltered from the prevailing winds and has two harbours, Le Palais which, when not overcrowded, is one of the best in Brittany, and Sauzon with its drying inner harbour, excellent for vessels which can take the ground. Sauzon also has an outer harbour with moorings and an anchorage outside, both comfortable except during the *vent solaire*, when they can be unpleasant.

   The Atlantic side of the island is rugged, deeply indented and has a profusion of rocks. It is picturesque and the island attracts many tourists. The only inlet on this side that provides some kind of harbour is the Port du Vieux Château (Ster Wenn), 1 mile S of Pointe des Poulains. This has no quay, roads or facilities, but has become a popular objective for yachts since attention was drawn to it in the first edition of this book. The danger is that here the Atlantic swell can rise and bar the entrance.

   The island has a long and interesting history. Owned at one time by the Counts of

Cornouaille, it was presented in the ninth century to the Abbey of St Croix at Quimperlé. An English fleet was driven off in 1548, but a raid was successful in 1573 after the monks had sold the island to the Retz family. Van Tromp attacked the island in 1673 and it was finally taken in 1761 by the British under Admiral Keppel. Two years later Belle Ile was restored to France by the same treaty that gave Nova Scotia to England. A number of Nova Scotian families returning to Europe settled in the island and introduced the potato some years before the vegetable became popular on the mainland.

Le Palais

Le Palais is a very good harbour, and there is a good anchorage outside in offshore winds. It can, however, become crowded and uncomfortable in July and August. The harbour itself has a narrow entrance facing SE but some swell can enter. Winds from the NE are worst; strong NE winds cause seas to break over the breakwater. Even strong NW winds

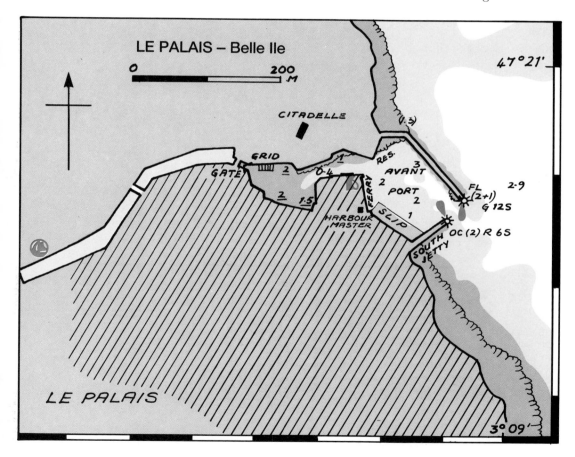

MLWS 0.7m; MLWN 1.9m; −0030(sp), −0005(np) Brest, Index 1, MTL 2.9m
Based on French Chart No. 5911 with corrections (No. 7032 supersedes). Depths in metres; right hand margin in cables

Le Palais entrance, approaching LW

can cause some swell in the harbour but it is well sheltered from the S and W. If the outer harbour becomes too uncomfortable it is possible to dry out in the inner harbour or go into the wet dock which has a marina. Once a principal sardine fishing port it is now mainly a holiday resort, though some fishing continues. It is very popular not only with yachts on passage but as an objective for the large fleet of yachts in Quiberon Bay so that in the afternoon the harbour fills rapidly especially at weekends. The town is the capital of Belle Isle, so there are shops of all kinds.

Approach and entrance
The Citadel makes identification easy and there are no dangers in the approach. Steer for the lighthouse on the end of the northern jetty. Keep a sharp lookout for the frequent ferries from Quiberon, which enter and leave at speed, taking up most of the channel. If the way is clear, enter giving a wide berth to the southern pierhead which has a rock at its base and to the northern one where the bottom is foul for some distance in along the wall.

By night
As by day, keeping a sharp lookout for unlit buoys which are sometimes moored near the entrance.

Anchorage and mooring
Outside the harbour, anchor to the east of the north jetty in 3m, keeping well clear of the fairway. This is a safe anchorage, with good holding ground, in offshore winds. Anchoring is prohibited between the Citadel at Le Palais and the approaches to Sauzon, because of cables, but the anchorage noted above is just clear of the prohibited area and two large mooring buoys have been placed here for visitors' use.

Inside the harbour, yachts secure fore and aft between three rows of mooring buoys and to the wall of the north jetty. The buoys are rather close together for yachts of 10m or more. Make sure that your neighbours are secured bow and stern. Use fendoffs and

Le Palais. Drying moorings in the inner harbour. There is a grid behind the fishing boat. The wet dock gate is far left

springs and check that spreaders will not foul as yachts are subject to movement from incoming swell. Yachts also secure in a cluster round the large mooring buoy to port inside the entrance, taking a line to the buoy and breast ropes to their neighbours.

Part of the inner harbour has been dredged but most of the berths are occupied by fishing boats. It is possible to dry out bow to the north wall, on either side of the grid, with a stern mooring if one is available. However, the bottom is foul along the north wall leading into the inner harbour (see plan). White stripes on the walls reserve spaces for fishing boats.

The wet dock gates are open for about 1 hour either side of high water. Beyond the wet dock and a lifting bridge opening daily at 0700 hours, lies La Saline marina, completely secure with water and electricity on the pontoons. Consult the harbourmaster before attempting to enter the wet dock and marina.

Facilities
Water, showers and toilets by the Capitainerie, also showers at the caravan park, up the hill beyond the marina. There is a fuel berth on the port hand side of the passage into the inner harbour. Haul-out facilities, marine and electrical engineers, chandlery, banks, hotel, restaurants, café/bars and a good selection of shops are available.

Communications
There is a frequent ferry service to Quiberon, and rail, bus and air links there. It is possible to hire bicycles and cars to explore the island.

Sauzon
Situated less than 2 miles SE of Pointe des Poulains, this once peaceful little harbour is now full of yachts in season, but is still a very pleasant place to visit and is a secure haven for vessels which can take the ground. The moorings in the outer harbour and the anchorage outside provide shelter from the S and W but no comfort when the *vent solaire* blows. There is some local fishing and active sailing.

Sauzon outer harbour. Some yachts are on moorings outside. One is secured stern to shore. The yellow beacon pole marking the ledge is behind her stern line. Most yachts secure bow and stern to the trot of buoys seen on the right

Approach and entrance

The harbour is not hard to identify except when the sun is behind it. The Gareau beacon tower (stbd) off the Pointe du Cardinal north of the entrance will be seen if approaching along the coast in either direction. The ends of the two outer breakwaters are marked by low white lighthouses with red and green tops, while behind them can be seen the old taller lighthouse, also white with a green top.

By night
The main light (**6**) (Q G 9m 5M) and the two jetty head lights (**7, 8**) (Fl G 4s and Fl R 4s) are obscured by the Pointe du Cardinal when approaching from the NW, but one can navigate by the Pointe des Poulains light (**2**) (Fl W 5s 34m 24M) until they open. Pick up a buoy on the west side of the entrance or enter with a good spotlight as the harbour is very crowded and ill-lit.

Anchorage and mooring

There are moorings outside the outer north mole with room to anchor outside them clear of the fairway.

Between the outer and inner moles on the east side there are some mooring buoys for

160

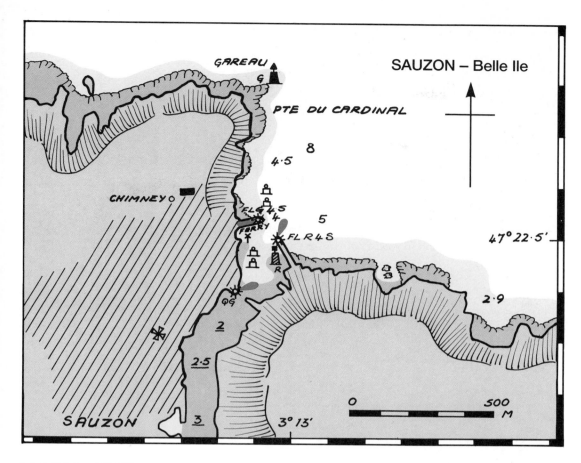

SAUZON – Belle Ile

GAREAU

PTE DU CARDINAL

8
4·5

CHIMNEY

FL G 4 S
FERRY

FL R 4 S

5

47° 22·5'

2·9

QG

2

2·5

SAUZON

3

3° 13'

0   500
                        M

MLWS 0.7m; MLWN 2.9m; −0030(sp), −0005(np) Brest, Index 1, MTL 2.9m
Based on French Chart No. 5911 with corrections (No. 7032 supersedes). Depths in metres; right hand margin in cables

single mooring with better shelter; the old port tower still stands there and the bottom round it is foul. Between the moles on the west side, the situation may not be immediately obvious: inside the ferry berth a yellow pole beacon, X topmark, marks the N end of a flat ledge about 5m wide, covered at half tide, and extending in about halfway towards the main lighthouse. Parallel to the ledge are two rows of mooring buoys. Depending on the number in the harbour, yachts may either moor bow and stern along the two lines of buoys, or moor E/W, the inner row having a bow line on a buoy and a stern line to a ring on the edge of the shelf, or a line to the rocks on the bank behind if the shelf is covered.

The inner harbour dries out, having a firm sandy bottom. Single keel yachts may find a space to lie against a wall after consulting the fishermen. Many French yachts are now fitted with legs or *béquilles* and the new verb *béquiller* is to take the ground and dry out (*échouer*) with legs. English yachts similarly equipped or with bilge-keels may join them by laying out bower and kedge anchors and adjusting the lie at low water if warps or chains

161

Sauzon entrance from the NE. The anchorage and moorings outside are exposed to the *vent solaire*

are over those of nearby boats. The estuary is over 500m long and if there is a crowd near the entrance there is plenty of room higher up for those prepared to dry out for longer each tide.

Facilities

There is a water tap at the root of the inner W jetty, and a water tap, municipal showers and toilets on the W wall of the inner harbour. Hotels and some good restaurants are available, as are some shops, but many have been converted to cater for a growing flood of tourists. Bicycles may be hired.

Sauzon inner harbour. Bilge keels or legs are a great advantage here as the outer harbour is most uncomfortable during a *vent solaire*. The bottom is sand and one can walk ashore

Les Poulains lighthouse, at the north end of Belle Ile, bearing about SW. It is near LW and Les Chambres rocks show clearly to the right of the island. These are now buoyed

Port du Vieux Château (Ster Wenn)

This anchorage is in a fjord on the west coast of Belle Ile, a little over 1 mile S of Pointe des Poulains. It was described, in the first edition of this work, as one of the most beautiful in France; in consequence it has also become one of the most overcrowded by day visitors. It has also been likened to a lobster pot: easy to get into and hard to get out of. The onset of bad weather, or heavy swell, which can be caused by bad weather elsewhere, would make the entrance a death trap.

The sailing directions and plan should be regarded with caution, as the largest scale chart published is on too small a scale to show much detail. The plan is much enlarged from the original chart. The names *Pointe Dangereuse* and *Pointe Verticale* are fictitious though appropriate; the name *Pointe du Vieux Château* (Beg en Nuet) is attached to what is believed to be the correct point – official charts differ.

Approach and entrance

In the approach from northward the dangers off the Pointe des Poulains must be avoided, and the tidal charts must be consulted as the streams are strong near the point and set across the rocks. A detour may be made round Poulains Basse Occidentale buoy (card W), and a yacht without auxiliary power should not risk being becalmed between this buoy and Port du Vieux Château with a northerly running stream. Alternatively, if the rocks of Les Chambres and Le Cochon are showing, as they generally will be, the Pointe des Poulains may safely be rounded close inside them.

The Port du Vieux Château is divided into two parts: the main inlet called Ster Vras which is seen from seaward, and a smaller inlet called Ster Wenn, which opens out on the south side of Ster Vras. Ster Vras is 400m wide and 900m long. Ster Wenn is only 50m wide and 500m long.

The entrance to Ster Vras is harder to locate than it appears on the chart, as there are several inlets looking similar from seaward, but on nearer approach it is easy to identify. The north side of Ster Vras is encumbered with rocks as much as 300m off Pointe Dangereuse, but the southern side is steep, there being 15m almost alongside. Pointe Verticale forms a vertical cliff on the south side of the entrance and it is this cliff which

163

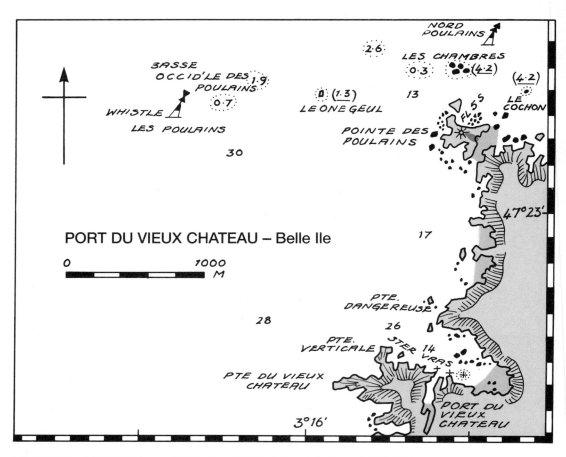

PORT DU VIEUX CHATEAU – Belle Ile

MLWS 0.7m; MLWN 2.9m; −0030(sp), −0005(np) Brest, Index 1, MTL 2.9m
Based on French Chart No. 135, enlarged, with corrections (No. 7032 supersedes). Depths in metres; right hand margin in cables

makes identification easy. Approximately 1km south of Pointe Verticale the Hôtel de l'Apothicairerie is conspicuous on the skyline.

Pointe Verticale, then, lies 1 mile SE from the Poulains Basse Occidentale buoy, but it is better not to approach the last ½ mile on this bearing for two reasons: because due allowance must be made for the stream which may be setting across the entrance to Ster Vras; and because approaching from a more westerly direction ensures that a good berth is given to the sunken rocks off Pointe Dangereuse and the northern arm of Ster Vras. The stream weakens as Ster Vras is entered, and so does the swell, especially in southerly winds.

The cliffs along the southern shore of Ster Vras may be skirted in safety. No sign or hint of the existence of Ster Wenn will be seen until, quite dramatically, the entrance opens up to starboard. Open Ster Wenn fully, when the course may be altered sharply to starboard to enter. If Ster Wenn is overcrowded, there is a possible day anchorage further up Ster

Vras but only in calm weather. Keep to starboard and look out for many rocks as the beach is approached. Most of the rocks occupy the northern half of the inlet and provide some shelter for local fishing boats.

Anchorage

Ster Wenn is deep near the entrance and shoals gradually up to a sandy beach after a small fork. A cable is slung across the inlet at the fork to provide moorings for small fishing boats. On the port-hand side iron rings are set into the rock above the high water line. Drop anchor in the middle of the inlet (1.5m or more) and take a stern line ashore to one of the rings. The holding is good but make sure that the anchor is well dug in before going ashore. On returning you may find several yachts rafted to you with slack cables and shore lines and their owners may require some gentle encouragement if you are to survive a *vent solaire* during the night.

The water is smooth in all winds except NW. It seems inconceivable that any sea can make the double turn to enter this snug retreat, even in a severe gale. It is stated, however, that surge enters when there is a heavy onshore wind, and therefore the anchorage is dangerous. Accordingly the anchorage must be regarded only as a fair weather one.

Facilities

There is a dinghy landing on the beach and a path leading up the valley to the road. Turn

Ster Wenn or Port du Vieux Château, from the N side of Ster Vras

left and Sauzon can be reached after a walk of some 3 land miles; turn right and visit the Grotte de l'Apothicairerie (nearly $\frac{3}{4}$ mile) a cave that is worth seeing, so named after the rows of cormorants that sometimes line the ledges looking like the jars of coloured liquid in an old chemist's shop. There is a tourists' shop by the cave, where supplies may be purchased, and a somewhat inactive hotel (1988).

Ster Wenn or Port du Vieux Château, looking out towards Ster Vras and Les Poulains lighthouse

32 Presqu'île de Quiberon

Charts: English BA 2353, 2646. Imray C38, C39.
French SHOM 7032 P, 7033 P. ECM Navicarte 545.
Tidal information, lights: See under the individual ports.

The name of Quiberon is familiar because it was the scene of the great sea-battle in 1759, when, in a November gale and gathering darkness, Hawke led his fleet into the bay to victory among the rocks and shoals and strong tides which will be described.

The peninsula itself is about 5 miles long and is joined to the mainland by a sandy neck which is little over 100m wide. North of this a narrow arm of sand dunes continues for some 3 miles before widening to merge with the broader mainland. The total length of the projection seawards is therefore about 8 miles and the geological formation continues for nearly 15 miles to the SE, in the shape of an archipelago of rocks, islets and shoals, between which are navigable passages, to be described in Chapter 33. Houat and Hoëdic are the only inhabited islands in this archipelago.

Presqu'île de Quiberon itself looks somewhat sinister from seaward; it is sandy in the north, but rocky towards the south and was formerly strongly fortified. Ashore, however, the whole peninsula is dotted with seaside resorts, for it has a long coastline and the sandy beaches are ideal for bathing. The town of Quiberon is the capital and there are two harbours a little over $\frac{1}{2}$ mile apart, Port Maria on the SW side and Port Haliguen on the NE. Quiberon has a population of about 4,000, a railway station, an airport and many shops, for it serves the whole district. Accommodation varies from the luxury hotel to the camping site.

Port Maria is closed to yachts except in an emergency. The harbour is very crowded with fishing boats and the ferries to Belle Ile. Port Haliguen, the yacht harbour for Quiberon, has all the facilities of a marina. The NE side of the peninsula is sheltered from the prevailing winds and there are several anchorages available in winds from NW to S. At Port d'Orange, $2\frac{1}{2}$ miles farther north, there is merely a jetty and a somewhat indifferent anchorage. There are oyster beds in parts of the NW corner of Quiberon Bay, marked by orange buoys.

Further north on the NE side of Quiberon peninsula is an almost landlocked bay, but it is very shallow, both in the bay and the approaches, except for a winding unmarked channel. Here is the Anse du Pô, which is only 1 mile from Carnac, where the standing stones form one of the greatest sites of the megalithic culture.

The only other harbour on the Quiberon peninsula is Portivi, on the west side. This is exposed to the west and, when there is a heavy swell, the sea is said to break nearly 1 mile to seaward. The anchorage is, however, a pleasant one in fine weather.

Port Maria

High water: −0020 Brest, Index 1, MTL 2.9m.

MHWS 5.1m; MLWS 0.7m; MHWN 3.9m; MLWN 1.8m.

Tidal streams: Some 4 miles SW of Port Maria the streams are rotary clockwise, the main strength being NE, 1½ knots at −0330. Brest and W, 1½ knots at +0240 Brest. There is no stream in the harbour.

Depths: Maximum about 2m, much of the harbour dries.

Lights:

1. Main light; Q WRG, 28m 15M White tower green lantern.
2. Leading lights 006.5°;
   Front: Dir Q G, 5m, 14M. White tower, black band and top.
   Rear: Dir Q G, 13m, 14M. White tower, black band and top.
3. East mole head; Iso G 4s, 9m, 7M. White tower, green lantern.
4. S breakwater head; Oc(2)R 6s, 9m, 7M. White tower, red lantern.

This is an artificial harbour, sheltered from all winds, situated just E of Beg el Lan on the SW extremity of the Quiberon peninsula. There is a conspicuous château with towers on this point. The harbour is used by many fishing vessels and is the terminal for the ferries to Belle Ile. Yachts are only permitted to enter in an emergency.

Approach and entrance

The approach is well marked. Coming from the W or NW a whistle buoy (card S) is left to port over ½ mile from the entrance. Then steer 070° until the leading marks, two BW masonry beacons E of the breakwater, come into transit, bearing 006°. Leave Les Deux Frères can buoy (R) about 150m to port and follow the transit carefully, as a drying rock has been reported close to it, about 200m N of the buoy. When the harbour entrance opens up behind the breakwater steer in.

By night

The main light (**1**) has five white sectors. Approach in the white sector where the light bears N or between 340° and 017° (an arc of 37°). In good time bring the leading lights in transit and steer so until the entrance between the S breakwater and E mole opens up.

Anchorage

The deep water, 1.4–2.2m, lies on the SE side of the harbour parallel with the southern mole, and rocks and rocky bottom lie on the landward side. There are rocks at the base of the mole, which should not be approached too closely. The berth at the E mole is used by the ferries to Belle Ile and considerably reduces the space available for anchoring. Much of that which remains is taken up by fishing boat moorings. In settled northerly winds it is possible to anchor clear of the fairway and W of the seaward leading light, subject to fishing boat and ferry wash. Yellow buoys define the swimming and pedal boat area. Do not anchor inside these.

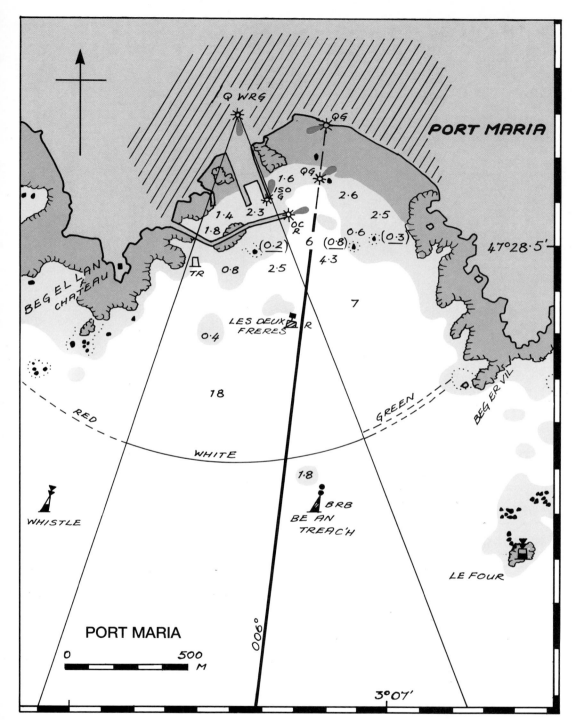

PORT MARIA

Q WRG

QG

QG

1·6

ISO G

QG

2·6

2·5

1·4 2·3

OC R

1·8

(0·2) 6 (0·8) (0·3)

0·6

TR 0·8 2·5 4·3

47°28·5'

7

LES DEUX FRERES R

0·4

18

BEG EL LAN CHATEAU

RED

GREEN

BEG ER VIL

WHITE

1·8

BRB

WHISTLE

BE AN TREAC'H

LE FOUR

PORT MARIA

0   500
                M

006°

3°07'

MLWS 0.7m; MLWN 1.8m; −0020 Brest, Index 1, MTL 2.9m
Based on French Chart No. 5352 with corrections (No. 7032 supersedes). Depths in metres; right hand
margin in cables   169

Port Maria. The lighthouse is bearing 015° and the Deux Frères buoy (port) is on the right of the picture. The church is conspicuous in the centre

Facilities
There is a water tap at the ferry terminal, several hotels, restaurants and shops of all kinds. There are ferries to Belle Ile and Houat, a bus service to Carnac and Auray, and a railway and airfield at Quiberon ($\frac{1}{2}$ mile). There is a good chandlery.

Port Haliguen
High water: −0010 Brest, Index 1, MTL 3.0m.
   MHWS 5.3m; MLWS 0.6m; MHWN 4.0m; MLWN 1.8m.
Tidal streams: Off the harbour the N stream begins +0445 Brest, the S stream at −0220 Brest, spring rates $1\frac{1}{2}$ knots.
Depths: The approach is deep. In the harbour there is up to 3m.
Lights:
   1. Port Maria, main light; Q WRG, 28m, 15–11M. White tower, green lantern.
   2. Marina. New breakwater head; Oc(2)WR 6s, 10m, 12–9M. White tower, red top.
   3. Old breakwater head; Fl R 4s, 10m, 5M. White tower, red top.
   4. NW mole head; Fl G 2.5s, 6m, 6M. White column, green top.
   5. Pier head; Fl Vi 2s, 5m. Purple column.

Port Haliguen is an expanding yacht harbour. A simple village encircles the old drying harbour. Every yachting facility is provided by the marina, there are excellent beaches handy and the resources of Quiberon are only $\frac{1}{2}$ mile away. It is a very pleasant harbour.

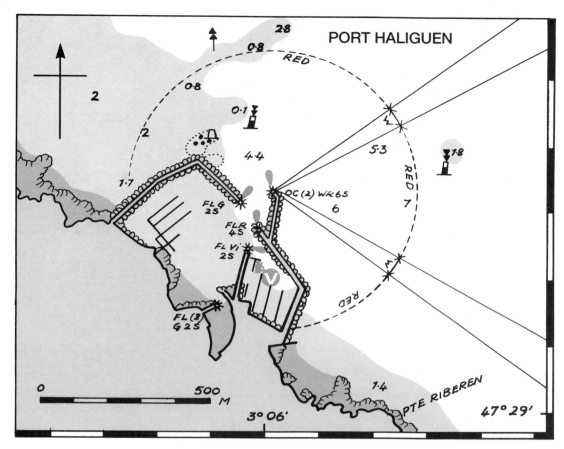

PORT HALIGUEN

28

0.8

RED

0.8

0.1

2

2

4.4

5.3

1.8

1.7

RED 7

FL G
2S

QC (2) WR 6S

6

FL R
4S

FL Vi
2S

V

RED

FL (3)
G 2S

0   500
                              M

1.4

3° 06'

PTE RIBEREN

47° 29'

MLWS 0.6m; MLWN 1.8m; −0010 Brest, Index 1, MTL 3.0m
Based on French Chart No. 5352, enlarged, with corrections (No. 7033 supersedes). Depths in metres;
right hand margin in cables

Port Haliguen entrance from the NE

Port Haliguen reception berth and fuel pontoon

Approach and entrance

The approach to Quiberon bay through the Teignouse is described in Chapter 33. Port Haliguen is situated less than 2 miles NW of the SE extremity of the Quiberon peninsula. The immediate approach is easy, keeping the Port Maria lighthouse bearing about W, leaving to starboard a YB (card S) buoy and a BRB buoy marking a wreck just outside the harbour entrance.

Enter between the breakwaters and leave the middle jetty to starboard. Secure to the short pontoon at right angles to the jetty. This is the reception berth, labelled *Ponton d'Acceuil*. Very large yachts can secure to a buoy in the NW section of the harbour. Report to the harbour office which will allocate a permanent berth if they wish you to move.

By night
Approach in the white sector of Port Maria light (**1**) 246°–252°, or in one of the white sectors of Port Haliguen Marina Light (**2**) 233°–241° or 297°–306°. Keep a lookout for unlit buoys and avoid the protective spur off the E breakwater head on entering.

Mooring

Anchoring is not permitted in the yacht harbour. Visitors normally secure to pontoons in the south-eastern basin. There are mooring buoys and pontoons in the north-western basin, accessible from the land north of the old drying harbour.

Facilities

The facilities are of a major marina. Water and electricity, showers and toilets are on the pontoons. There are also a fuel pontoon, slip, crane, engineers, club. Bread is available at a café at the port; a 15 minute walk on the road towards Quiberon is a large supermarket with fish and oysters on sale outside. Hotels, restaurants, banks and all shops are in Quiberon, 1 mile away, where there are connections by bus, train and plane to all parts. This is a good place for a change of crew.

33 La Teignouse, Le Béniguet, Ile aux Chevaux, Les Soeurs (passage notes)

Charts: English BA 2353, 2646. Imray C39.
French SHOM 7033 P. ECM Navicarte 545, 546.

Tidal streams:

La Teignouse: NE begins −0610 Brest, SW begins −0005 Brest, spring rates 4 knots.

Le Béniguet: NE begins +0535 Brest, SW begins −0045 Brest, spring rates 3 knots.

Ile aux Chevaux and Les Soeurs: NNE begins +0535 Brest, SSW begins −0050 Brest, spring rates 2¾ knots.

Depths: All four channels are deep.

For a distance of some 15 miles SE of Quiberon there are reefs of rocks, shoals and the two islands of Houat and Hoëdic. Between the reefs and rocks there are several navigable passages, but only four which are suitable for the stranger. The Passage de la Teignouse is the big ship route, well lit at night; it is about 3 miles from Quiberon. In addition to the main channel, some short cuts are described, formerly rated *severe* (see page 16). The Passage du Béniguet, which lies close NW of Houat, is narrow but quite straightforward by day; there are no lights at night. The Passage des Soeurs lies between Houat and Hoëdic; it is wider than Le Béniguet, but also unlit. The Passage de l'Ile aux Chevaux is the short route between Le Palais and Hoëdic.

Passage de la Teignouse
Lights:

1. Port Maria main; Q WRG, 28m, 15–11M. White tower, green lantern.
2. La Teignouse; Fl WR 4s, 19m, 15–11M. White sector 033°–039°. White round tower, red top.
3. Goué Vas Sud (card S) by; FlQ(6)+L Fl, 15s.
4. Basse du Milieu Lanby; Fl(2)G 6s.
5. Goué Vas Est (lat port) by; Fl(3)R 12s.
6. NE Teignouse (lat stbd); by Fl(3)G 12s.
7. Basse Nouvelle (lat port); by FlR 2.5s.
8. Port Haliguen; Oc(2)WR 6s, 10m, 12–9M, white tower, red top.

This is a well-marked channel, ¼ mile wide, and small vessels have plenty of margin, as there is deep water on either side of the marked channel. There are no difficulties other than those caused by bad visibility or bad weather. The strong tides cause a steep sea when wind and tide are opposed, so that with a contrary wind the passage should be taken as near slack water as possible.

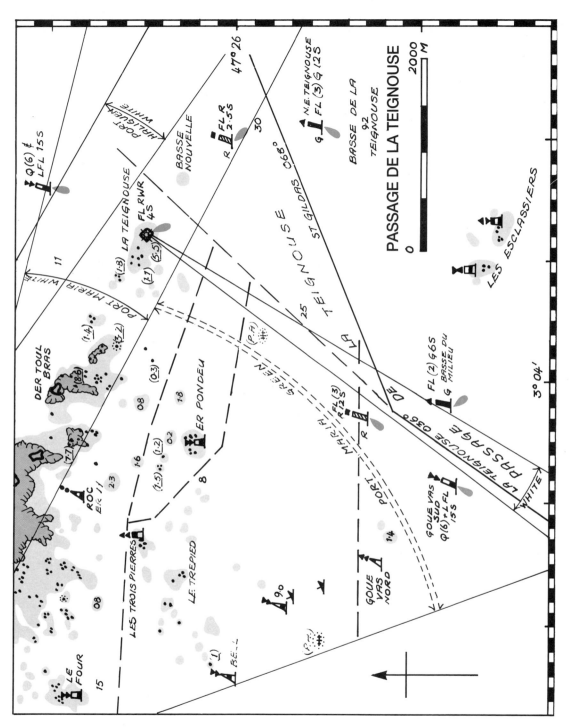

PASSAGE DE LA TEIGNOUSE

Based on French Chart No. 5352 with corrections (No. 7033 supersedes). Depths in metres; right hand margin in cables. The alternative passages (1, 2, 3, 4), shown hatched, are feasible but are not described

174

La Teignouse, bearing about NW, near LW. Note the outlying rock on the channel side

From the south west
Bring the white lighthouse on La Teignouse to bear 036°. This line leads S of Goué Vas Sud buoy (card S), which must not be confused with Goué Vas NW buoy (card N), situated ½ mile to the NW of it. Steer on this course, 036°, leaving:

Goué Vas Sud by (card S) 200m to port,
Basse du Milieu Lanby stbd 200m to starboard,
Goué Vas Est buoy (port), 200m to port.

When this last buoy is abeam alter course to 068°. The official lead for this is the church at St Gildas, 10 miles away, bearing 068°, but all that is necessary is to steer out between Basse Nouvelle buoy to port and La Teignouse NE buoy to starboard.

From the east
Plot these courses on the chart (BA 2353 is good for this) and reverse.

By night
Enter the white sector, 033° to 039°, of La Teignouse light (2) before Port Maria main light (1) turns from white to green. Steer in this sector between the buoys. When the vessel is approximately between Basse du Milieu (4) and Goué Vas Est (5) buoys alter course to 068° to pass between the two eastern buoys (6 and 7).

From the east or north
Avoid the dangers off La Teignouse by keeping in the white sector of Port Haliguen light (8) 299°–306°. Enter between the two eastern buoys (6 and 7) and steer 248° to pass between Basse du Milieu and Goué Vas buoys (4 and 5). Steer out 216° between the buoys in the white sector of La Teignouse light (2). When Port Maria main light (1) turns from green to white all dangers are past.

Several short cuts can be taken by day (see chart, page 174), making allowance for conditions of wind and tide. While these have not been included in the present edition, they can still be explored with the assistance of a large-scale chart such as BA 2353.

Passage de Béniguet
For the plan of this passage see under Houat in Chapter 34.

This is an easy daylight passage lying immediately to the NW of the island of Houat, and is often used by yachts going between Belle Ile and Houat.

Coming from the SW leave Le Rouleau tower (card W) about 600m to starboard and steer about 030° to pass between Le Grand Coin tower (card E) and Bonen Bras tower (card W). Keep closer to Le Grand Coin tower and well clear of Bonen Bras and the

Passage du Béniguet, passing Men er Broc rock, with Houat behind. Bonen Bras tower (card E) bears 205°, with SE point of Belle Ile on the horizon. (Motorboat to the right of Bonen Bras tower)

shoals with a least depth of 1.5m which extend 600m to the NNE of it. Le Grand Coin tower bearing 240° (and in transit with Le Palais Citadel, if the visibility is good) clears these shoals.

Use this transit when leaving Quiberon Bay and alter to 210° when Le Grand Coin is 400m distant.

Passage de l'Ile aux Chevaux
No plan is given, chart BA 2353 is sufficient.

This is the direct fine weather route from Le Palais to Hoëdic, and is an attractive alternative to Le Béniguet for reaching Houat.

Steer E from Le Palais for the Ile aux Chevaux. The Pot de Fer, 1 mile NNW of Ile aux Chevaux, must be passed on either side. It is marked by a BRB spar buoy and can be safely cleared by keeping the northern tangent of Ile aux Chevaux clear to the N or clear to the S of Hoëdic. Keep 400m N of Ile aux Chevaux; the outlying danger dries 5.7m and hardly ever covers.

Bound for Houat steer for Try Men, the steep to isolated rock off the south end of Houat. Pass this closely; there is a rock with 1.3m over it about $\frac{1}{2}$ mile to the SE. Beg Pel and the rocks north of it are steep to and can be passed at 100m. Thence leave the Men er Houteliguet BRB tower 100m to starboard. To port will be seen the dramatic sweep of Tréac'h er Gouret, one of the sights of Brittany.

It is a magnificent beach for bathing. BA 2353 marks it as a prohibited anchorage but ECM Navicarte 546 shows an anchorage and in July 1988 *Capelan* joined over 100 yachts in the bay. The evening was delightful, but 0130 saw navigating lights come on and riding lights extinguished as the fleet weighed and stood out to clear the lee shore in a violent *vent solaire*.

Cross the bay if proceeding to Port de St Gildas, leave the rock Er Yoc'h (23m high) 100m to port, the beach on the point Enthal well to port and round Er Genetau (16m high), leaving it 100m to port to enter Port de St Gildas.

Bound for Hoëdic, leave Men er Vag shoal, marked by a BRB spar buoy to starboard. The clearing mark is Le Palais breakwater open N of Ile aux Chevaux astern. Thence leave Les Soeurs tower (card W) to starboard and follow the direction for the Passage des Soeurs given below.

Passage des Soeurs
No plan is given for this passage; chart BA 2353 is adequate.

Bound north east
Make a point 400m W of Er Palaire tower (card W), which is itself 1 mile W of Hoëdic. If the visibility is good this will bring the church of St Gildas in transit with Er Rouzès tower (card E) bearing 019°. If St Gildas church, which is on the mainland 10 miles away, cannot be seen, bring Er Rouzès tower three or four times its own height to the left of Les Soeurs tower (card W). Leave Les Soeurs tower 100m to starboard. The channel is quite wide and it is not necessary to follow the alignments closely. Having passed Les Soeurs tower steer out as required.

Bound for Hoëdic do not bring Les Soeurs tower to bear more than 255° until the west side of Hoëdic is shut in behind the Pointe du Vieux Château, bearing 175°. This point is the NW headland of Hoëdic and shoals extend northwards of a line between the point and Les Soeurs.

Bound north leave Er Rouzès tower (card E) at least 200m to port.

Charts: English BA 2353, 2646. Imray C39.

French SHOM 7033 P. ECM Navicarte 546.

High water: −0020 Brest, Index 1, MTL 3.0m.

MHWS 5.2m; MLWS 0.6m; MHWN 4.2m; MLWN 1.9m.

Tidal streams: The tidal stream in Passages du Béniguet and des Soeurs are given on page 173. North of Hoëdic the NE stream begins at +0600 Brest, the SW stream at −0020 Brest, spring rates 2 knots. Half a mile E of Les Grands Cardinaux the flood runs NNE, the ebb SW, spring rates $2\frac{1}{2}$ knots.

Depths: In the harbour at Houat there is 2–2.5m near the breakwater; the southern side of the harbour dries. Half the harbour Argol on Hoëdic dries, but there is 2m in the entrance.

Lights:

1. Houat, Port de St Gildas north mole; Oc(2)WG 6s, 8m, 8–5M. White tower, green top.
2. Hoëdic, Port de l'Argol breakwater head; Fl WG 4s, 10m, 10–7M. White tower, green top.
3. Grouguègues (Les Grands Cardinaux); Fl(4)W 15s, 28m, 13M. Red round masonry tower, white band (2M SE of Hoëdic).

English yacht encounters French yacht with island looming out of the mist.

Englishman: 'What is that?'

Frenchman: 'That is WHAT!'

(Told by a French yachtsman who pronounced the 'a' as in 'hat'.)

Houat

Houat is a strangely shaped island about 2 miles long, lying 7 miles E of Le Palais and 10 miles S of La Trinité. At its eastern end there are long promontories; En Tal on the NE is low, the southern one is higher, with offlying rocks. Between these headlands lie the remarkable sands of Tréac'h-er-Gouret, and the old Port er Berg, destroyed by a violent tempest in 1951; the new harbour, Le Port de St Gildas, lies to the west of En Tal. This harbour is very snug and well protected from the swell, but it is small and the local fishing boats nearly fill it. As it is a popular objective for a weekend sail from the mainland, it becomes very overcrowded and should only be visited mid-week during the season.

Approach

The easiest approach is from the north and east. From the north one will try to come down with the ebb stream, but it is better to avoid arriving near low water, so as to have room to manoeuvre inside the harbour.

From the north steer towards the eastern end of the island. Nearly 1 mile N of it is the conspicuous rock La Vieille, 19m high. Once this is identified it is easy to locate the

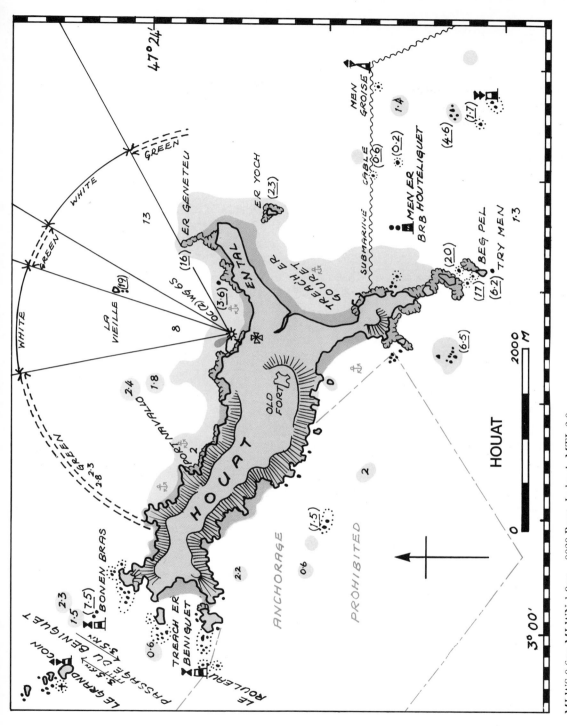

MLWS 0.6m; MLWN 1.9m; −0020 Brest, Index 1, MTL 3.0m
Based on French Chart No. 135 with corrections (No. 7033 supersedes). Depths in metres; right hand margin in cables

179

Houat harbour bearing 230°, right centre. Some yachts are at anchor to the left of the picture

harbour, which bears 200°, ¾ mile from it. Pass either side of La Vieille; it is clean to the N and E, less so to the SW and shoals extend about 200m to the S. A convenient lead passing W of the rock is to keep the church in transit with the breakwater lighthouse.

From the east the outer NE rock Er Geneteu, 16m high, can be passed at a distance of 100m. There are rocks near the direct line from it to the harbour, and a yacht should stand well out into the bay before shaping up for the harbour.

By night
Green sectors of the breakwater light (**1**) cover La Vieille and also the dangers to the east and west of the harbour. Approach in either white sector and anchor off the harbour, or enter if there is enough light to berth.

Entrance and mooring
There are two rows of moorings for yachts running parallel to the breakwater which is reserved for fishing boats. The bottom shoals behind the second row of moorings and a rock must be avoided if they are to be approached. Enter between the breakwater and the first row of moorings if there is room to pick one up or raft to another yacht. If the harbour is full, anchor in the bay to the east in 2m. The holding here is not good and in fine weather it is exposed to the *vent solaire*. Port Navalo, a small bay 1 mile to the west, offers better holding, as does the next bay west which has a sandy beach.

Many yachts anchor off Tréac'h-er-Gouret and Tréac'h-Salus despite being shown as prohibited on English charts because of high tension cables. Tréac'h-Salus offers good protection from the *vent solaire* in fine weather. The anchorage in Tréac'h-er-Béniguet is also attractive, sheltered from N through E to S.

Facilities
Water is from the public tap in the village centre, toilets are on the pier. The shops can supply simple needs, but they are limited; there are three hotels and cafés. Good shrimping and cockling is off Tréac'h-er-Gouret. The island is noted for its succession of wild flowers: roses in May, carnations in June, yellow *immortelles* in July and sand lilies in August. There are excellent beaches on the north side of En Tal, at Tréac'h-er-Gouret in the east, Tréac'h-Salus in the SE and Tréac'h-er-Beniguet in the west.

Hoëdic

This island, rather over 1 mile long and ½ mile wide, lies about 4 miles SE of Houat. There are many detached rocks off its west, south and east coasts. There are two harbours. Argol harbour, on the N side, is very small; most yachts will prefer to lie outside. The southern, drying, harbour and its approaches are dangerous in winds from the S and E, but in settled fine weather offer the best anchorage.

Approach

From the north make for the centre of the island, taking care to avoid La Chèvre in the close approach (see below). From Houat, leave Men Groise beacon (card E) and Er Rouzès tower (card E) to starboard. Thence steer for the north side of the island, keeping Houat church open to the S of Er Rouzès tower; this line passes SW of La Chèvre. From the east, making for the north side of the island, leave Beg Lagatte, the NE point of the

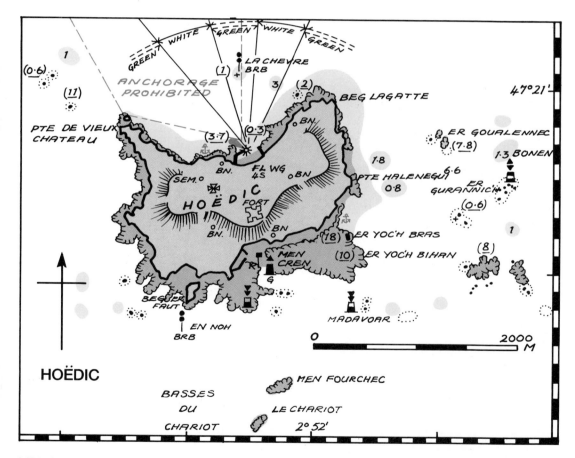

MLWS 0.6m; MLWN 1.9m; −0020 Brest, Index 1, MTL 3.0m
Based on French Chart No. 5482 with corrections (No. 7033 supersedes). Depths in metres; right hand margin in cables

181

Houat, Tréac'h er Gouret bay. A beautiful evening anchorage for 150 yachts. At 0300 the following morning came the *vent solaire*! (See p. 180)

island, about 400m to port to clear a drying rock, marked by a N cardinal beacon, NW of the point and continue into the bay.

La Chèvre, a small group of rocks drying 1m, marked by a BRB beacon, forms the principal danger on this approach.

For the approaches from the south and west see Chapter 33.

By night

Approach in one of the white sectors of the harbour light (**2**). Green sectors cover La Chèvre and dangers to the east and west of the approach.

L'Argol harbour, Hoëdic, looking W

Southern harbour, Hoëdic, near LW. Men Crenn tower (stbd) on left of picture

Anchorages

L'Argol harbour has room for 20–30 visiting yachts in settled weather. To avoid sunken rocks in the approach and outside anchorage, do not bring the head of the eastern jetty to bear more than 180°. The bottom shoals steadily; anchor in 2m, 60m from the beach, just inside the entrance to port or raft in less water with other yachts, using two small mooring buoys. A road leads to the village.

The southern harbour is best approached using a French chart (ECM 546 is suitable). The harbour itself dries 2.8m and is often crowded; most yachts will prefer to anchor outside, where there is good shelter from the *vent solaire* in fine weather. If the French chart is not on board, approach with the S cardinal tower Madavoar, (see chart, page 181) in transit with the right-hand edge of the fort, bearing 320°. On close approach leave the tower to starboard and make for a point to the S of Men Cren starboard beacon tower fetching a slight curve northwards to avoid rocks which must be left to port SE of Men Cren. Anchor S of Men Cren tower. Yachts which can take the ground, and others at neaps, can pass between Men Cren tower and the port hand beacon and anchor beside other vessels. Thence the way to the harbour is open.

There is an anchorage suitable for a visit by day off a sandy beach north of Er Yoc'h Bras, a rock 18m high which rises out of rocky flats which cover (see chart, page 181). This is approached from Beg Lagatte (Beg Lagad on BA 2353), the NE point of the island, keeping 300m offshore and avoiding a rocky spur extending SE from the northern headland of the bay (Pointe Halenegui). Anchor with soundings on sand, avoiding any patches of weed. This and other anchorages round the island are frequented by French yachts from the mainland but room to anchor can usually be found.

Facilities

It is best for a yacht to be fully provisioned and watered before visiting Hoëdic. The island boasts one small hotel, one grocery store, two crêperies, two cafés and a couple of 'Chicken take-away' establishments (not McDonalds!). There is a shower and toilet block on the right on the way up from the harbour.

Charts: English BA 2353, 2358, 2646. Imray C39.
          French SHOM 7033 P. ECM Navicarte 546.
High water: −0015 Brest, Index 1, MTL 3.0m.
  MHWS 5.4m; MLWS 0.7m; MHWN 4.2m; MLWN 2.0m.
Tidal streams: The currents outside vary from point to point; 4 miles south of La Trinité the
  flood sets NNE, the ebb SW, spring rates 2 knots.
Depths: The river is deep in the channel until the last reach, approaching the quay, where there
  are patches with only 2m.
Lights:
Leading lights on 347°:
  1. Front; Q WRG, 10m, 11–9–8M. White tower, green top.
  2. Rear; Q W, 20m, 17M. White tower, green top.
  3. Le Petit Trého by; Fl(4)R 15s.
  4. La Trinité-sur-mer dir lgt 347°; Oc WRG, 9m, 14–11M. White tower.
  5. S pier head; Oc(2)WR 6s, 7m, 10–7M. White tower, red top.
  6. No. 12 by; Fl R 2s.
  7. No. 5 by; Fl G 2s.
  8. No. 7 by; Fl(3)G 4s.
  9. No. 9 by; Fl G 2s.
  10. Marina pierhead; Iso R 4s. White framework tower, red top.

General

La Trinité, situated 1½ miles up the river Crac'h on the west side, is one of the most
popular yachting centres in the Bay of Biscay. It is not in itself exceptionally pretty, but it

La Trinité harbour and bridge; in the foreground, Eric Tabarly's hydrofoil trimaran, *Paul Ricard*

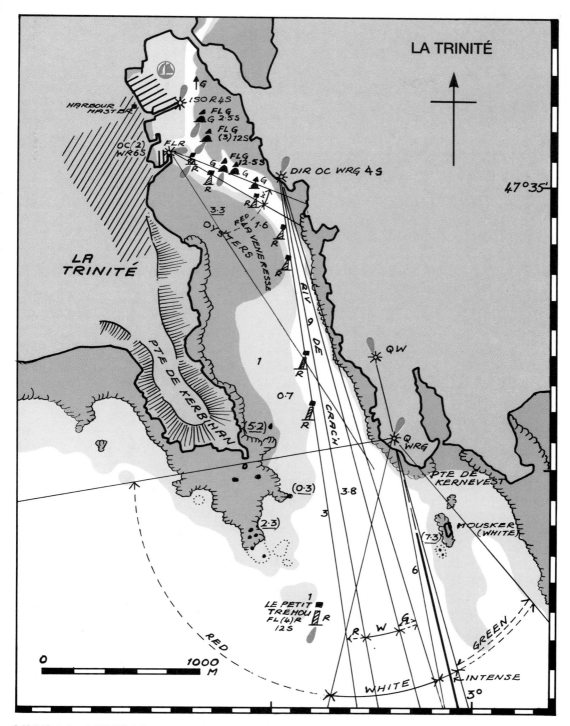

LA TRINITÉ

47°35'

LA TRINITÉ

HARBOUR MASTER

ISO R 4S
↑ G
FL G
G 2.5S
FL G
(3) 12S
OC (2)
WR 6S
FL R
G FL G
12.5S
R
R G G
R W
DIR OC WRG 4 S
3.3
RED 1.6
RA VENERESSE
OYSTERS
R
R
R

RIV 9 DE

PTE DE KERBIHAN

QW

1

0.7

(5.2)
R

CRAC'H

Q WRG

PTE DE
KERNEVEST

(0.3)

3.8

3

2.3

(7.3)

MOUSKER
(WHITE)

6

LE PETIT
TREHOU
FL (4) R
12 S
R

R W G

RED

GREEN

INTENSE

WHITE

3°

0   1000
            M

MLWS 0.6m; MLWN 2.0m; −0015 Brest, Index 1, MTL 3.0m
Based on French Chart No. 5352 with corrections (No. 7033 supersedes). Depths in metres; right hand
margin in cables

185

has good facilities, good communications and is the centre for a remarkably interesting cruising area, which also affords good courses for racing. It is, in consequence, more of a place to yacht from than to visit, though visitors are made welcome and all reasonable needs can be met.

In the marina the shelter is excellent from all except strong S and SE winds which send in a sea near high water when La Vaneresse, the sandbank protecting the harbour, is covered. In addition to its yachting activity it is a great centre for oyster culture. Anchoring is prohibited in the main channel between the entrance to the river and the town. Speed limit is 5 knots. Power vessels over 20m overall, barges, and tows of oyster-culture vessels have priority over all other vessels.

Approach

The entrance to the river is not conspicuous. It is most easily identified by the rear leading lighthouse, although this is masked on some bearings.

By day, approaching from La Teignouse, the wooded hill about 30m high will be seen to the west of the entrance. La Trinité nestles behind it, but there are some villas on it. To the east the lighthouse will be seen. Some 2 miles S by W of the entrance lies Le Souris BRB spar buoy; this must not be confused with Le Rat BRB spar buoy, situated about 1 mile to the NNW of Le Souris. From a position 500m E of Le Souris buoy Le Petit Trého buoy (lat port), 1½ miles due N will be easy to find; this buoy marks the outer dangers on the port side of the entrance to the river.

From the S or SE leave the island of Méaban 1½ miles to starboard, leave the Basse de Buissons buoy (card S) to starboard and make for the leading line, the two lighthouses in transit bearing 347°. Many of the dangers on the east side of the leading line are marked by beacons, but Roche Révision, with 0.2m over it, is unmarked.

Entrance

The river is entered between Mousker rock 7.3m high, painted white on top, to starboard, and Le Petit Trého buoy to port. Follow up the channel which is well marked by buoys, as shown on the plan. Near no. 3 buoy (stbd) there is a shoal with about 2m over it; yachts of deep draught should consequently keep close to no. 10 buoy (port) near low water.

By night
Approach with the leading lights (**1** and **2**) in transit, bearing 347°, or in the white sector of the directional light (**4**) . When the pier head light (**5**) turns from red to white continue in the white sector of that light, with due regard to buoys, lit and unlit.

Mooring

Anchoring is forbidden below the bridge (clearance 10m at HWS). Visitors berth at the marina on the first or second pontoons above the breakwater. A marina launch will normally meet a visiting yacht and direct her to a berth.

Facilities

Water and electricity are on the pontoons, showers and toilets at the Bureau du Port.

There is a launderette, ice, fuel and all the facilities of a busy yachting centre; crane, travel-lift (25 tonne) chandlers, shipyard, repairs of all kinds, but charges are high. There is a good but very busy Volvo agent, and a scrubbing berth, with a level concrete bottom, by the Yacht Club.

In the town are banks, hotel, restaurants and all shops, a good fish market at the head of the marina. There is a bus to Auray and other localities.

Charts: English BA 2358. Imray C39.
          French SHOM 7034 P. ECM Navicarte 546.
High water: (Port Navalo) as Brest, Index 0, MTL 2.8m.
   MHWS 5.0m; MLWS 0.6m; MHWN 3.8m; MLWN; 1.7m.
   Note that HW Vannes is HW Navalo +0100.
Tidal streams: Outside, in the middle of the bay, the streams are rotary: SSW at +0300 Brest
   and on to NNE at −0300 Brest, they then swing anticlockwise to N at HW Brest and back to
   SSW at +0300 Brest, spring rates 1–2 knots. Nearer the entrance the streams strengthen. Off
   Port Navalo the flood begins −0400 Brest, the ebb at +0055 Brest, spring rates 7 knots.
Depths: The approach and entrance is deep.
Note: Tidal information for the interior of the Morbihan is given below under the headings
   Auray river, Vannes channel and southern and eastern Morbihan.
Lights:
   1. Port Navalo; Oc(3)WRG 12s, 32m, 16–12–11M. White tower and house.
   2. Port de Crouesty; Leading lights Dir Q W on 058°.
      Front; R panel with vert W stripe. Rear; white tower.
   3. Crouesty N jetty head; Oc(2)R 6s, 9m, 7M. White square tower, red top.
   4. Crouesty S jetty head; Fl G 4s, 9m, 7M. White square tower, red top.
   5. Gd Mouton beacon (stbd) QG, 4m, 3M.
   6. Grégan; Q(6)+L 15s, card S tower.

General

This inland sea, which receives the waters of three rivers, though it is fed mostly by the
tide, has an area of about 50 square miles. Since the megalithic era the land has sunk, or
the sea level has risen, according to S. Baring-Gould, some 10 metres and a partly
submerged stone circle can be seen on the islet Lannic to the south of Gavrinis island. Just
south of this circle is another, fully submerged, which could present a hazard. Today the
islands of the Morbihan are said to be equal in number to the days of the year, but in fact
there are no more than 60 and this figure includes the isolated rocks. Many are wooded
and all, with the exception of Ile aux Moines and Ile d'Arz, are privately owned. Most are
uninhabited and, in these cases, landing is not objected to. Ile Berder is a convalescent
home and if one wishes to go ashore it is usual to ask permission. Ile aux Moines with its
pine woods, restaurants, good shops and beach is the island most visited. Ile d'Arz has
picturesque walled farms, such as Ker Noel. The Séné peninsula (known as L'Angle and
lying east of Boëdic) was the home of the Sinagots, a separate community of fishermen.
On Gavrinis, a guide will conduct visitors round the celebrated carved tumulus.

As a cruising ground the Morbihan is exceptionally interesting and offers innumerable anchorages in sheltered water. Only near the narrow entrance off Port Navalo is it open to the sea. Within the entrance, off Grand Mouton rock and south of Ile Longue, Gavrinis and Ile Berder the streams attain 8½ knots at extreme spring tides. They are fierce in the narrows between the islands, but farther from the entrance they moderate and in the upper reaches are not strong.

Navigation in the Morbihan is not as difficult as it appears on the chart as the islands are easy to identify. There is deep water in the main channels and dangers are marked by beacons and buoys. Chart BA 2358 is recommended if it is intended to explore the more out-of-the-way channels. The best time for cruising is at neaps, but even then the navigator will have to be quick in his pilotage, as with a fair stream the speed scross the ground will be greater than he expects.

It is a help to plot courses on the chart and to tick off the landmarks as they pass.

The tidal streams are often fast enough for their direction to be seen from their surface appearance. In 1951 *Isabel*, an 80 tonne ketch, under sail, was spun through 360° south of Gavrinis and it is reported that, some years later, the Brixham trawler *Provident* went up the channel like a carousel. However, except in the vicinity of Le Grand Mouton, the streams tend to follow the directions of the channels. Sometimes they run on one side of the channel and there is a slack or reverse eddy on the other, with a clear dividing line between them. Using the eddies, those with local knowledge can make surprising progress against a foul tide. If you leave the main channel, begin to turn in good time, or you will be swept past your destination.

Approach and entrance

The outer approach to the Morbihan presents no difficulty. Peering above the trees is Port Navalo lighthouse, on the east side of the entrance, with a second tower like a lighthouse close to it; more conspicuous from the south-west are the Petit Mont, a hill 42m high, on the peninsula 1 mile to the SE of it, and the white lighthouse within Crouesty marina.

Golfe du Morbihan entrance, with the leading marks almost in line on 001°. Baden spire and Le Petit Veisit beacon are half way between the Port Navalo lighthouse and the right hand white sail

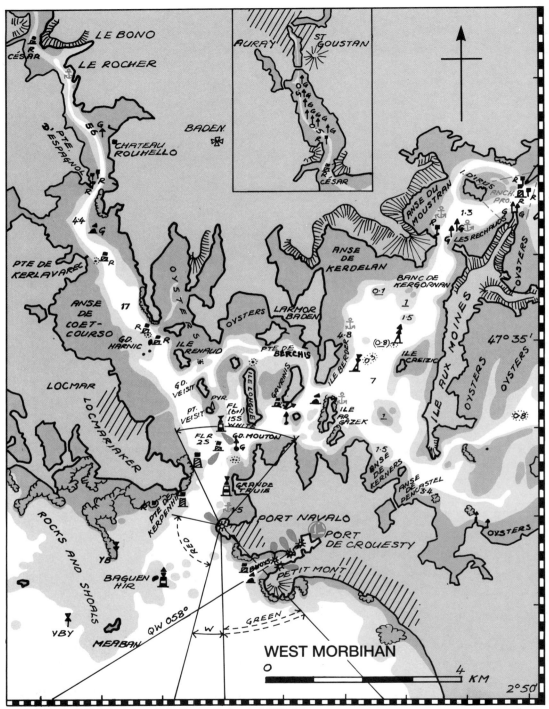

MLWS 0.6m; MLWN 1.7m; 0000 Brest, Index 0, MTL 2.8m
Based on French Charts Nos. 5420 and 3165 with corrections (No. 7034 supersedes). Depths in metres;
right hand margin in cables. Gd Mouton QG. Delete buoy light Fl R 2s

190

Make Basse de Méaban S cardinal buoy and, leaving it to port, approach the entrance and identify the leading marks. They are: the white pyramid on Le Petit Veisit in transit with Baden church spire 3 miles behind it, bearing 001° (see photograph). Follow this transit through the narrows, leaving Petit Mont ¾ mile to starboard, Baguen Hir E cardinal tower ½ mile to port and Port Navalo lighthouse 200m to starboard. This transit leads close to the Pointe de Navalo and, on the ebb, there can be a strong eddy, running along the shore from the entrance to Crouesty marina and round the point, which facilitates passage into Port Navalo bay to await the flood.

The flood sweeps past the Pointe de Navalo, then swings across towards the Pointe de Kerpenhir, then back towards Le Grégan tower. The approach is rough on the ebb if there is an onshore wind. The entrance channel is marked on its western side by two towers, Kerpenhir (port) and Goëmorent (port), and on its eastern side by the Grande Truie tower (card W), on the northern side of Port Navalo bay.

For further directions for the Auray river see page 193, and for the Vannes channel see page 198.

A gale warning light is shown by day from Port Navalo lighthouse: Int Qk Fl for force 6 to 7; Qk Fl for force 8 and above, between July 1 and September 15.

By night

There are no lights in the Morbihan. If it is not quite dark it is possible to use the Port Navalo lighthouse to get into Port Navalo and wait for daylight, but it is easier to enter Crouesty marina which has leading lights.

For Port Navalo: enter the white sector of Port Navalo light (**1**) on about 010° and keep on the west side of the sector. Petit Mont (42m) will be left to starboard and, when the Crouesty leading lights are in transit, bear a little to port, just into the red sector. Round the lighthouse at a distance of 150m and, passing through the white sector of the light, pick up a vacant mooring clear of the pier in 1m or less. The bay is full of moorings and it is not advisable to anchor without light.

For Le Crouesty: enter the white sector of Port Navalo light (**1**) as before on about 005°. When the Crouesty leading lights (**2**) come into transit on 058°, turn to starboard on to this transit and steer into the marina, securing to the pontoon along the starboard wall or to a waiting pontoon under the Capitainerie.

Le Crouesty

This marina has been built in the bay south of Port Navalo and is useful if one arrives at the entrance to the Morbihan at the wrong tide. It also has a large supermarket at the head of the north basin with a fish market outside. This is excellent for storing ship before entering to explore the Morbihan and there is a fuel berth on the pontoon on the starboard side on entry.

The entrance opens on passing Petit Mont and it is only necessary to follow the buoyed channel, carrying 1.5m, to pass between the outer piers. Leading marks are the lighthouse and a red panel with a vertical white stripe.

Crouesty marina entrance

Facilities
Water and electricity are available on the pontoons, and showers, toilets, a good launderette. The bank is open Friday and Tuesday. There are cafés and food shops round the marina, and an excellent supermarket, chandlers, engineers, crane, travel lift (45 tonne). There is a post office at Arzon ($\frac{1}{2}$ mile).

Golfe du Morbihan. Looking out to the entrance with the tide running. Port Navalo is to the left of the picture and Le Grand Mouton beacon (green) is just clear to the right of the point. This presents a real hazard as the current will set the unwary onto it. The beacon is now lit

Port Navalo at LW

Port Navalo

There is a tolerable anchorage, in depths of 1.5m off the end of the pier, but it is exposed to the S and W and disturbed by the wash from ferries. The shoaling bay is full of moorings and in may be possible to arrange to borrow one further in near neaps.

Facilities

One may land at all tides at the outer jetty, but dinghies must not be left blocking the way for passengers on the ferries. At tide time, land at the eastern jetty by the village. There are simple shops and restaurants, and ferries to Auray and Vannes.

Departure

When leaving on the flood to enter the Morbihan, steer boldly out into the stream to avoid being set on to the Grand Mouton (see page 189).

Auray river

High water Auray: +0025 Brest, Index 1, MTL 3.0m.
   MHWS 5.2m; MLWS 0.7m; MHWN 4.0m; MLWN 1.9m.
Tidal streams: Flood begins −0510 Brest, ebb begins +0025 Brest, spring rates 3–3½ knots.
Depths: The river is deep as far as Le Rocher, though the last mile of the deep channel is narrow, so that it may be better to regard it as carrying 1m. Above Le Rocher it shoals rapidly and the bottom is only just below datum. The mooring area at Auray in midstream has been dredged to 3m, and more in places, but the quays dry.

Auray river. Anchorage off le Bono creek

This fine river on the west side of the Morbihan provides 8 miles of varying scenery. The town of Auray, at the head of the navigable river, stands on a steep hill on the west side of the river with the old port of St Goustan on the east side. Auray is quite a large town, much of it fifteenth century, with the steeples of the church and chapel standing on the hill. The old port of St Goustan is now small, but at one time had a substantial trade. Benjamin Franklin landed here from America to negotiate a treaty with France during the War of Independence. The river runs southwards between wooded shores, through a narrow cleft at Le Rocher, then gradually widens out between mud banks and oyster beds, until near the entrance it merges into the Morbihan scene of islands and fast tidal streams.

The river is often visited by English yachts, but is relatively less popular with the local people, so that one can easily find quiet spots away from the crowds. Auray has good communications, making it a good place for changing crew.

The river

In passing the Morbihan entrance (see page 191), keep nothing E of the 001° transit of Le Petit Veisit pyramid and Baden church. When the tide is up a bit one can pass fairly close to Goëmorent tower (port), but there is only 1.4m some 300m E of it and near LW the leading line must be strictly held.

The tidal set over Le Grand Mouton at the entrance to the Vannes channel presents a real hazard at this point whether a vessel intends to proceed up to Auray or to Vannes.

If bound for Auray, it is desirable to alter to port when Goëmorent is abeam and to leave Le Lieu buoy (lat port) to *starboard*, there being 3m depth up to 300m W of the buoy. From Le Lieu a course of 332° leads to E Harnic buoy (lat port). Beyond Le Lieu the tides

194

Auray river. Looking upstream towards St Goustan. The bridge, completed 1989, has a clearance of 14m

set fairly up and down the channel, except for local sets between the islands on the east side, particularly north of Grand Veisit.

Steer for Grand Harnic, easily recognized by two conspicuous clumps of trees, leaving Le Gréguan tower (card S) 300m to starboard. Petit Veisit, Grand Veisit and Ile Renaud will also be left to starboard and, when E Harnic buoy (lat port) has been identified, leave

Anchorage out of the stream SE of Ile Longue. The yacht in the stream is making good 10 knots over the ground

Er Lanic with its half-submerged stone circle. There is another circle fully submerged in the foreground. The tomb on Gavrinis is far right of the picture

it close to port and pass between N Grand Harnic buoy (lat port) and a green (lat stbd) beacon off Pointe du Blair.

North of this the channel is wide, though there is a big shallow bay, the Anse de Coët Courzo, to port. A course of 325° will take the yacht to the port hand buoy off the Pointe de Kerlavarec and on to the Catis buoy (stbd). Here the channel is narrower and there are extensive mud flats on either hand. The yacht should be steered in a gradual sweep round the mud on the starboard hand until she heads for the middle of the narrows off Pointe d'Espagnol (SE of Kercado BA 2358) with the Château Rouhello (conspicuous with a lawn in front and trees on either side) well open. Steer for the château when it bears 025°, leaving the two red (port) beacons on the end of Pointe d'Espagnol (the first marking the end of a long slipway) to port. The withies on the oyster beds help to identify the channel. Above Pointe d'Espagnol the deep water lies on the east side of the river off the château. Then, as the Anse de Kerdreau opens, the channel bears to port towards the narrows seen ahead. The shallow Anse is left to starboard, together with the green beacon marking the edge of the mud. The deep channel now crosses to the other side. This is the narrowest part of the river which becomes much prettier, passing between steep rocky shores and thick woods to Le Rocher.

The deep part of the river ends above Le Rocher and it can only be navigated up to Auray with sufficient rise of tide. The channel almost dries, but there is plenty of water in the pool at Auray. The channel is clearly marked, the trickiest part being where it crosses the remains of a Roman bridge ½ mile above Le Rocher. There is a drying shoal in midstream, marked by Caesar, a red buoy which should be left well to port. The only visible remnant of the bridge is a flat square of turf over stones on the bank to port.

Anchorages

One of the beauties of the Morbihan is that it is possible to find an endless variety of anchorages according to weather and individual preference for solitude or company, steep banks or saltings. Some well-known anchorages are given but many others can be found.

Locmariaker

This village is on the west side of the river near the entrance opposite the Veisit islands. There is a channel to it, with about 0.6m, marked by port hand beacons, but it is narrow and used by the ferries. The quay dries 1.5m. Yachts can take the ground between the village quay and the vedette jetty. It is possible to anchor off the entrance and go in by dinghy, but this anchorage is rather exposed and subject to strong tides.

Larmor Baden

This village lies 1 mile to the east of the Auray river, between it and the Vannes channel. It is approached from the Auray river by passing between Grand Veisit and Ile Renaud, leaving Ile Radenec to starboard and keeping in the northern half of the channel to avoid a rock and a drying patch 200m N and 200m NE of Radenec. It can also be approached from the Vannes channel by passing close east of Ile Longue, or more simply between Gavrinis and Ile Berder. It is possible to anchor near Pointe de Balis or farther to the east and closer to the pier, but there are many moorings here and it might be more convenient to arrange to borrow one. The tides run hard through the channel (flood E, ebb W), and it is best to work into one of the bays as far as draught and depths allow.

Le Rocher

Once an excellent and popular anchorage, but now full of permanent moorings. If one is available, land at the small inlet downstream on the east side.

Port du Bono

An inlet to starboard just north of Le Rocher. There is 1m as far as the jetty and 0.5m at the quay but the holding is bad. The new bridge, but not the old, has ample clearance. A dinghy excursion can be made to the hamlet and chapel of St Avoye; land on the port side ½ mile above the old bridge at Le Bono.

St Goustan

A new road bridge was under construction in 1988 just below the port; clearance should, by report, be 14m at HWS. There are moorings in the middle of the river opposite the quays and visitors' fore and aft moorings further down. There is enough water at most tides over a considerable length. The water shoals rapidly on the turn to the old bridge and, especially at springs, the ebb pours violently through the bridge and eddies make the upper end of the deep water an uneasy berth. The quay should only be used as a temporary berth at high water and the large floating restaurant-cum-sight-seeing vessel must be given plenty of room to manoeuvre and berth. There is a dinghy pontoon near the old bridge which is useful at LW.

Facilities

All shops and restaurants at Locmariaker, Larmor Baden and Le Bono but nothing at Le Rocher. At St Goustan a Bureau du Port was under construction in 1988. There are simple shops and restaurants on the quay, a good fishmarket in the square and all the facilities of a substantial town up the hill at Auray, including a marine engineer. Market day is Monday. There is a good train service, though the station is some way from the town and further from St Goustan. There are buses to all parts, including La Baule for the airport and Carnac for the megaliths.

Vannes channel

High water: (*Vannes*) +0200 Brest, Index see below, MTL 3.0m.

   MHWS 4.7m; MLWS 1.3m; MHWN 4.0m; MLWN 2.1m.

   The tide tables in this book will not give very good results for Vannes, as the tide wave is distorted in passing up the channels. The Index varies from 0 at neaps to −3 at springs. Chart datum is the level of LAT at the *entrance*; coming up the channel even the lowest do not fall below 0.4–0.9m above this level.

Tidal streams: Inside the entrance the stream divides, a weaker portion running up the Auray river. Part of this sweeps past Larmor Baden and rejoins the main Vannes Channel at the south end of Ile Berder, where it causes turbulence and a back eddy close to the shore. The main torrent follows the main channel; the spring rate is about 8 knots. The irregularities of the channel produce whirlpools and the yacht's head is thrown from side to side, but not so as to make it difficult to keep in the channel. The way the water climbs up the Grand Mouton is remarkable. Once through the narrows south of Ile Berder the rate decreases a little, but the stream continues in a narrow jet towards Ile Creizic, and thence near the Ile aux Moines to the narrows NW of that island. Here the stream is fierce, sweeping across from the Pointe des Réchauds in a wide curve along the mainland side and south of Ile d'Irus. This sets up an eddy, so that NW of Ile aux Moines the current runs SW almost continuously. After passing the narrows north of Ile aux Moines the stream fans out and becomes weaker, nowhere exceeding 4 knots. The ebb stream roughly reverses the flood, but it is important to keep towards the south side of the narrows between Ile Berder and Ile ar Gazek (Ile de la Jument) if one does not want to be swept up the channel west of Ile Berder to Larmor Baden. It is important to realize that, not only is high water progressively later as one goes up the channel (2 hours between Port Navalo and Vannes), but the streams do not turn until about $1\frac{1}{2}$ hours after local high water or low water.

Depths: The channel is deep to Ile aux Moines; thence deep water can be carried to Ile de Boëdic, but the deep channel is very narrow in places and it is easier to regard it as carrying 0.7m. Thence to Conleau it carries 2.5m, after which it shoals progressively (but see the note above on low water levels).

Vannes, looking N at the marina and Cathedral. The pontoon bridge is open for entry

The channel

Before entering the Morbihan it is advisable to plot the succession of compass courses up
to Vannes on the chart. This will make it easier to identify the islands and the relevant
gaps between them as the vessel speeds up the channel. Tick the islands off on the chart as
they flash past. Note that some of the names on BA 2358 do not match those on the
French charts. The latter are used in this pilot.

After passing the entrance (see page 191), immediate steps must be taken to avoid being
swept by the tide onto the Grand Mouton rock, which lies to starboard and is marked by
a green beacon with a green conical topmark. Steer to leave Le Lieu buoy (port) close to
port and turn sharply to starboard only when the Grand Mouton is safely passed. The
channel is now clear before you. Leave Ile Longue to port, a beacon (stbd) and the islet of
Er Lanic to starboard, Gavrinis to port (there is a landing place here marked by
beacons), a buoy (stbd) and Ile ar Gazek to starboard, and Ile Berder to port.

A wide expanse of water, some of it shallow, now opens, but it is best to keep in the jet of
the tide setting towards the small Ile Creizic. Leave to port the two cardinal buoys
marking middle grounds, steering midway between the second and the N end of Ile
Creizic. After passing this, turn towards the north, keeping fairly close to (but not less

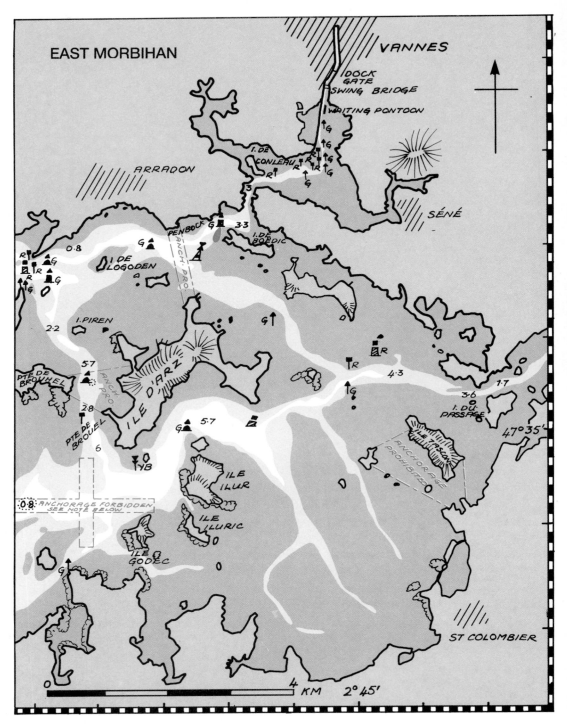

Roughly MLWS 1m; MLWN 2m; +0100 Brest, Index 0 (np), −1(sp), MTL 2.9m but see text
Based on French Charts Nos. 5420 and 3165 with corrections (No. 7034 supersedes). Depths in metres;
right hand margin in cables

than 200m off) the Ile aux Moines shore. This avoids the Kergornan shoal which dries 1m in places.

The stream sets strongly through the narrows between Ile aux Moines and the mainland, and Les Réchauds rocks, marked by two beacons (stbd), are left to starboard. Thence the channel is straightforward, the critical points being well marked.

Leave:

  Ile d'Irus to port,
  Two beacons (stbd) on Pointe de Drec'h to starboard,
  A tower (port) and a beacon (port) on La Truie to port,
  A buoy (stbd) off Pointe d'Arradon to starboard,
  The yachting centre of Arradon to port,
  Steer to leave the green (stbd) beacon W of Ile de Logoden 100m to starboard and
    round Le Petit Logoden, leaving it 100m to starboard,
  Drenec buoy (stbd) to starboard.

An alternative and rather shorter channel carries 1.8m. After passing Pointe de Drec'h leave Holavre tower (stbd) to starboard and pass south of Ile de Logoden, rejoining the other channel N of the next buoy (stbd).

After leaving Penboc'h pier to port there is a shoal in the centre of the channel carrying only 0.7m in places. There is a very narrow deep channel north of it, and a wider but tortuous channel south of it. However, even extreme tides here never fall to within 0.5m of datum and, as one will usually be sailing here near high water, having come up on the flood or being bound down on the ebb, this shoal should not normally present a hazard.

The channel continues in a curve to the north east, leaving a cardinal W buoy and Roguédas tower (stbd) to starboard. North of Ile de Boëdic the continuation of the channel is not obvious from a distance. As one passes north of Boëdic the narrow gap opens up dramatically. When it is fully open turn sharply to port and steer through it.

Approaching the Roguédas narrows. Boëdic chapel is right centre and Roguédas tower (stbd) is left centre

Coming out of this narrow passage the yachting centre of Conleau is to port and a wide expanse of shallow water lies ahead. The channel through this is marked by beacons; at the far end it takes a very sharp turn to port and its bottom is only just above datum. Thence the channel is very narrow, though well marked by beacons, and there is only just room to pass oncoming traffic. The channel gets progressively shallower and is about 1.2m above datum when it reaches the vedette quay on the port bank.

A short distance past the vedette quay is a swing bridge. This is operated from the Capitainerie at the Vannes wet basin. Closed circuit television cameras show the situation on the road and in the channel. If the bridge is not open, secure to the waiting pontoon on the starboard side.

The gate for the wet basin at Vannes is open between 0800 and 2200 in season for a maximum of 5 hours depending on the requirement to maintain a depth of 2.4m at the pontoons. As a rough guide, according to the harbourmaster, it will open at HW Navalo. Regulations state that the bridge will open for 10 minutes every half hour while the gate is open. In fact the harbourmaster may operate the bridge at his discretion, depending on road traffic, should there be vessels waiting to pass. Harbour office listens on Ch. 9.

Lights
Red: stop; yellow: boats that can, proceed under bridge; flashing green: get ready; green: go.

The visitors' pontoon in the wet basin is on the starboard side, but a launch may direct you to a vacant berth on arrival.

Anchorages
With the large-scale chart many anchorages can be found; some of the better known ones are:

Ile Longue
There is a NE facing bay on the SE end of this island where the water is slack when the tide is running hard in the channel. The bottom shelves rapidly but there is room to anchor on soundings. Some use the 4.9m (rocky) patch (see BA 2358) where the water is still. The island is private and landing is not allowed.

Larmor Baden
See page 197.

Ile ar Gazek
(Ile de la Jument on BA 2358). On the east of the island out of the tide. A good place to wait for a fair tide.

Ile Berder
To the SE of the island, NW of the card S buoy, or farther north in the Mouillage de Kerdelan. A good anchorage with little stream. Yachts on moorings indicate the best areas.

Ile aux Moines

There is a small marina on the NW corner with a few berths for visitors and some visitors' moorings. It is also possible to anchor to the NE of the moorings. It is worth working out the depths carefully, because the bottom slopes very gently for a long way before suddenly dropping into deep water. To have more than just enough water one has to go a long way out with a deep draught vessel and so tend to be more in the tide, though the tides are not too strong if one gets well into the bay. There is no official information about tidal constants for this point. If the tide tables in this book are used take high water as +0100 Brest, Index 0 at neaps, −1 at springs, MTL 2.9m; these constants are only estimates and some margin should be allowed. A fine weather anchorage exposed to the W and SW is south of Pointe de Toulindac, the NW tip of the island.

Anse de Moustran

This is the bay just north of Port Blanc on the opposite side of the narrows to Ile aux Moines. The best spots are occupied by moorings, so that one is pushed out into deeper water where the tide is strong. If the wind comes up against the tide the yacht sheers about and, as the bottom is sharp sand, galvanizing can be lost from the anchor chain.

Arradon

A popular yachting centre. There are moorings for visitors or anchor outside the moorings. It is rather exposed in southerly weather near high water.

Penbock

Anchor east of the jetty; again it is rather exposed.

Ile de Boëdic

There is a pleasant, secluded, sheltered anchorage in the bight at the NW end of the island. The island is private and there is no landing.

Conleau

The inlet to the SW of the peninsula is full of moorings. The best available anchorage is in the bight on the port side just before the far end of the narrows. There are usually some fishing boats here. The restaurant on the Ile de Conleau is recommended.

Vannes

Entry has already been described above. Port signals: green light, departure prohibited; red light, entry prohibited; red above green, entry and departure prohibited.

A timetable for the gate operation is available at the Capitainerie on the W bank (telephone: 97 54 16 08 or 97 54 00 47; VHF Ch. 9).

The wet dock, 600m long, has a pontoon bridge for pedestrians half way up which is broken when the gate is open. The quieter pontoons are on the W bank below the pontoon bridge.

Facilities

There are no facilities at all at Iles ar Gazek, Berder and Boëdic. Facilities are very limited at Arradon and Penbock. At Port Blanc (Anse de Moustran) fuel and water are available, with a Capitainerie and tourist bureau. On Ile de Conleau there is a good restaurant. At Ile aux Moines there are all the usual village shops and hotels and restaurants near the quay.

Vannes is an attractive cathedral city of historic interest with banks, hotels, restaurants and all the facilities of a large town. Market day is Tuesday. Water and electricity are on the pontoons, showers and toilets by the Capitainerie, which provides a good regional Meteo. Yacht yard with fuel berth outside the gates and chandlers in the town.

Communications

Vannes is a main rail centre and communications by rail and bus are good, making it a good place for a change of crew. Buses from Conleau and Vannes marina pass the railway station. There is an airfield north of the city and a regular service of ferries from below the swing bridge to Conleau, Ile aux Moines, Port Navalo, Auray and other points in the Morbihan.

Southern and eastern Morbihan

Tides: There is a lack of official information. Tidal heights can probably be calculated approximately, using the tables in this book and taking high water as +0100 Brest (later at Ile du Passage), Index 0 (neaps) or −1 (springs), MTL 2.9m, but these figures are guesses and a margin should be allowed.

An interesting alternative after passing between Iles Berder and ar Gazek is to proceed S of Ile aux Moines. Beyond the narrows the channels, though well marked, wind between mudflats and are probably best taken by a stranger on a rising tide. The tidal streams are not so fierce as in other parts of the Morbihan. Between Ile aux Moines and Ile d'Arz the flood runs to the S.

Anchorages

Anse de Kerners
Anchor outside the local boats. There are water, showers and provisions in season.

Anse de Pencastel
Anchor outside the moorings.

Anse de Penhap
This is a peaceful anchorage in the south of the Ile aux Moines. Get in as far as draught and soundings will allow to be right out of the streams.

Between Ile aux Moines and Ile d'Arz

Those requiring solitude may find it south-west of the anchorage shown on BA 2358 south of Ile de Spiren (Ile Piren on the French charts). Shallow draught vessels must keep clear of the oyster beds. There is a landing at the Pointe de Brouel and at the slip W of Pointe de Brouel. All shops are available on Ile aux Moines in the Bourg, 1 mile walk. Ile d'Arz is more primitive but has shops.

Ile du Passage

This is the last anchorage where one can lie afloat. However, in 1988 a yacht drawing 2m could only get within 400m of the narrows before grounding and reported another yacht grounded nearby. Anchor midstream in the narrows to the north of the island; the tide is strong. Quiet and rural, it has no supplies. This used to be the base for the Sinagots, fisherman living at Séné, who sailed an individual type of brown-sailed lug-rigged schooner with conspicuous skill. A few of these survive, sailed as yachts.

37 Penerf

Charts: English BA 2353, 2646. Imray C39.
      French SHOM 7033 P. ECM Navicarte 546.
High water: −0010 Brest, Index 2, MTL 1.9m.
    MHWS 5.5m; MLWS 0.6m; MHWN 4.2m; MLWN 1.9m.
Tidal streams: Between Pointe du Grand Mont and the river mouth the flood has a spring rate of
   1 knot, the ebb 1½ knots. In the passes the streams run 3 knots springs when the rocks are
   uncovered, but only 2 knots ENE and WSW when the rocks are covered.
Depths: In the central pass 0.5m, in the east pass 4.5m. Inside, the river is deep as far as Cadenic.

This quiet and unspoilt river, 6 miles west of the entrance to La Vilaine, is sheltered from the Atlantic swell by groups of rocks and the peninsula on which Penerf is situated. The village is small, combining oyster culture with being a minor holiday centre. A fair number of yachts and fishing boats are moored off the village of Penerf and others off Cadenic on the other side of the river ½ mile further up. There is still plenty of room for visitors. There are many rocky ledges near the entrance. They are well marked with beacons, but the channels are very narrow in a wide expanse of water; it is not safe for the stranger in bad weather or poor visibility as an error could have serious consequences.

Loss of trees during the storm of October 1987 has made the main leading mark, the spire of Le Tour du Parc, visible once more. It was for some years obscured from view and this may well recur at some future date.

Penerf quay, looking towards Pen Cadenic

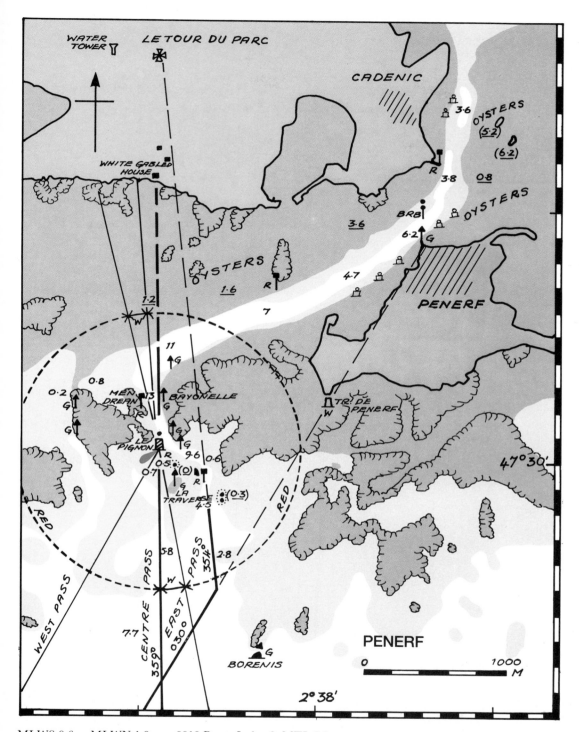

WATER TOWER

LE TOUR DU PARC

CADENIC

3·6

OYSTERS

(5·2)

(6·2)

WHITE GABLED HOUSE

R

3·8

0·8

B.R.B

OYSTERS

3·6

6·2 G

OYSTERS

1·6

4·7

PENERF

R

7

11 G

0·8

0·2 G

MEN DREAN 13

BAYONELLE G

Tr. DE PENERF

G

W

LE PIGNON

R

9·6 0·6

0·5

0·7 (0)

R

LA TRAVERSE (0·3)

4·5

47°30′

RED

RED

5·8 2·8

WEST PASS

CENTRE PASS 359°

EAST PASS 354° 030°

W

7·7

PENERF

0   1000
                 M

G

BORENIS

2°38′

MLWS 0.6m; MLWN 1.9m; −0010 Brest, Index 2, MTL 3.0m
Based on French Chart No. 5418 with corrections (No. 7033 supersedes). Depths in metres; right hand margin in cables

207

Approach

Pointe de Penvins, 1½ miles SW of the entrance, is easy to identify. It is low, with a conspicuous octagonal mosque-like chapel on it; ½ mile SSE of Penvins chapel is the Penvins buoy (lat port) which is left to port. To the ENE of Penvins chapel are Le Pignon tower (red) and the Tour de Penerf, looking like a chess castle and painted white.

Enter the bay with the Tour de Penerf roughly in transit with the left-hand side of the village of Penerf, bearing about 030°.

Approaching on this transit, identify:

1. Le Pignon red beacon tower,
2. a conspicuous water tower to the north,
3. a prominent white house with a single gable on the shore to the right of the water tower,
4. the steeple of Le Tour du Parc church above the trees to the right of the white house.

Beware of heavy fishing netting in the approach.

Entrance

There are three passes into Penerf. The west pass can be disposed of by saying that, although it is preferred by the local fishermen in strong westerly winds, it is not well enough marked for strangers, who should not enter this port in strong westerly winds. The central pass is the easiest, but is not deep enough to be used at low water. The east pass is less easy to follow but is deep.

Penerf entrance, using the centre pass. La Traverse is astern to starboard, Le Tour du Parc spire bears 358° and Le Pignon (red) tower must be left to port

Central pass

This pass carries a least depth of 0.5m. If the steeple is clearly visible, bring the steeple in line with Le Pignon tower bearing 000°. Should the spire become obscured, Le Pignon in transit with the white house, bearing 359°, will serve. These transits will leave Borenis spar buoy (stbd) 800m to starboard and La Traverse beacon 150m to starboard, with a port hand beacon for the east pass beyond it.

On close approach to Le Pignon tower, bear to starboard and leave the tower 40m to port. Thence steer to leave the Bayonelle beacon (stbd) 20m to starboard; this course leaves to starboard two beacons (stbd) on the S end of Le Petit Bayonelle rocks and Men Drean beacon to port. The Bayonelle beacon pole replaces a beacon tower which was destroyed but is still shown on some charts.

After passing between the Bayonelle beacon and Men Drean beacon hold the same course for nearly 200m, until another starboard hand beacon has come into transit with Penerf village. Then alter course to steer ENE for the boats on moorings off the village over 1 mile away. Leave the beacon (stbd) 100m to starboard, and a beacon (port) half way to the village about 200m to port as it is well up on the mud.

East pass

This pass carries 4.5m if the directions are followed, but the pass is narrow and there are rocky shoals to the east of it which it is essential to avoid. Before finally committing the yacht to the pass, that is to say before passing the outer port hand beacon, the following marks should be positively identified:

The port hand beacon on the east side of La Traverse, and the Men Drean beacon (port) beyond Le Pignon tower;
the starboard beacon replacing the former Bayonelle tower east of Men Drean; and
the two starboard beacons opposite Le Pignon.

Approach on the transit (030°) of the Tour de Penerf with the left hand edge of the village of Penerf. Having identified the Tour du Parc steeple and the port hand beacon, La Traverse, they will come into transit on 354°. Turn onto this transit to enter the pass. If La Traverse port hand beacon has not been identified by the time Borenis spar buoy (stbd) is abeam, distant about 600m, go back.

The transit leaves very close to starboard a rock with 1.3m over it. When within 100m of La Traverse beacon alter course to leave it 20m to port. After passing it continue to steer about 355° for another 100m until a course of 300° will lead between Le Pignon tower (port) and the southernmost of the two green beacons (stbd) on Le Petit Bayonelle to the east of Le Pignon. Steer this course and alter as necessary to leave the two green beacons 30m to starboard and Le Pignon to port. Thence, passing between Bayonelle beacon (stbd) and Men Drean beacon (port), follow the directions given above for the central pass.

When leaving by the east pass it is important to bring La Traverse beacon (port) in transit with Le Tour du Parc steeple quickly in order to avoid contact with the eastern rocks.

By night
Le Pignon is lit (Fl(3)WR 12s, 6m, 9M), with white sectors covering the central channel. However, a fair amount of light would be needed to go up the river and strangers are not recommended to attempt a night entry.

Anchorage
The most convenient anchorage is off Penerf slip, the end of which is marked by a green beacon (stbd), but moorings now extend down river for several hundred metres below the slip as well as above it. There is a line of visitors' moorings outside the local moorings above the slip in 6m. These are in the tide and one must aim off accordingly when going to and from the shore in a dinghy. About 200m upstream is an isolated danger beacon (BRB) which should be left to port by visitors. North of this the channel tends to the west bank where there is a slip, the end marked by a red beacon (port) with moorings in 3.5m, mostly occupied by the fishing boats of Cadenic. A green buoy (stbd) on the other side of the channel marks the edge of the extensive mud flats and oyster beds on the east side of the river. A quiet overnight anchorage may be found upstream of the Cadenic moorings, but some report that the tide runs hard and the holding is not good.

Facilities
All shops, café and restaurant are at Penerf. There is a café but no shops at Cadenic, but a travelling shop calls daily; orders for it could be left at the café.

Charts: English BA 2353, 2646. Imray C39.
French SHOM 7033 P. ECM Navicarte 546. ECM Carte Guide: Navigation Fluviale Voies Navigables de Bretagne.

High water: −0010 Brest, Index 2, MTL 3.0m.
MHWS 5.4m; MLWS 0.6m; MHWN 4.2m; MLWN 1.9m.

Tidal streams: Normal for an estuary of this size. Above La Roche Bernard and up as far as Rennes the river can be closed to navigation for a time after heavy rain.

Depths: The closure of the Arzal Dam has caused silting in the estuary and the line of the buoyed channel is subject to alteration. In 1988, 1m could be found over the bar south of Pointe de Penlan and a least depth of 2m in the channel to Arzal. Above Arzal, vessels drawing 1.3m can proceed up to Rennes with an occasional drive through soft mud. A vessel drawing 1.2m can usually navigate from Rennes to Dinan except in a dry summer.

Lights:
1. Basse Bertrand; Iso WG 4s, 6m, 9–6M. Green tower.
2. Penlan; Oc(2)WRG 6s, 26m, 15–12M. White tower, red bands.
3. Pointe du Scal; Oc(3)G 12s, 8m, 6M. White square tower, green top.
4. Tréhiguer; Oc(4)R 12s, 21m, 11M. White square tower and dwelling.
5. Channel bys;
    No. 1: Fl G 2.5s.
    No. 2: Fl R 2.5s.
    No. 4: Fl(2)R 5s.
    No. 5: Fl(3)G 6s.
    No. 6: Fl(3)R 6s.
    No. 8: Fl(4)R 7s.

On a summer's day few places are prettier than La Vilaine, running between meadows where cows ruminate, or between rush-covered banks or rocky cliffs.

Above the Arzal dam there is a tideless lake. This is not a tidal power scheme like that on the Rance in north Brittany, with its rapid changes of level. The intention is to improve the river for drainage and navigation and to reactivate the port of Redon. So far no commercial traffic to Redon has developed.

At Redon the river connects with the Breton canal system, by which shallow draught vessels can travel between the Bay of Biscay and St Malo.

Approach and entrance

In the approach to La Vilaine the depths on the outer bar are not less than 1m, except for La Varlingue, a rock drying 0.3m, situated only ½ mile off Pointe du Halguen, which

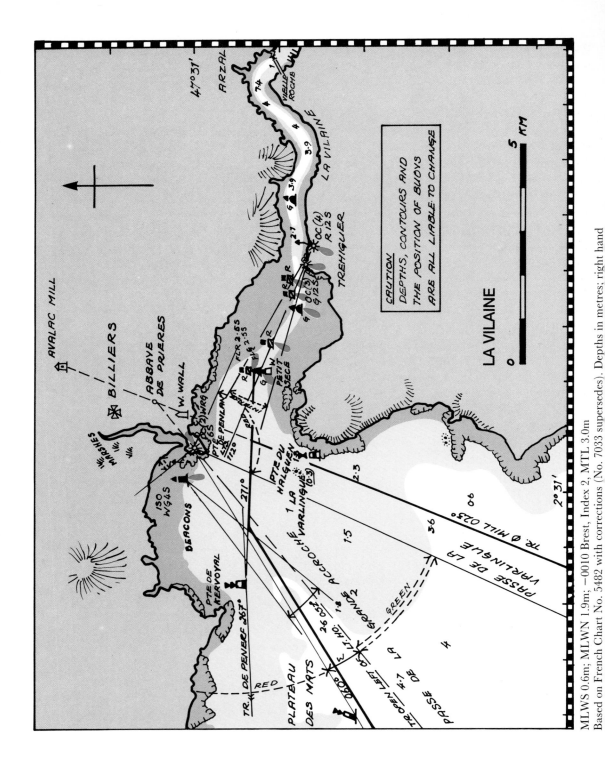

MLWS 0.6m; MLWN 1.9m; −0010 Brest, Index 2, MTL 3.0m
Based on French Chart No. 5482 with corrections (No. 7033 supersedes). Depths in metres; right hand

212

marks the SE side of the entrance. In good weather, with a sufficient rise of tide, it is only necessary to steer a mid-channel course.

With any sea or swell conditions are rough on the bar, especially on the ebb, and it is better to enter or leave on the last of the flood. Directions for the three recommended passes across the bar are given below, for use when the conditions call for them.

The western pass, Passe de la Grande Accroche, carries 1.5m least water and is lit, but the sea breaks heavily in it in strong onshore winds. Passe de la Varlingue, the eastern one, carries 1.3m and is not lit, but is preferable in heavy W or SW weather as the shallow part is inshore and gets some protection from the Grande Accroche bank to seaward. The landmarks shown on the charts and described in earlier editions of the Pilot are virtually impossible to see from a yacht due to the growth of trees. For the Passe de la Grande Accroche and for the SW approach one must employ the Pointe de Penlan Lighthouse. The Passe de la Varlingue should only be attempted if the leading marks can be positively identified.

Passe de la Grande Accroche

Make the Plateau des Mâts (card S) buoy and, leaving it 300m to port, steer on 060° for Pointe de Penlan Lighthouse. Leave Pointe de Kervoyal tower (card S) about 600m to port and la Grande Accroche (1.8m) shoal about 300m to starboard.

When the Pointe de Kervoyal tower bears 271°, with the Tour de Penerf (white tower with castellated top), if it can be seen, just open to the left, make good 091° into the estuary to pick up the port and starboard buoys that mark the Channel.

From the SW

Pass Ile Dumet on either hand and steer for Pointe de Penlan Lighthouse bearing more than 025°, to leave La Varlingue (dries 0.3m) off Pointes du Halguen and Cofreneau, to starboard and less than 040°, to leave La Grande Accroche (1.8m) shoal to port. When Pointe de Kervoyal tower (card S) bears 271° proceed as in the Western approach.

This leads in 0.8m to the outer pair of small port and starboard channel buoys north of the Petit Sécé tower. This tower is shown as white on the charts, but looked very dark in 1988 and may in fact be green. Follow the narrow channel defined by nos 2, 4, 6, 8 port buoys, with starboard buoys nos 1 and 5 opposite nos 2 and 6. Note that the Tréhiguier lighthouses in transit define a line which now dries. East of Tréhiguier there is one starboard buoy which should be left 100m to starboard after which the deep water tends to be nearer the north bank, with drying mud banks along the south bank. Mussel beds occupy the mud flats on either side of the channel. For a short distance below the Arzal lock the channel is marked by beacons.

By night

Approach in the white sector of Penlan light (**2**), between 052° and 060°. The sectors of Basse Bertrand light (**1**) can be disregarded. When the intensified sector of the rear light at Tréhiguier (**4**) opens red, at 106°, steer E to pass between the first pair of red/green channel buoys (**5**). Disregard the Tréhiguier light transit line (**3**, **4**), and follow the channel buoys to Tréhiguier, beyond which the channel is unlit. Due to channel changes a night entry should only be attempted when weather and tide conditions are very favourable.

Passe de la Varlingue

This pass carries 1.3m to the bar and leads through a narrow channel between a card W tower off Pointe de Cofrenau and La Varlingue (dries 0.3m); the transit must be closely held. The leading marks are the tower of Abbaye de Prières in transit with a white wall beacon (in front) and Avalec Mill ($1\frac{1}{2}$ miles behind), bearing 023°; the wall beacon is not easy to locate. Follow this transit until the Petit Sécé tower (green?) bears 105°, then steer to make good 090° until nos 1 and 2 starboard/port buoys N of Petit Sécé are picked up.

Should there be doubt in the identification of the Abbaye square tower, an alternative is to pass outside La Varlingue by keeping Billiers church clock tower in transit with Penlan lighthouse bearing 025°. Make the alteration in good time and use the SW approach if Billiers church tower is not seen, with Pointe de Penlan Lighthouse bearing more than 025°.

The river

The lock is on the north side of the river, adjacent to the conspicuous control tower. The approach channels from above and below are buoyed and the danger area above the dam

Bouëxière Lock on the Vilaine river

214

spillway is marked off by yellow buoys with a cross topmark. The lock is worked in daylight hours between 0700 and 2000 except on public holidays, such as 14 July and 15 August. The sill level is 2m below datum, but there is only 1m just outside, preventing use close to LW; the level above the lock is is maintained at 4.5m above datum (3.5m during floods). At high water springs there may, therefore, be a small drop on passing through the lock into the river. The road bridge above the lock is raised as necessary to allow masted vessels to pass. Securing in the lock is awkward as there can be substantial turbulence. If alongside the wall, rather than rafted to a boat that is so secured, pass bow and stern warps round the chains hanging down the walls and tend them and your fendoffs as the level rises or falls. Do not be in a hurry to unmoor as there will be further turbulence when the gates open and salt and fresh water mix.

The river is very beautiful for some distance above La Roche Bernard. Farther up the hills draw away and the scenery is less interesting. Masted vessels can go all the way up to Redon, which is a town of some character. There is a swing bridge at Cran, which is often slow to open, and has been known to stick altogether in very hot weather. Sound three blasts on your horn on approach or telephone in advance ((99) 90 21 93).

Above the dam a mid-channel course should be followed. Be careful not to cut corners, rather tend to keep to the outside. A few special dangers are marked on the lateral system.

Anchorages and facilities

Tréhiguier
A convenient anchorage is near the entrance, exposed to W and NW winds. Anchor outside the moorings of local craft in soft mud. Land at the slip; a restaurant is available.

Vieille Roche
This is an excellent anchorage, completely sheltered, on the starboard bank just below the dam. Anchor outside the moorings. There is a landing slip, but it is about a 2 mile walk to the shops.

Arzal
There is a marina (Camoël) on the south bank with a substantial extension (Arzal) nearing completion in 1988 on the north bank. There are all the facilities of a large marina with water and electricity on the pontoons, showers and toilets on both sides, Capitainerie at present on the south bank, fuel berth on the north side at entrance to lock, haul-out facilities, repairs and laying up under cover on the north side. The villages of Arzal and Camoël are both about 2 miles by road but food supplies may shortly be available in the marina, which has a good restaurant.

La Roche Bernard
Excellent anchorage and several moorings in the river. There is a marina in the small inlet on the starboard side, but the berths are often all reserved. There is another marina in the river below the bridge, and many mooring buoys.

La Roche Bernard: the bridge, with abutments of earlier bridges

Water and fuel are on the quay, and hot showers and launderette at 'Le Camping'. There is a chandlery and marine engineer. All shops are in the town, ¼ mile walk up the hill, with a number of excellent restaurants.

Foleux
Some 4 miles above Roche Bernard, in peaceful surroundings, by the old ferry slips are moorings and pontoons on both sides of the river with a restaurant on the north bank.

Redon
A small marina has been built in the old dock, surrounded by picturesque old warehouses. At present there is no commercial traffic. Rather basic showers and toilets are by the Capitainerie on the port hand side of the entrance. There is a fuel berth nearby, and a crane for masting on the other side, and a good chandlery at the top of the basin on the port hand side. All shops, banks, hotels and restaurants are in the town, which is a major rail centre offering good communications.

The Breton canals
The canals offer a convenient route for shallow draught yachts which do not relish the long haul round the western end of France, where the seas can be rough. Any yacht which can safely reach the Channel Islands can easily get from there to St Malo and thence have a most pleasant rural passage to the interesting and relatively sheltered waters of Quiberon Bay.

The passage is especially attractive to motor yachts, but there are cranes at each end which the crew can use to lay the mast of a sailing yacht on deck; the crew should be sufficiently experienced to do this without calling on outside help. For limits of size, width must not exceed 4.5m and headroom above the waterline 2.7m. Permissible draught varies, but will never be more than 1.3m and 1.2m or 1.1m are more usual official limits. If rainfall has been low, 1.0m draught may be difficult.

The normal, and quickest, route is from St Malo to Rennes by the Canal d'Ile et Rance,

216

Lock on the Canal d'Ile et Rance

from Rennes to Redon by La Vilaine Canalisé and thence to the sea via the lower reaches of the Vilaine, about 130 nautical miles with 62 locks. The locks are worked from 0630 to 1930, with a short lunch break. There are speed limits of 6 km/h ($3\frac{1}{4}$ knots) in the canal north of Rennes, and 10 km/h ($5\frac{1}{4}$ knots) in the river between Rennes and Redon. By travelling reasonably fast the passage can be made in 5 days. It is also possible to turn aside at Redon and go up to Josselin, from there over the hill to Lorient. The draught limit is 0.8m. For Nantes, leave the Vilaine at Bellions lock below Redon; the canal direct from Redon is now closed.

At present no permit is required, nor is any charge made for a single or return journey, but enquiry should be made from the French Government Tourist Office (179 Piccadilly, London, W1V 0AL) for a list of dates of *Chomages* when sections of the canals are closed for maintenance. It is also desirable, before setting out, to obtain an up-to-date copy of the *Carte Guide: Navigation Fluviale de Voies Navigables de Bretagne*, produced by ECM. This has strip maps of the canals with directions in French, English and German and can be obtained from the Continental Bookshop in Regent Place off Regent Street if it is not available in a local chandlers or bookshop.

Building sand appears now to be transported by road and there was no sign in 1988 of the sand barges that once provided uneasy companionship in the locks of the Vilaine.

The lock-keepers are careful when letting in the water, and with ordinary care no

Rennes. Pleasant for a short stay. Noisy at night. Shopping centre 300m off picture, right foreground. The lock into the Vilaine is beyond the moored yachts and goes under the road. Fuel can be obtained from a garage on the left bank after passing through the lock

damage is to be expected. Small motor tyres with, perhaps, a plank and an apron to protect the ship's side are preferable to normal fendoffs which will get very dirty. There are strong currents as a lock fills and the yacht must be securely moored and the lines tended as the water rises; moor near the lower gates if possible, but somebody has to be in front if two or three yachts share a lock.

It may help to fit blocks at bow and stern so that the mooring lines can be led to the cockpit and tended by one person who could use the sheet winches in a sailing yacht. Officially the lock-keepers are not required to help with mooring lines and north of Rennes a crew member should be put ashore before entering the lock to handle the lines; help with the gates is appreciated and will speed the passage. South of Rennes the locks are larger, it is less easy to get ashore and the lock-keepers will usually help willingly with the shore lines.

There are cranes to help in masting at Dinan and Redon, the limits which can be reached by masted vessels; there are cranes at St Malo and La Roche Bernard, but these deprive one of some pleasant sailing; there are also cranes at Nantes and Lorient for those using these variants.

218

The route

St Malo–Dinan

This is accessible to masted vessels. The lock at Le Châtelier is only available for about four hours during the high water period in the Rance. Information on the times of operation of the Barrage and Le Châtelier locks may be obtained in St Malo. The upper reaches are shallow out of the channel, but this is clearly marked.

Dinan–Rennes

Ile et Rance canal is a straightforward canal section, with 47 locks, of which 11 in quick succession (*l'escalier*) climb to the top. Yachts of draught near the maximum will have trouble with soft mud in places. This mud is carried in by water courses joining the canal. If you begin to drag try to see which side the flow has come in; the best water will be near the opposite bank. Having found it, open up the engine and force a way through; the bad patches are not very long. The engine water-cooling intake should be inspected regularly as it may become blocked with weed or grass cuttings from the tow-path.

Fuel at Dinan and refuel at Rennes; the fuel berth at Tinténiac has closed.

Dinan Port from the Viaduct

Rennes–Redon

This is the canalized portion of the river Vilaine. There are 12 locks. The river is wider and the best water is usually about one-third of the way from the towpath bank (left bank to Pont Réan, right bank thereafter). There is a channel of the requsite depth all the way, but it is easy to get out of it and go aground. In some places the distance of the channel from the bank is indicated by notices on the towpath with an arrowhead and a figure indicating the distance in metres. However, there are other shallows, and if an echo sounder is available it is as well to use it regularly between Boel and Mâlon. Do not trust the advice of fishermen; they have seen shallow draught vessels travelling in parts of the river outside the proper channel and imagine that all boats can take the same course. Beware of the fisherman who can sometimes leave four rods and lines poking out through the reeds, expecting yachtsmen to avoid them. It is a courtesy to slow down when passing fishermen in full view; to quote the English translation in an old guide: 'Anglers would otherwise have their feet watered, and you would hear everything but congratulations ...!'

The river is closed to navigation in times of flood.

Entering Redon you will come to a stop-gate for flood control. Check to see that it is open before passing through. The locks on either side directly below the stop-gate are no longer in use. After passing the stop-gate, turn sharp right at the junction if you want to enter the dock, straight on and turn left for the sea.

Facilities

Nearly all the villages on the route have a café-restaurant which can supply a very adequate meal at a reasonable price; one is off the tourist route and does not have to pay tourist prices. Food shops are also available, but some close for a month in the summer and a whole village has been found to be closed for August. A number of the lock-keepers are pleased to sell farm and garden produce. Water can be had at the camping site at Tinténiac (where it sometimes tastes of chlorine) and Pont Réan, the quays at Guipry, Port Roche, Rennes and Redon and by hose at Beslé. There are hot showers at Pont Réan, cold at Tinténiac. Some hotel/restaurants will provide a shower while your meal is prepared (at Guipry for instance). There is a launderette near the yacht berths at Rennes and washing facilities at Tinténiac and Pont Réan.

The main road runs alongside the canal in Rennes and there is traffic noise all night, but it is well worth making a stop for supplies and fuel by day. There is an excellent supermarket and banks in a shopping precinct on the right bank close to the yacht berths, and a garage from which fuel may be obtained on the left bank after passing through the lock into the Vilaine.

39 Le Croisic and La Turballe

Charts: English BA 2353, 3126, 2646. Imray C39, C40.
   French SHOM 7033 P. ECM Navicarte 546, 547.
High water: −0020 Brest, Index 1, MTL 3.2m.
 MHWS 5.6m; MLWS 0.6m; MHWN 4.3m; MLWN 2.0m.
Tidal streams: In the middle of the Rade du Croisic the streams are rotary clockwise and weak, at HW Brest the direction is SE and at LW Brest it is N, spring rates 1 knot. Between the Pointe du Croisic and the Plateau du Four the pattern is similar, but the rates are greater, the greatest rate being $2\frac{3}{4}$ knots SW at +0250 Brest. The streams in the entrance to the harbour are very strong; west of the Mahon rocks they exceed the reputed 4 knots at springs.
Depths: On the leading line the channel is dredged to 1.2m as far as the 'zeroth entrance' (see below), to 0.5m as far as the second entrance. From there a narrow channel *dérocté à 0.5m* runs some 30m out from the wall to the upper end of the fifth entrance which leads in to the Port de Plaisance which dries 1.7m.
Lights:
Le Croisic
1. Jetée du Tréhic head; Iso WG 4s, 12m, 12&10M. Grey tower, green lantern.
2. Basse Hergo tower; Fl G 2.5s, 5m, 3M. Green beacon tower.
3. First leading lights on 156°; Dir Oc(2+1) 12s, 10&14m 18M. Fluorescent orange rectangles on white pylons.
4. Intermediate leading lights on 174°; Q G, 5&8m, 12M. Fluorescent white rectangles with vertical green stripe on white and green pylons.
5. Final leading lights on 134.5°; Dir Q R, 6&10m, 11M. Red and white chequered rectangle, front on white pylon, red top, rear on fish-market roof.
6. Le Grand Mahon tower; Fl R 2.5s, 6m, 5M. Red beacon tower.
La Turballe
7. Jetée de Garlahy (west breakwater head); Fl(4)WR 12s, 13m, 10–7M. White metal frame, red top.
8. Leading lights on 006.5°; Dir fixed violet. White masts, orange tops.
9. Digue Tourlandroux (northern end); Fl G 4s, 7m, 6M. White tank, green top.

The harbour of Le Croisic is situated in the SE corner of the Rade du Croisic. The town is a popular holiday resort with a busy fishing harbour, and is associated with Batz and La Baule to the eastward to form a district noted for its bathing sands and holiday amenities. A large yard for building GRP fishing trawlers was under construction in 1988 and a substantial new fish-market building was already in use. There is a yacht builder and much yachting activity.

Yachts that can take the ground may use the basin of the Port de Plaisance and there is a good sheltered anchorage outside, though the best spots are occupied by permanent

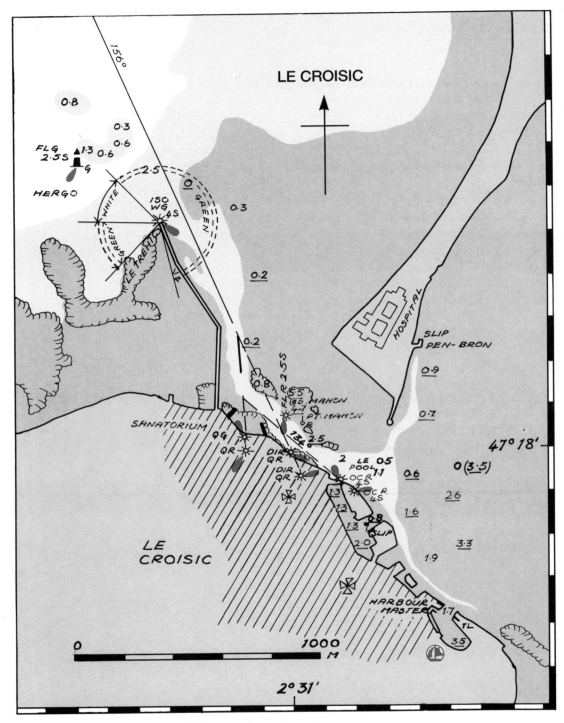

MLWS 0.6m; MLWN 2.0m; −0020 Brest, Index 1, MTL 3.2m
Based on French Chart No. 139 with corrections (No. 7033 supersedes). Depths in metres; right hand margin in cables

Le Croisic breakwater head, with Hostel for the disabled behind. The primary leading marks are just to the left of the church belfry, left centre

moorings. The entrance channel is shallow, exposed to the W and NW, and in fresh onshore winds is rough owing to the shallow and irregular bottom. If approached on the flood with sufficient rise of tide it presents no difficulty.

Approach

The streams are strong and for this reason the best time for entry at springs is within the last hour of the flood, when they are weakening. It is difficult to enter against the ebb. At neaps there is more latitude and, by following all the transits, a yacht can use the channel at any state of tide.

Final leading marks, rear one on fish market roof

Drying yacht basin with pontoons, left. Harbour office and toilet cabin, centre. Fin-keel yacht alongside wall, far right. Viewed from new fishing trawler yard

Approaching from the west or north west, steer into the bay until the leading marks are identified. The church tower with an unusual near-Byzantine belfry is conspicuous behind the primary leading marks. Also conspicuous are the broad white three-storeyed building with grey roof and central spire to the west of the roof of the Jetée du Tréhic (a hostel for the disabled) and the long white building with central belfry of the isolation hospital on the Pen Bron peninsula to the east of the entrance.

Approaching from the south, the extensive Plateau du Four with its conspicuous lighthouse lies on the west side and the Pointe du Croisic with off-lying rocks to the east. Near the eastern side of this passage is the Basse Castouillet, with a least depth of 0.3m. This shoal is marked on its western side by a buoy (card W). After leaving this buoy to starboard steer about 045° towards La Turballe, which lies ahead conspicuously, until the leading marks for Le Croisic (a pair of fluorescent orange rectangles bearing 156° with the church tower behind) are in line.

Entrance

Steer in with the church belfry bearing 157° until the orange leading marks have been identified and then bring them into transit bearing 156°. On close approach the Hergo green tower (stbd) will be left 300m to starboard and the transit leads in about 100m E of the end of Jetée du Tréhic. To port the sands dry. Proceed up the channel inside the breakwater on the transit of the leading marks. This transit crosses a rocky patch, which dries 0.8m, NW of Le Grand Mahon tower (port) and, except near high water, it is advisable to alter to starboard on passing the bend in the breakwater and steer 174° on the transit of the intermediate leading marks, a pair of fluorescent white rectangles with a green vertical stripe, 100m to the left of the lifeboat station.

Approaching the lifeboat slip, if the intermediate line is being followed, the final leading marks (a pair of red and white chequered rectangles) will be seen beyond Le Grand Mahon tower (port). The rear mark is on the fish-market roof with the front mark on the quay. Turn onto their transit of 134.5°.

Hold this transit until close to the fishing quay to avoid a rocky patch (drying 2.5m) to port; then steer to leave the quays about 50m to starboard if bound for the yacht basin. A training wall of stakes on the port side of the narrow channel to the yacht basin is marked by red beacon poles. If looking for a mooring, turn to port when the fish-market is abeam to starboard and search the pool.

If one is late on the tide one meets an ebb which runs like a torrent off the Grand Mahon at springs.

By night
Follow the transits as by day (**3**, **4**, and **5**). Notice particularly that the white sector of Le Tréhic light (**1**), which leads clear of the distant dangers, such as Le Four and Ile Dumet, leads right onto the nearby rocks, and the close approach must be made in the green sector.

The street lighting on the quays is good and there is no difficulty once they are reached.

Looking downstream from trawler yard at LW. Note the row of training fence stakes. Fish market to left of picture. Le Pool moorings, centre

Moorings and anchorage

'Le Pool' is a fair size, and provides good anchorage, though much of it is occupied by yachts on moorings. Mussel beds cover the drying banks of Le Grand Traict, but the narrow and steep-sided Chenal de Pen Bron runs up the east side of the peninsula, containing more moorings and a possible anchorage. There are no visitors' moorings but it might be possible to borrow a mooring in Le Pool or Chenal de Pen Bron or to anchor after taking soundings, clear of the moorings and with a trip-line, as the bottom is foul with old chain. The ebb runs very hard in the Chenal and even in the anchorage the streams are strong.

The harbour has a curious pattern of islands called *jonchères*, with backwaters behind them called *chambres*, in which vessels lie. The original character has been changed by the building of bridges to the islands so that only one remains in its original isolated state. The old first entrance is now blocked, so that it is convenient to call it the 'zeroth' entrance; when first seen it looks as though it is going to be an entrance; it is only as it opens up that it is seen to be blocked. Scouring sluices have been left in the base of the block, so be ready for a set in or out.

The first entrance gives on to the first, *La Grande Chambre*. To port there is a patent slip and scrubbing hard. At one time a good place to try for a drying berth was just inside on the right, where one could set up a line to hold the yacht against *Le Quai des Yachts*. Fishing boats occupy most of the town side of this *chambre* and the new fish market hall or *Halle de Criée* has been built on the *Jonchère de Lenigo*, making it a busy quay to moor alongside.

It is probably advisable to avoid the first four entrances and make for the Port de Plaisance in the *Chambre des Vases*. Deep keel yachts can dry out against the wall outside on a hard, level bottom and those that can take the ground can enter and secure bow to a pontoon with a stern mooring. The Capitainerie with a shower and toilet cabin is on the wall at the entrance.

Facilities

The facilities are those of a holiday resort and a fishing and yachting port. There are banks, hotels, restaurants and all shops, water and electricity on the pontoons, water from the quays. At present there is no fuel berth for yachts, but fuel may be obtained from a garage in the town. There is a yacht yard with haul-out facilities, marine engineer and good chandlery. Ice is from the *Criée*.

La Turballe from the W. Breakwater head far right

La Turballe marina entrance

Communications
There is a railway station and buses to La Baule, where there is an airport.

La Turballe
La Turballe is a busy fishing port 2 miles north of Le Croisic with a fishing fleet of some 60 trawlers. Yachts may lie afloat at the entrance on the west side under the breakwater, attached to a large white iron mooring buoy or *ton*, but as the fishing boats come in at high speed this is most uncomfortable.

However, the inner harbour has recently been dredged (to 1.5m probably) and developed so that half of it is now a small fishing boat harbour and the other half converted into a yacht harbour, with pontoon berths for some 280 yachts; 20 pontoon berths are available to visitors in addition to the six on the *ton* in the outer harbour.

Entry is possible in winds of Force 5 or 6 from the east through south to south west and the land provides good shelter from stronger winds from the west through north to north east.

Approach and entry
Rocky shoals extend offshore to the north of the harbour which should be approached from the SW. Seen from the west, the long white-walled fish-market, with a water tower some distance behind, makes a good landmark and a red beacon tower is situated just west of the entrance. South of the entrance there is 2m to within 300m of the long sandy beach.

Entry is made on a course of about 005° (the leading lights being on 006.5°), as the deep water appears to be nearer the west breakwater. Once past the breakwater head turn sharply to starboard to enter the yacht harbour.

By night
Approach in the white sector of the W jetty head light (**7**), steering to leave it to port and enter in the intense sector of the violet leading lights (in line on 006.5°) (**8**). After passing

227

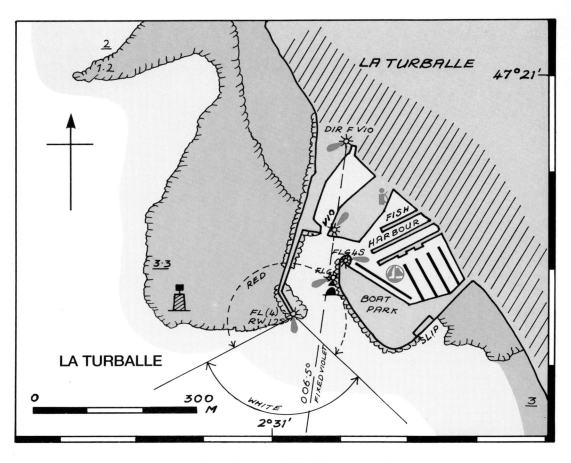

MLWS 0.6m; MLWN 2.0m; −0020 Brest, Index 1, MTL 3.2m
Based on information provided by the harbourmaster. Scale of metres and margin scales approximate

the W breakwater head make a sharp turn to starboard round the light flashing green every 4s marking the starboard side of the entrance to the yacht harbour (**9**).

Facilities
Water and electricity are on the pontoons, and there are also fuel berth, showers and toilets, 16 tonne crane, 140 tonne travel lift and slipway.

The boatyard can take yachts of up to 16m; wood or glass fibre and engine repairs are undertaken. There are chandlers, banks, baker, restaurants and bars close to the marina in the old town.

La Turballe is developing as a holiday resort with quite a large summer population and provides all facilities. There are good sandy beaches to the south east of the harbour. Access to the marina in La Turballe is easier than entry to Le Croisic, making it a useful stopping place on this part of the coast.

La Baule: 40 Le Pouliguen and 41 Pornichet

Charts: English BA 3216, 2353, 2646. Imray C39, C40.
   French SHOM 6825 P. ECM Navicarte 547.
High water: − 0035 Brest springs, −0020 Brest neaps, Index 1, MTL 2.9m.
   MHWS 5.4m; MLWS 0.5m; MHWN 4.1m; MLWN 1.7m.
Tidal streams: The tidal streams in the offing are irregular in direction, the flood running generally in the easterly quadrant and the ebb in the westerly quadrant, rates up to about $1\frac{1}{2}$ knots. In the north of the bay itself the tide runs always westerly. In the Pouliguen river the tidal streams can attain 4 knots at springs.
Depths: The Pouliguen channel dries and the rocky sill should be assumed to dry 1.6m. In the pool there is water to float vessels drawing up to 1.8m. The marina at Pornichet has 2.8m in the main berths.
Lights:
   1. Les Guérandaises by (lat stbd); Fl G 2.5s.
   2. Penchâteau by (lat port); Fl R 2.5s.
   3. Les Petits Impairs; Fl(2)G 6s, 6m, 6M. Green tower.
   4. Le Pouliguen, S jetty; Q R, 13m, 9M. White column, red top.
   5. Pornichet, W breakwater head; Iso W G 4s, 9m, 11–8M. White tower, green top.
   6. Pornichet entrance west; Fl G 2s.
   7. Pornichet entrance east; Fl R 2s.

La Baule is a sophisticated international beach resort with a casino and innumerable hotels and restaurants of all grades. It may be reached by train and by air to St Nazaire or its own smaller airport. There are two harbours, Le Pouliguen and Pornichet. The approach to the former dries out and it is essential for strangers to enter around high water. Pornichet is a modern marina providing 1,100 berths for yachts of all sizes, and available at all states of the tide. The bay is sheltered from northerly and westerly winds and is often smooth in summer. Both harbours are very crowded in high season and vessels of over 10m are often turned away from Le Pouliguen.

Approach to Le Pouliguen
Le Pouliguen is situated in the NW corner of the bay of the same name, and is some 4 miles E of Le Croisic. The best approach from any direction is the western passage between the Pointe de Penchâteau red pillar buoy on the west side of the bay and the ledges and rocks to the SE which extend nearly 4 miles to the Grand Charpentier lighthouse. Even from the east it is better to approach south of the Grand Charpentier along the Chenal du Nord in the entry to the Loire. There is an inshore passage which can be followed using BA 3216 or a French chart; this channel joins the western channel south of La Vieille beacon (stbd).

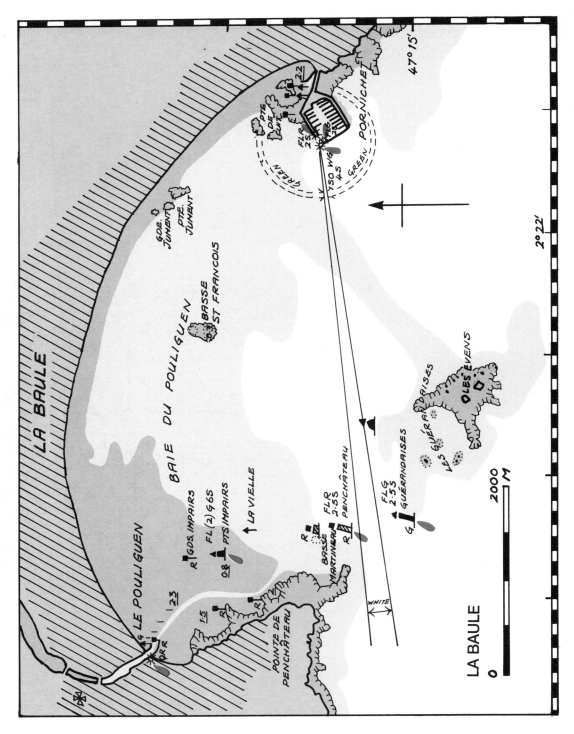

LA BAULE

BAIE DU POULIGUEN

LA BAULE

LE POULIGUEN

POINTE DE PENCHÂTEAU

POINTE JUMENT
G.DE. JUMENT
BASSE ST FRANCOIS
LA VIELLE
GDS. IMPAIRS
FL(2) 9.6S
PTS.IMPAIRS
BASSE MARTINEAU
PENCHÂTEAU
FLR 2.5S
LES GUÉRANDRISES
G. GUÉRANDRISES
FLG 2.5S
LES EVENS
PTE DE L'UTE
GREEN
GREEN PORNICHE
ISO WG 4S
FLR 2.5S

WHITE

LA BAULE

0   2000
         M

47°15'

2°22'

MLWS 0.5m; MLWN 1.7m; −0035(sp), −0020(np) Brest, Index 1, MTL 2.9m
Based on French Chart No. 547 with corrections (No. 6825 supersedes). Depths in metres; right hand

230

The approach to Le Pouliguen, with beacons on each side. The slender white lighthouse is left to port

The approach is sheltered from the N, through W to SW, but southerly swell breaks in the shallow water, and it is fully exposed to the SE. The sands shift and if the available margin of depth is very small, it is worth seeking the advice from local yachtsmen or the club boatman.

Leave the Penchâteau red pillar buoy 100m to port. Thence steer 020° to leave the Basse Martineau buoy (lat port) also to port. There is an anchorage about 400m NNW of this buoy where a yacht may await the tide in good weather.

Entrance

Shortly before high water proceed towards the entrance, leaving La Vieille beacon (lat stbd) and Les Petits Impairs tower (stbd) well to starboard, and two red beacons 150m to port. Close to the harbour entrance are four black beacons followed by one green beacon, all to be left to starboard and one red beacon to be left to port (the black beacons may by this time be green). The channel usually lies closer to the red beacons than to the starboard ones.

Approach the entrance with the church spire open between the pierheads. The lighthouse on the west pier head is a very slender white structure with a red top. This is left to port and the vessel then proceeds between stone embankments. Special care must be taken on near approach to the entrance as the channel is narrow between high sands on either side. On the starboard side a slender wooden beacon marks the end of a training wall; it lies well inside the line of rather thicker iron beacons marking the approach and must not be overlooked.

The first quay to starboard, showing the moorings

By night
The lights are few in number and some local knowledge is desirable for a night entry.

Mooring

Deeper draught yachts moor fore and aft to buoys on the La Baule (east) side near the entrance. Shallower draughts and those which can take the ground moor and warp to pontoons farther up. Berths are allocated by the club boatman. Visitors should moor temporarily to the first quay on the starboard hand (where the fuel pumps are) and ask for a berth to be allocated.

Facilities

Water is by hose at the pontoons, fuel berth on starboard side on entering; there are all the facilities of a sophisticated yachting centre. The yacht club is a large and clearly labelled building on the La Baule side above the first road bridge. It is hospitable to visitors and its boatman acts as harbourmaster. There are all shops handy in Le Pouliguen, and yacht yards, chandlers and marine engineers are all close at hand. There are many hotels and restaurants.

Approach to Pornichet

From the Penchâteau and Guérandaises light buoys the white lighthouse at the end of the outer mole can be made out amongst the buildings at the eastern end of La Baule, bearing 083°, and course should be altered towards it. An unlit green conical buoy marking the northern extremity of the Guérandaises shoal is left to starboard.

Entrance

The entrance faces north and it is not until close approach that the red and green beacons marking the underwater projections from the pierheads will become clear, and course must be altered to pass between them.

By night

The approach is covered by the white sector of Pornichet pierhead light, which can be seen from 081° to 084°. This sector just excludes the Penchâteau light buoy and the Guérandaises unlit buoy (lat stbd); the Guérandaises light buoy lies 400m S of this white sector. The beacons in the entrance show flashing red and green lights.

Pornichet marina: the entrance, looking E

Mooring

There are ten pontoons, A–J, on the southern side of the harbour and four, K–N, on the northern. The heads of all these are allocated to visitors, together with the whole of pontoon J and the west side of pontoon I, although these are only suitable for boats of under 6m length. All the main berths carry a depth of 2.8m and as the bottom is soft mud, vessels of deeper draught will sink their keels into it and remain upright. Charges are substantial (fr115 per day for 10m, 1989).

Facilities

This is one of the best equipped marinas on the coast. (VHF, Ch. 9, 0800–2000). Fuel pontoon is immediately to port on entry; water and electricity on the pontoons; showers, toilets, ice, restaurant and chandlery shop (chart agent) are in the marina, with groceries and a good wine merchant. There is a yacht yard with 24 tonne travel lift and slip. Across the bridge to the mainland there are many shops, hotels and restaurants.

Charts: English BA 3216, 2646. Imray C40.

        French SHOM 5039 P. ECM Navicarte 547.

High water: −0035 Brest springs, −0010 Brest neaps, MTL 3.0m.

  MHWS 5.4m; MLWS 0.7m; MHWN 4.1m; MLWN 1.7m.

Tidal streams: Outside the flood runs E, the ebb W, springs rates $1\frac{3}{4}$ knots. The streams in the harbour are weak.

Depths: There is 1.5m to the fairway buoy but the marina entrance may dry if dredging is irregular. Inside the marina 2.0m. The depths shoal rapidly at the entrance to the old harbour and the channel to the inner basin dries 1m, the basin itself drying from 1.3 at the north quays to 1.8m at the south quays.

Lights:

1. Pointe de Noëvéillard; Oc(3+1)WRG 12s, 22m, 13-9M. White square tower, green top, white dwelling.
2. Marina elbow; Fl(2+1) 7s, 4m, 3M. Grey pole.
3. Off Marina SW breakwater head; Q(2)R 6s, 4m, 2M. Red column.
4. Off Marina E breakwater head; Fl G 2s, 4m, 2M. Green column.
5. Gourmalon breakwater head; Fl(2)G 6s, 4m, 8M. Green mast.
6. Fairway buoy (RW); L Fl 10s.
7. Inner basin entrance; QR to port, QG to starboard.

Gourmalon yacht moorings and breakwater, looking SE

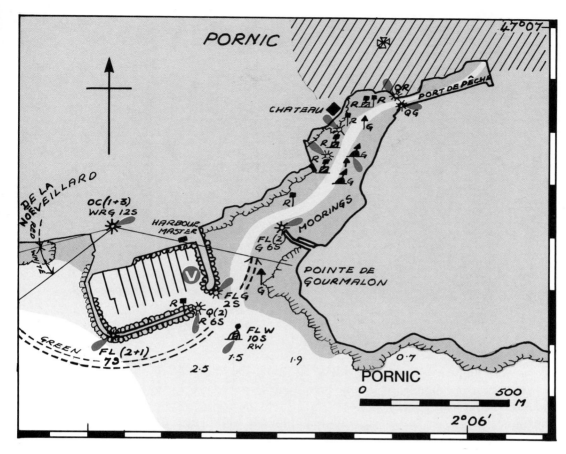

MLWS 0.7m; MLWN 1.7m; −0030(sp), −0027(np) Brest, Index 2, MTL 3.0m
Based on French Chart No. 5039 with corrections. Depths in metres; right hand margin in cables

The Baie de Bourgneuf is a big wide bay east of the Loire, formed between the mainland to the north and east and the Ile de Noirmoutier on the south. The bay is exposed to the west and shallows progressively. There is plenty of water for yachts and although there are many shoals and rocks, they are, with the exception of the Kérouars bank in the northern part, well marked, so that there are few navigational difficulties except in thick weather. There is no exit from the bay to the south between Ile de Noirmoutier and the mainland except for shallow draught vessels at high water, as there is a causeway, drying at low water across which there is insufficient depth at any state of the tide.

The harbours, however, are poor except for Pornic and L'Herbaudière. Those on Noirmoutier are described in Chapter 43. Pornic harbour, situated half way along the northern shore of the Baie de Bourgneuf, is rather off the route for foreign yachts. The harbour is easy of access in reasonable weather and supports considerable local yachting activity. It is a pretty little place which is well worth a visit. Bluebeard's castle overlooks the harbour just seaward of the quays.

Pornic, looking upstream past Bluebeard's Castle

Approach

In the outer approach from the SW the outlying dangers to the north of Ile de Noirmoutier are well marked by a series of buoys and towers. From the NW care must be taken to avoid the Banc de Kérouars, which is unmarked except for a buoy, La Couronnée (stbd), one of the channel buoys for the Loire entrance, 1 mile off its western end and Nord Couronnée buoy (card N) marking a rock which dries 1.9m. The least depth near the eastern end is 1m and is unmarked. To the north of the bank there is a passage over $\frac{1}{2}$ mile wide and $\frac{1}{2}$ mile off the land, or entry can be made south of the bank if it is not safely covered.

Leave the tower of Notre Dame (BRB topmark two spheres; but B, dirty brown, B with topmarks missing 1988) about $\frac{1}{2}$ mile to starboard and steer for the RW fairway buoy at the entrance to Pornic, leaving it to starboard on arrival.

Entrance

Marina
Do not attempt entry within $1\frac{1}{2}$ hours either side of low water at springs. Enter the marina between the two red (port) and the green (stbd) steel columns. These columns and their associated lights are placed in the entrance and not on the breakwater heads. Once inside keep clear of the south wall which is lined with submerged rocks. The east breakwater head is also foul, with a partly submerged knuckle extending diagonally into the marina. Manoeuvring among the pontoons is not easy in an onshore wind. There are 165 berths for visitors. Yachts of up to 10m length can secure to pontoons P2 and P3; those over 10m to P1 and the ends of the other pontoons.

Pornic. The marina entrance is bearing about 020°. A confusion of water towers and spires makes Pornic hard to locate from afar. A radio mast to the west is of some assistance and the masts in the marina are conspicuous once Notre Dame tower (BRB) is abeam to starboard

Facilities
(VHF, Ch. 9.) Water and electricity are on the pontoons, as well as showers, toilets and ice, and there is a fuel berth and 20 tonne travel lift. Café-restaurant and food shops can be found in the marina, and engineers and a sailmaker in the town.

Old port
The inner harbour dries about 1.3m and it is assumed that no attempt will be made to go up the harbour unless the tide has risen sufficiently to float the yacht there. On this basis there is sufficient water in the outer part of the harbour provided that course is set roughly near the centre. Just beyond the marina a beacon (stbd) marks a rock to starboard. The breakwater, which extends from the E side of the entrance (Pointe de Gourmalon), is marked at its end by a green beacon.

Above the breakwater the channel is marked by red and green beacons and buoys. The beacon posts should not be confused with various other posts, mostly white, erected for swimmers to dive from. There is a silting problem in the harbour east of the marina entrance. The RW fairway buoy must be left to starboard and entry should not be attempted near LW.

By night
The white sector of the main light (**1**) clears the Banc de Kérouars and Notre Dame rock. The marina and Gourmalon yacht harbour can be reached, but strangers should not attempt to go up the harbour.

Anchorage and mooring
Berth in the marina; yachts which can take the ground can use the Gourmalon yacht harbour.

Yachts can also berth alongside the quays in the inner harbour. The quay on the north side of the entrance to the inner harbour is prohibited, and immediately inside the entrance to port is the berth reserved for the Noirmoutier ferry. The north side is the best, though it is principally used by fishing vessels. Not only is the water deeper here (dries 1.3m) but the quay is stone faced with many recessed ladders. On the south side, where the local yachts mostly berth, the mud dries about 1.8m, and the quay is faced with vertical wooden rubbing piles, though there are again plenty of ladders.

Facilities
There are all the facilities of a small holiday town, all shops, several restaurants and hotels, marine engineer, diesel at the south quay, petrol close by. Communications are by bus and branch railway line. There is a club house and showers at Gourmalon yacht harbour.

43 Ile de Noirmoutier

Charts: English BA 3216, 2647. Imray C40.
French SHOM 5039 P. ECM Navicarte 549.

Tidal information is given below for the NE side of the island; for Fromentine see page 244.

High water: −0020 Brest, Index 2, MTL 2.8m.
MHWS 5.4m; MLWS 0.3m; MHWN 4.0m; MLWN 1.6m.

Tidal streams: In the middle of the entrance to the Baie de Bourgneuf the tide is rotary clockwise: at +0450 Brest N, ½ knot springs; at −0300 Brest E 1 knot; at −0100 Brest S, ½ knot; at +0250 Brest W, 1½ knots springs. In Chenal de la Grise, at the NW end of the island, NE begins at −0615 Brest, 2 knots springs; SW begins −0145 Brest, 3 knots springs. Off Bois de la Chaise SE begins −0545 Brest, NW begins −0040 Brest, spring rates 2 knots.

Depths: L'Herbaudière has 1.5m–2.2m at the pontoons, the entrance channel is dredged to 1.5m. Bois de la Chaise has about 1.5m. Noirmoutier dries about 2.5m.

Lights:

1. Ile du Pilier; Fl(3) 20s, 33m, 29M. Grey stone tower.
   Auxiliary light; Q R, 10m, 11M. On same structure covering Les Boeufs.
2. Pointe de Saint-Gildas; Q WRG, 23m, 11–6M. Metal framework tower on white house.
   Radio beacon, call NZ, 289.6 kHz, 50M. 1/6, start H+01.
3. Basse du Martroger; Q WRG, 10m, 9–6–6M. Card N beacon tower.
4. Passe de la Grise card S by; Q(6)+L 15s.
5. La Pierre Moine; Fl(2) 6s, 14m, 9M. Isolated danger tower.
6. L'Herbaudière: West jetty head; Oc(2+1)WG 12s, 9m, 10–7M. White column and shelter, green top.
7. East jetty head; Fl(2)R 6s, 8m, 5M. Red tripod.
8. Lifeboat slip; Fl R 2s. Red casing.
9. Entrance channel bys; 2 lat stbd Fl G; 1 lat port Fl(2)R.
10. Pointe des Dames; Oc(3)WRG 12s, 34m, 19–15M. White square tower.
11. Port de Noirmoutier, jetty head; Oc(2)R 6s, 6m, 7M. White column, red top.

The Ile de Noirmoutier is a long, narrow, sandy island measuring about 9 miles from NW to SE. It is separated from the mainland by the narrow Goulet de Fromentine. North of the Fromentine bridge is a causeway carrying the old road from the mainland to the island. This is so high that, although it covers at high water, it is not safe for a deep keel boat to attempt to cross over.

The island, which was invaded by the English in 1388, by the Spanish in 1524 and by the Dutch in 1674, is now invaded only by crowds of summer holiday-makers. L'Herbaudière in the north has a marina in a rather bleak spot. It is, however, a

239

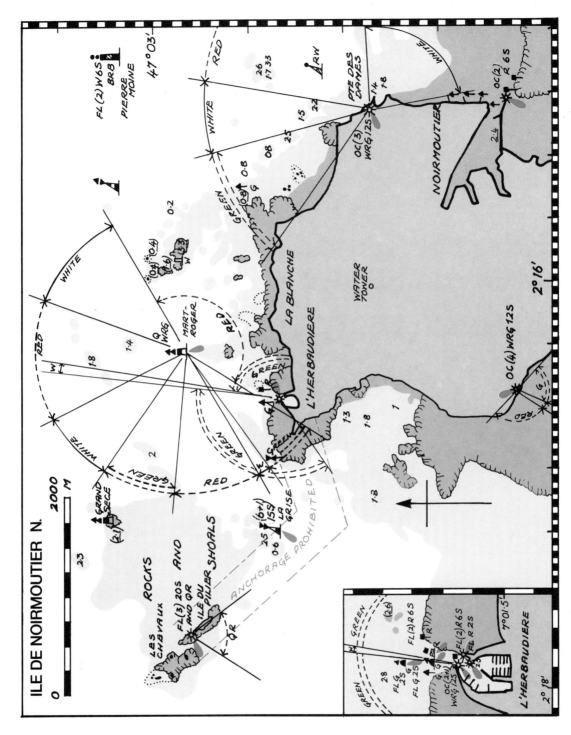

ILE DE NOIRMOUTIER N.

MLWS 0.3m; MLWN 1.6m; −0020 Brest, Index 2, MTL 2.8m
Based on French Chart No. 5039 with corrections. Depths in metres; right hand margin in cables

convenient passage anchorage. Bois de la Chaise is an open anchorage, though with enough shelter to be the summer base of many yachts. Noirmoutier town dries and can only be reached near high water (high water springs for deep draught yachts) and Fromentine, on the mainland by the bridge, is approached over a shallow bar exposed to westerly winds and swell, though it is easily accessible at high water in offshore winds. There are shoals and rocks extending a long way off the island; they are adequately marked, but call for care in the approach.

Orins des casiers
South of the Loire one must keep a good lookout for the *nombreux orins des casiers* which start to appear round the N and W coasts of Noirmoutier. To the north, a line of lobster pots is marked by a dan buoy at each end. From Noirmoutier to the south a line of very small floats will be seen to stretch between the two dan buoys and, if under power, one should avoid crossing the line.

Approach and entrance
The island is well placed in the middle of the French charts, SHOM 5039 and ECM 549, but lies on the overlap of the two English charts, BA 2646 and 2647. BA 2646 is adequate for entry to L'Herbaudière from the north.

Approaching from the N, the landmarks to look for are: the tall, twin lighthouses on Ile du Pilier, the conspicuous red and white radio mast on the NW tip of the island and an easily identified water tower, with a wide tank and a flat conical top painted red, to the SE of L'Herbaudière. Although there are a number of shoals – Le Four, La Blanche, La Lambarde, Keŕouars – to avoid, they lie in the approaches to St Nazaire and the Loire and are consequently very well marked.

If making for L'Herbaudière, the entrance lies 500m E of the radio mast. Steer for Basse du Martroger tower, leaving Grand Sécé cardinal N tower $\frac{3}{4}$ mile to starboard. $\frac{1}{2}$ mile NW

L'Herbaudiere entrance is well marked on close approach. The lifeboat station on the left and the radio mast, out of the picture to the right, are conspicuous at a distance

of Martroger tower, when the radio mast bears 195°, the harbour can be identified by a slender chimney close to the west and the large red roofed lifeboat house to the east of the entrance. From here the entrance channel should bear 190°, marked by a lateral port and starboard buoys and port hand beacons.

Bound for Bois de la Chaise, it is best to pass at least 1½ miles N of Martroger tower to avoid the Banc de la Blanche with a least depth of 1.8m. Passing close to the south of Banc de la Blanche buoy (card N) steer for Pierre Moine BRB tower and alter to leave Basse des Pères buoy (card E) close to starboard, with Pierre Moine tower 1.3 miles to port. From this point Noirmoutier spire is conspicuous bearing 182° and a course of 153° should lead to the small RW buoy marking the Bois de la Chaise anchorage ½ mile NW of the Pointe des Dames. A wooden pier projects from this headland which is steep, tree covered, and with only the top of the lighthouse showing above the trees.

Approaching from the S or SE, unless going to Fromentine, it will be necessary to clear Les Boeufs, after which one can pass through the Chenal de la Grise. This channel carries 3.3m. It is marked on its NW side by a buoy (card S) and on its SE side by a beacon, marking Rocher Patou (card W) off Pointe de L'Herbaudière, which should be given a berth of at least 200m. Basse du Martroger tower (card N), in transit with the Rocher Patou beacon, bearing 050°, clears all the dangers of Les Boeufs. A mid-channel lead is the tower of Ste Marie church, on the mainland, in transit with Martroger tower, bearing 058°. In the channel, pass rather closer to the buoy than to the beacon and continue until the entrance of L'Herbaudière harbour has been identified by the large red roofed lifeboat building on the east side and the slender chimney behind. Steer for the entrance when it bears 190°.

If proceeding to Bois de la Chaise, steer to leave the Basse du Martroger tower 200m to starboard. There are shoals to the E and ENE of Basse du Martroger; although there is a thin pole beacon on these shoals it is ½ mile inside the northern edge. A safe course is to keep the Rocher Patou beacon off Pointe de l'Herbaudière in transit with Martroger tower, bearing 230° astern, until the Basse des Pères buoy (card E) bears 090° when alter course to pass 200m south of it. Thence steer to give the Pointe des Dames a reasonable berth. The anchorage is described above.

By night
The following directions lead to L'Herbaudière.

From the north-west
Approach in the white sector of Basse du Martroger light (**3**), bearing 124° to 153°, and thence in the white sector of L'Herbaudière light (**6**) bearing 187.5° to 190°. Finally leave the Fl G light buoy (**9**) close to starboard.

From the south
Go through the Chenal de la Grise in the white sector of Basse du Martroger light (**3**), bearing between 055° and 060°. When L'Herbaudière light turns white, steer in this sector on 187.5° to 190°, leaving the Fl G light buoy (**9**) close to starboard.

Bois de la Chaise. *Black Jack* is lying on a mooring, but later in the season there might be no mooring free. Pointe des Dames lighthouse shows just over the treetops

L'Herbaudière

There are two starboard hand buoys and one port in the near approach together with two port hand beacons. The channel is no wider than the entrance so do not stray. Alter to starboard on passing the west breakwater and then round the slipway and lifeboat station to port to enter the marina. The visitors' pontoon (F) is on the west side in the entrance of the marina with 2.5m depth.

Facilities

Water and electricity are on the pontoons, and there are also fuel berth, 25 tonne crane, slipway and grid, showers, toilets, launderette, telephones, ice, café/restaurant, and superette with provisions, fruit and wine. Engineers and chandlers. In the village there are shops, but no bank (1988). There is a large camping site on the west point.

Bois de la Chaise

This open anchorage is sheltered from the W and S. It is exposed to the N and E, but the fetch is not more than 5 miles, and in summer many yachts lie on moorings here. It is an attractive situation though the facilities are limited. There are some moorings for visitors and four lines of private moorings with space to anchor outside, keeping clear of the wreck some 300m E of the pier and possibly marked by a red beacon. Land at the steps half way along the pier; the end must be kept clear for the ferries.

Facilities

There are two restaurants, a paper shop and a pâtisserie (which does not sell bread); good shops are in Noirmoutier, a 1½ mile walk. There is a big camp site behind the beach to the south. In the summer a general shop opens to serve the camp, and a butcher in July and August. To reach them it is easier to land on the beach to the south of the anchorage rather than to walk round from the pier.

Noirmoutier

This port is reached by a long, straight, narrow channel. It should be regarded as drying 2.5m and is therefore not accessible to deep draught yachts at neaps.

South of the channel training wall a rocky shelf, covered with oyster beds, stretches out

Noirmoutier harbour at LW. The quay on the right is the best place to moor

some 4 miles to the ENE, with several passages marked by beacons. The old approach runs north of a curving line of 5 red (port) beacons on the northern edge of the shelf. This approach does not dry as far in as the second beacon out from the training wall (Atelier), but since there is a drying 2.5m patch at the entrance, it is more convenient to wait until there is sufficient water in the channel and use the line of green beacons to approach along the shore.

Coming south from the Bois de la Chaise anchorage, when there is considered to be enough water, keep about 500m offshore, passing over a sandy bottom (drying 1.6m) inshore of a mussel bed. A line of green (stbd) beacons will be seen along the shore, curving to starboard into the entrance of the channel. While taking soundings, follow the line of beacons round to the entrance and from thence continue up the marked channel to the town.

Moor to the first quay on the starboard hand, before the crane is reached. Farther up, the quays are shallower. The mud is very soft so that the keel will probably sink in, leaving the yacht upright.

Facilities

All shops are available, as are restaurants and hotels, shipyard and marine engineer. This is a pleasant town.

Fromentine

High water: −0020 Brest, Index 1, MTL 2.9m.
   MHWS 5.3m; MLWS 0.5m; MHWN 4.0m; MLWN 1.8m.
Tidal streams: Ingoing stream begins +0600 Brest, 4 knots springs; outgoing begins −0220 Brest,
   5½ knots springs.
Depths: The bar varies in position and depth; it dries about 1.5m.
Lights: No lights are included here. It is not advisable to attempt entry at night.

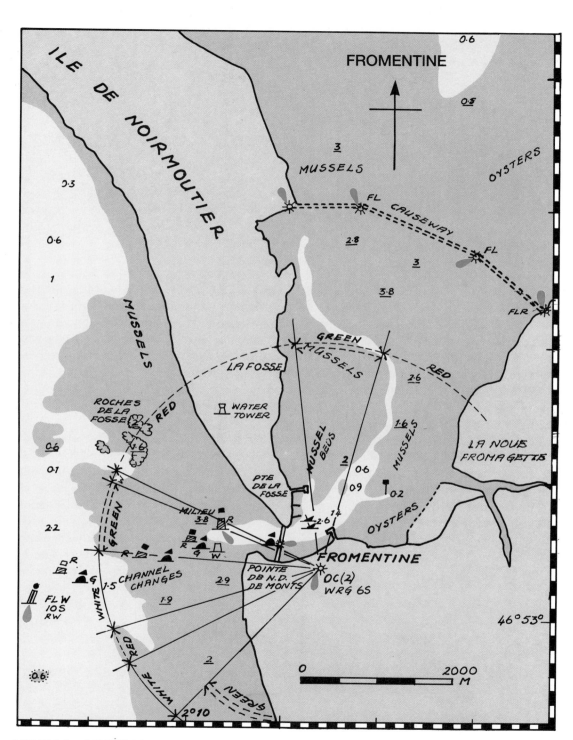

MLWS 0.5m; MLWN 1.8m; −0020 Brest, Index 1, MTL 2.9m
Based on French Chart No. 147 with corrections (No. 5039 supersedes). Depths in metres; right hand
margin in cables

Cohoe III indicates the best anchorage, just eastward of the cable area, looking E

The Goulet de Fromentine, between the south of the Ile de Noirmoutier and the mainland, does not have a very good reputation among yachtsmen, as the entrance is on a lee shore if the wind is in any westerly direction and the bar of sand dries and shifts in position. The streams are very strong in the narrows and run seaward for nearly 9 hours, from about $1\frac{3}{4}$ hours before high water to 1 hour after low water. The channel is, however, well buoyed and, as it is used all the year round by the Ile d'Yeu ferry, it may be regarded as fit for navigation in reasonable weather conditions.

Approach and entrance from the NW

Deep draught vessels must on no account approach from the Baie de Bourgneuf as there is a causeway which dries 3m with guide posts and raised refuges between the island and the mainland. In 1987 Mr Paul Dane surveyed the passage in a bilge-keel ketch drawing 1.1m and has kindly supplied the directions included in this edition.

The coast of Noirmoutier and the mainland south of it merge together into a line of sand dunes when viewed from seaward. There are several windmills painted white with black tops on the Noirmoutier side, and a very conspicuous water tower. At Fromentine there is Notre Dame des Monts lighthouse and in the background a water tower; $\frac{1}{2}$ mile seaward of the bridge are two beacon towers, the northern one red and the southern one white.

The sea shoals some 6 miles west of the entrance, before the landmarks can be located if the weather is at all thick. Accordingly it is best to fix the vessel's position precisely on the buoys SW of Les Boeufs, Réaumur (card W) and Le Bavard (card S) if approaching from the NW .

Although the Ile d'Yeu ferry uses the port near HW, strangers would be unwise to attempt it in a strong onshore wind, or if there is a swell high enough to break on the shoals. If it is not rough and the approach is made during the last 2 hours of the flood there will be plenty of water over the outer shoals, the shallowest being Basse de l'Aigle with 2.9m over it. The landfall buoy (RW, bell) is situated 1.95 miles at 264° from

Fromentine lighthouse. From this buoy pairs of red and green buoys mark the channel across the bar to the red and the white beacon towers. Passing between them the channel deepens and a starboard hand buoy indicates the channel to the main navigation arch of the bridge which is clearly marked (clearance 27m). A red buoy (lat port) marks the lead of the channel to the Fromentine pier. To the north of this buoy are two wrecks exposed at LW.

Approach from the SW

This really starts from the Basse de l'Aigle buoy, from where set course for the landfall buoy, LFl 10s (spherical RW with radar reflector) 46°53.1′N 02°11.6′W. On the flood tide there is a set to the south. Before reaching the landfall buoy you will see a large water tower on the S end of Noirmoutier and the very large new bridge, joining the mainland and the island. The channel is well buoyed and most of the buoys have radar reflectors. Buoys are changed when necessary by the ferry operators. The centre span of the bridge is lit.

Anchorage

Depending on draught, either off the jetty on the E side of Pointe de la Fosse (Noirmoutier) with less tidal stream, or off the shore just west of the ferry jetty off Fromentine and just east of the cable area, or pick up one of the buoys. The chains are substantial. The buoys to the E of the Fromentine ferry jetty are not too suitable, there being a lack of water at LWS. The streams in the fairway are very strong, about 5 knots, but they moderate towards the shore. Anchor as far in as draught and tide will allow. Owing to the strength of the tide it is said to be unwise to leave a yacht unattended while at anchor, and this would certainly be true at the top of springs. If going in to the Pointe de la Fosse side, beware of the E boat wrecks just N of the channel; they lie between the first and second red buoys after you pass under the bridge, so either turn in before the first red buoy or after the second. It is not practical to row across the stream to Fromentine in the dinghy and the bridge is a long way round.

Facilities

Water at both ferry jetties, ask the ferry operators. Fromentine is a small holiday resort with hotels, restaurants and small shops. There is a ferry to Ile d'Yeu. At Pointe de la Fosse, on Noirmoutier, there is a small hotel, which combines a bar/restaurant, tobacconist, and a small shop for bread etc., about 3 min walk from the ferry office. Alternatively take a walk or taxi over the bridge to Fromentine.

Passage north from Fromentine over Causeway

French directions state that there should be more than 1.5m over the causeway 2 hours before HWS but but not more than 1m at HWN.

The directions below are compiled from Mr Paul Dane's survey in *Pampa Mia*, a bilge-keel ketch drawing 1.26m, in July 1987. The chart used was French, SHOM 5039 P, but ECM Navicarte 549 might be preferred.

The causeway is about 2 miles long and 30m wide, constructed of stones and small rocks. The roadway is pavée about 10m wide. It is the highest object in the immediate area and calculations put the height as being 2.64m above St Nazaire datum. (*Note:* SHOM 5039 shows sand drying 3m S of the eastern *bal à hune* and drying 2.7m N of the refuge.)

There are three refuges or *bal à hune* on the causeway. On either side of the eastern refuge are beacons to indicate the best place to cross. The starboard beacon is west and the port beacon (to be left to starboard going north) is east of the refuge which is a wooden structure mounted on a stone and concrete plinth the top of which is 2.1m above the level of the causeway. From this it follows that, when the plinth is just covered, the causeway may be crossed between the refuge and the port hand beacon with a minimum depth of 2.1m.

The tide makes from the south, comes in quickly and runs over the causeway, across the sands, to meet the tide rising on the north side. From a position 100m off the end of the Fromentine ferry jetty make good a course of 030° up the channel to pass 15m to the east of a spar which is located approximately 400m from the eastern *bal à hune* on a bearing of 199°. Do not borrow east as there is a training wall further E, covered at HW. After passing the *bal à hune* set course to make good 355° to clear the oyster beds. On the port bow you will see a prominent water tower bearing 351° from the *bal à hune* and on the starboard bow, north of Pornic, another water tower with a RW radio mast close west bearing 002° from the *bal à hune*. This course crosses La Préoire rocky plateau, drying 2.9m, and to avoid it turn onto 040° 2½ miles from the *bal à hune*, when the water tower on the southern end of Noirmoutier bears 205°. This course will lead to Le Fain channel, where there is sufficient water to leave Goeland lateral starboard buoy to starboard (although it is a starboard hand channel buoy when going south) and a green (lat stbd) beacon to port.

The way is then clear to Pornic. As an alternative, those equipped with ECM Navicarte 549 can find their way across the extensive rocky shelf south of the port of Noirmoutier to an anchorage off Bois de la Chaise.

44 Ile d'Yeu

Charts: English BA 2647, Imray C40.
       French SHOM 6853 P. ECM Navicarte 549.
High water: −0050 Brest, springs, −0020 Brest, neaps, Index 0, MTL 3.0m.
  MHWS 5.2m; MLWS 0.8m; MHWN 4.1m; MLWN 2.0m.
Tidal streams: There is considerable variation in the directions and rates of the streams round
  the island and tidal charts should be consulted. There are local variations close inshore.
Depths: The principal harbour, Port Joinville, is dredged to 1.5m with a wet basin (3.7m) and a
  marina (2.5m) has been excavated. Port de la Meule dries, but there is an anchorage outside
  that can be used in offshore winds, as can that further east in Anse des Vieilles.
Lights:
1. Grand Phare or Petite Foule; Fl 5s, 56m, 24M. White square tower, green lantern.
   Siren 1 ev 60s. Radio beacon; call YE 312.6 kHz contin.
2. Les Chiens Perrins; Q(9)WG 15s, 16m, 8–4M. Beacon tower cardinal W.
3. Pointe des Corbeaux; Fl(2+1)R 15s, 25m, 20M. White square tower, red top.
4. La Sablaire by (card S); Q(6)+L 15s.
5. Port Joinville NW jetty head; Oc(3)WG 12s, 9m, 11–9M. White metal frame, green top.
6. Leading lights bearing 219°; sync Q R front 9m, rear 16m, 5M. Front metal frame tower,
   rear pole.
7. Passerelle de Galiotte inner end; Fl(2)R 5s.
   Gare Maritime pierhead; Iso G 4s; 7m, 6M.
8. Port de la Meule; Oc WRG 4s, 9m, 9–6–5M. Grey square tower, red top

The Ile d'Yeu, situated about half-way between Belle Ile and La Rochelle, is the furthest
from the mainland of the outlying islands off the coast of the Bay of Biscay. It measures
about 5 miles long and 2 miles across. The only deep harbour, Port Joinville, is an
important fishing port, especially for tunny, with good berths at the quays and an
anchorage outside sheltered from the prevailing winds. The town is a pleasant one with
excellent facilities as the island is a popular one for visitors.

The south coast of the island is very rocky and deeply indented by the action of the
Atlantic seas. There are two bays that can be used as temporary anchorages in offshore
winds. In one of these is the narrow winding inlet which forms Port de la Meule which,
although very small, is the only other harbour in the island. The other is Anse des
Vieilles, near the SE corner of the island. The bay west of the ruined château looks
inviting, but from the land it is seen to be full of rocks.

Despite its lack of good harbours Ile d'Yeu appears very prosperous, perhaps because
the fishing industry is so active. The houses are whitewashed with brightly painted doors
and shutters. The whole island seems trim and well cared for; it is high, wind-swept and
bracing.

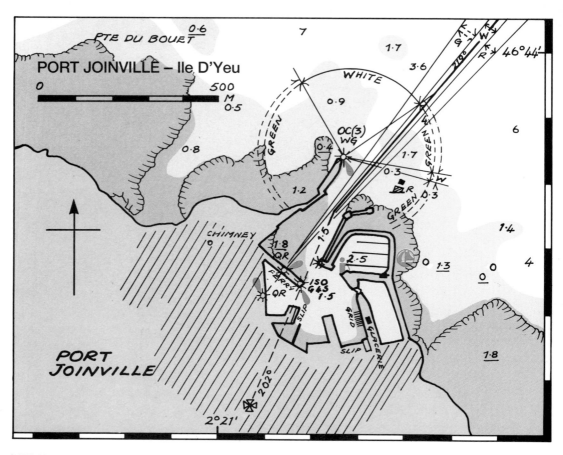

MLWS 0.8m; MLWN 2.1m; −0050(sp), −0020(np) Brest, Index 0, MTL 3.0m
Based on French Chart No. 6613 with corrections (No. 6853 supersedes). Depths in metres; right hand
margin in cables

The coastline is magnificent, especially on the southern side where, overlooking a rock-studded bay, there are the ruins of an eleventh-century castle, much attacked by the English, complete with dungeons and moats. In recent history, Marshal Pétain was imprisoned near Port Joinville, and his simple tomb is to be seen in the cemetery there. The island is well worth a visit, and although the marina is very crowded in the summer it provides a convenient port of call when bound for La Rochelle.

Port Joinville

This harbour, on the north side of the Ile d'Yeu, is exposed to N and E winds, though the extension to the NW mole has improved the shelter. Swell enters in strong winds from these directions, and there is sometimes a surge during gales from other directions. None of this, however, affects the berths in the yacht marina or in the wet basin which are completely sheltered. It is the only safe harbour in the island.

Port Joinville, yacht basin; entrance and fuelling pontoon to right of picture

Approach and entrance

The high water tower will be seen just behind the town; in the distance this is more conspicuous than the island's main lighthouse. The town and breakwaters at the harbour entrance are easy to locate from seaward; an approach with the water tower bearing 224° will lead in.

On the east side of the entrance is the Passerelle de la Galiotte, a walkway on concrete columns, with an elbow giving the outer half a lead of ENE, outside of which is a 0.2m drying patch and a red can buoy 100m NE of the head. The NW breakwater arm has

Port Joinville entrance on a hazy day. The chimney (right) and water tower (centre) are conspicuous from seaward

been extended and the light has been moved to a metal frame tower. The old light tower is still in position, but no longer lit.

Enter the harbour leaving the NW breakwater head 50m to starboard and, on reaching the Passerelle elbow, bear to port (as the western side of the outer harbour dries 0.5m) and round the inner end of the Passerelle to enter the marina.

By night
Approach in the white sector of the NW breakwater light (**5**) and enter the harbour with the leading lights in line (**6**) bearing 219°.

Anchorage and mooring
There is an anchorage in 3–4m (sand and mud) 700m east of the port in Anse de Chalon, a bay with rocky outcrops on either side, Rocher Ronde to the W drying 3.2m, and some rocks in the sand close inshore. Should the marina and the wet basin be full, it is possible to anchor in the basin west of the Jetée de l'Est with its large ice factory building. Beware of the grid beside the jetty whose position is marked by red lines on the wall.

There are only three pontoons in the marina which was full in the afternoon, mid week in June 1988, and overfull by nightfall after a severe thunderstorm. The harbourmaster likes visitors to telephone (51 58 38 11) to arrange a berth before arrival, or to call on VHF, Ch. 9. Entry to the wet basin is possible 2 hours either side of high water. It is intended for the fishing fleet, but yachts may moor by arrangement with the harbourmaster. Keep clear of the west side of the harbour and the ferry terminal. Marina charges are higher than average.

Facilities
Water and electricity are on the pontoons, and a fuel berth at the entrance to the marina, with toilets, showers, telephones, in the marina. Ice is from the factory, and there is a 5

Ruined château on the S coast

tonne crane, slip, grid, shipyard, marine engineer, chandlery at fishermen's cooperative, sailmaker (who is, however, more used to trawlers' riding sails than yacht work). In the town are banks, hotels, restaurants, all the usual shops, a good supermarket and, also, several bicycle-hire firms.

There is a regular ferry service to Fromentine on the mainland and also, in summer, to St Gilles sur Vie and Croix de Vie and less frequently to Les Sables d'Olonne.

Port de la Meule

This is a picturesque but tiny fishing harbour on the south side of Ile d'Yeu, which is rewarding to visit if one is lucky enough to get the right conditions of offshore wind, but is to be avoided in unsettled weather. The harbour is crowded with small fishing boats, with the occasional trawler at anchor in the entrance. The fishermen much prefer yachts to anchor outside and report that, in the summer, there will be ten or more yachts at anchor during *le week-end*.

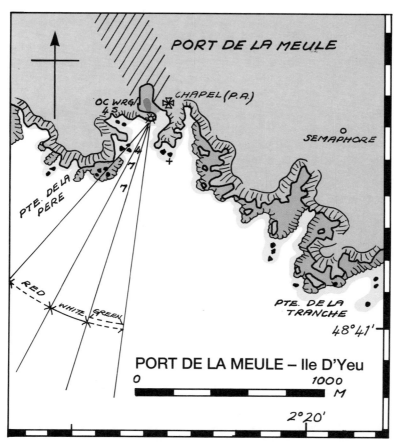

PORT DE LA MEULE – Ile D'Yeu

MLWS 0.8m; MLWN 2.1m; −0050(sp), −0020(np) Brest, Index 0, MTL 3.0m
Based on French Chart No. 147, enlarged, with corrections (No. 6853 supersedes). Depths in metres; right hand margin in cables

Approach and entrance

The entrance is not conspicuous, but lies between two fairly prominent headlands, La Panrée, with a white stone cross, 1½ miles to the west, and Pointe de la Tranche, ¾ mile to the SE, behind which there is, on high ground, a conspicuous white semaphore tower. Another landmark is the ruined castle 1 mile to the W. The ruins are of similar rock to the cliffs behind them, but can be made out on a clear day.

From seaward the entrance has little to distinguish it from the other inlets on this coast until it is opened up, when the white panel on the side of the lighthouse and the white chapel at the NE end of the inlet can be seen. The bay in which Port de la Meule is situated is clear of offlying rocks, except for those off the headlands or in the immediate vicinity of the cliffs. Steer for the lighthouse, bearing 022°, allowing for any set of the tide.

On near approach a headland on the west side of the entrance will lie to port. This has rocks off the south end which are well off the line of approach, but there is also a reef projecting eastward almost facing the headland on the opposite side. These rocks can usually be seen as the swell breaks on them, but an incoming vessel should borrow to starboard to give them an offing.

The headland on the east side, which is an island (Tête Jaune) at high water, does not project seawards so far as does the west headland. There are rocks off its southern extremity, which it is convenient to regard as a short underwater continuation of the headland.

Thus, in the near approach, first give reasonable clearance to the reef of rocks to port, then keep the inlet between the lighthouse and the cliff on the east side open, steering parallel with the eastern side of the inlet. When within the entrance, where there is 4m, lobster pot buoys will be seen on the west side, which are an aid to navigation, as the outer ones are usually laid where they may be treated as port hand marks, to be left close to port. On the opposite, east, side there are a few rocks at the foot of the cliffs, one of which

Port de la Meule entrance. Chapel, centre, light tower with white square, left centre

Le Meule harbour at HW

lies close to the channel. Hence, if proceeding to the quay, a vessel should now keep rather W of the centre and turn sharply to port round the point on which the lighthouse stands.

There is shelter at the quay in normal conditions with the wind from W through N to E, but if the wind goes into a southerly quarter the swell will surge right in and the harbour is untenable. In southerly gales even the local boats move round to Port Joinville.

By night
Night entry cannot be recommended to a stranger.

Anchorage and mooring
In settled offshore winds it is practicable to anchor in the entrance, though some swell comes in even in NE winds. The bottom is rocky and there is little swinging room so that two anchors are necessary.

The harbour dries; the fishermen are helpful but say that there is really no room for a yacht. It would be wise to seek their advice before entering. There are three slips and the best walls to lie against are between the first and second (although there are said to be some stones on the bottom here) or between the second and third, where it will be necessary to keep clear of the chain moorings for fishermen's dinghies. The bottom is rocky off the first slip and above the third.

Facilities
There are two restaurants, but almost no other facilities. There are paths over the hills and the cliffs to east and west. The ruined castle 1 mile to the west is interesting.

Charts: English BA 2647. Imray C40.

       French SHOM 6853 P, 6523 P. ECM Navicarte 549, 1022.

High water: −0020 Brest, Index 1, MTL 3.1m.

  MHWS 5.3m; MLWS 0.8m; MHWN 4.1m; MLWN 2.1m.

Tidal streams: The streams are weak in the offing, but strong in the harbour itself, the ebb reaching nearly 6 knots in the narrow parts. The ebb is increased and the flood reduced (or even fails to occur) after heavy rain.

Depths: The channel is said to be dredged to 1.5m, so that both fishing harbours and the yacht marina should be accessible at all states of the tide. There is, however, a serious silting problem, with continuous dredging to prevent two sand bars forming.

Lights:

1. Pointe de Grosse Terre; Fl(4)WR 12s, 25m, 17-13M. White truncated conical tower.
2. Leading lights; bearing 043.5°; sync Oc(3+1)R 12s.
       Front: 7m, 13M. White square tower, red top.
       Rear: 28m, 13M. White square tower, red top.
3. Pilours by, card S; Q(6)+L 15s, bell.
4. NW jetty head; Fl(2)WR 6s, 8m, 10-7M. Red column, white shelter. Reed (2) 20s.
5. SE jetty head; Iso WG 4s, 7m, 8-5M. green tower.
6. Lit channel bys in harbour; 3 red (port) and 4 green (stbd).

This harbour is formed by La Vie river; the entrance is protected by moles on either hand. The entrance faces SW, and is therefore unsuitable for entry during strong onshore winds or if there is a swell. As the ebb tide can reach 6 knots at springs, conditions for entry are impossible when a strong wind opposes this and it is safer to make both entry and exit before high water.

St Gilles Croix de Vie, looking upstream past fishing quays to marina

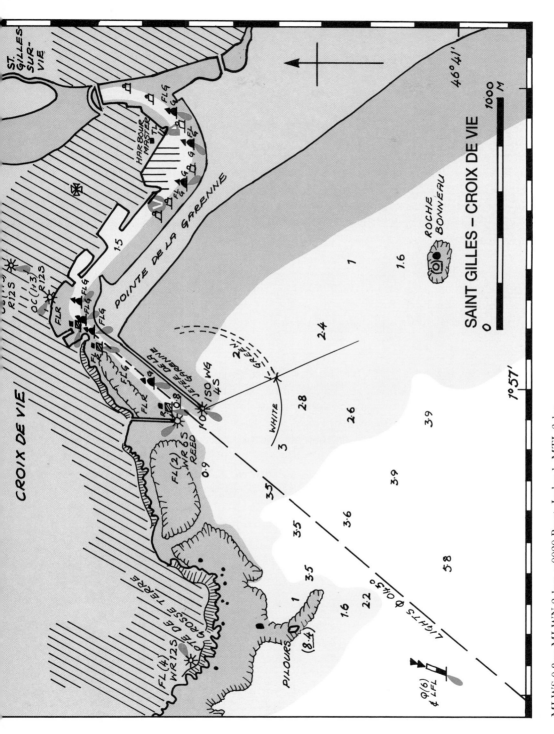

SAINT GILLES – CROIX DE VIE

MLWS 0.8m; MLWN 2.1m; −0020 Brest, Index 1, MTL 3.1m
Based on French Chart No. 6613 with corrections (No. 6522 supersedes). Depths in metres; right hand margin in cables

257

Within the river there are two enclosed basins for the fishing fleet on the north side; above these lie the pontoons of the yacht marina. There are also quays further up the river at St Gilles sur Vie on the southeast side. Croix de Vie is a substantial town and the fish quays near the railway station are very busy. There is much yachting activity in the port with 800 permanent berths and 60 for visitors. There are also mooring trots along the river opposite the marina and on up to the bridge.

Approach

In a rather featureless sandy coastline, with churches and three water towers in the background, the entrance can be located by the low rocky headland of Grosse Terre on the north side, with many houses and a lighthouse, the two church spires and the high lighthouse of Croix de Vie. On nearer approach the Pilours, a low reef of rocks like a small island, will be seen, marked by a pillar light buoy (card S), with the entrance and the leading lighthouses beyond.

Approach should be made, preferably shortly before high water, with the leading lighthouses in transit bearing 043°. This approach leaves the Pilours buoy (card S) 250m to port and, further in, the end of the Pilours reef 160m to port. Soundings fall gradually from 6m opposite the buoy to 1m, 250m off the pierhead. Thence the channel should be dredged to 1.5m, but some silting may have occurred.

Entrance

The entrance lies between the two outer breakwater heads, and the transit leads on the SE side of the entrance following close to and parallel to the SE mole (Jetée de la Garenne). This line is out of the dredged channel so that incoming vessels should if possible borrow to port and keep in the buoyed channel after the mole head is passed. Four lit starboard hand buoys lead up the channel and into the sharp curve to starboard. To port are two port hand buoys, then the old Grand Môle with a stone tower and a ferry landing on the head. The stream runs very hard here and the buoys should be given a good berth as they are moored on the high ground beside the channel. After a 90° turn to starboard, the channel passes the fishing boat basins to the reception (*accueil*) berth on the port side. Secure here to obtain a berth from the harbourmaster, but beware of the strong tides passing the ends of the pontoons.

Departure should be made before high water, as the strong ebb quickly raises a sea at the entrance.

By night

Provided weather conditions are suitable, entry is easy at night. As by day, avoid entry when a strong tide is running.

Anchorage and mooring

Anchorage in the channel is prohibited. The berths near the shore ends of the marina pontoons may dry out, but the mud appears to be soft and boats remain upright. If no marina berths are available in this popular harbour, there are mooring buoys on the

St Gilles Croix de Vie entrance with the leading lighthouses in transit bearing 043°

south side of the channel opposite the marina; it may also be possible to berth below the bridge, further upstream, by the quay to starboard at St Gilles sur Vie, where the streams are not so strong.

Yachts which can take the ground could enquire if a berth is available at, or just off, the pontoons of the sailing club just inside the Grand Môle.

There is an anchorage outside in offshore winds, about 400m off the pierheads, keeping clear of the leading line. There is no convenient landing place for dinghies except at the harbour moles. The ebb could set up a nasty sea for dinghy work.

Facilities
Water and electricity can be found on the pontoons, with showers and toilets at the Capitainerie. Fuel berth is by the travel lift at the upstream end of the marina. There are shipbuilders, marine engineers and a chandlery. All shops are nearby, with bank, hotels and restaurants, the best of which will be found at Boisvinet, to the west of Croix de Vie. The railway station is just by the harbour. Croix de Vie is an important fishing port with all facilities for fishing vessels.

Les Sables d'Olonne

Charts: English BA 2648, 2647, 3640. Imray C40.

French SHOM 6523 P, 6522 P. ECM Navicarte 1022.

High water: −0020 Brest, springs, +0015 Brest, neaps, Index 0, MTL 3.1m.

MHWS 5.3m; MLWS 0.8m; MHWN 4.2m; MLWN 2.1m.

Tidal streams: In the offing the streams are weak, rarely exceeding ½ knot; they are rotary clockwise, N at LW Brest, S at HW Brest. In the Rade the streams are negligible and in the harbour itself they are normally weak.

Depths: The harbour is dredged to 1.5m and the marina to 2m.

Lights:

1. Les Barges; Fl(2)R 10s, 25m, 17M. Grey tower, red lantern.
2. L'Armandèche; Fl(2+1)W 15s, 42m, 23M. White hexagonal tower, red top.
3. La Petite Barge buoy, card S; Q(6)+L W 15s.
4. Le Nouch S buoy, card S; Q(6)+L W 15s (same as La Petite Barge).
5. Passe du SW Leading lights 033°; sync Iso R 4s shown throughout 24 hrs.
   Front, 14m, 16M. Metal mast.
   Rear, 33m, 16M. White square masonry tower.
6. Jetée Saint Nicolas, head; UQ(2)R 1s, 16m, 10M. White tower, red top. Horn (2) 30s.
7. Leading lights 320°;
   Front, Jetée des Sables, head; Q G, 11m, 8M. White tower, green top.
   Rear, Tour de la Chaume; Oc(2+1)W 12s, 33m, 13M. Large grey square tower surmounted by white turret.
8. Leading lights 327°; Dir FR.
   Front, 6m, 5M. Rectangle with WRW vertical stripes over white pedestal.
   Rear, 9m, 11M, intens 323.5°–330.5°. Rectangle with RWR vertical stripes over white tower.

Yachts bound south for La Rochelle pass within sight of Les Sables d'Olonne, which is situated some 35 miles NW of their destination. It is a convenient staging point, although on a small-scale chart the entrance appears shallow, beset with rocks, and a lee shore to the prevailing winds. With a large scale chart, however, the approach is found to be easy and the harbour and town provide excellent facilities. The approach is rough in strong SE, S or SW winds, especially if there is a swell, owing to the shoals. In bad weather the SE approach is the safer, and given plenty of rise of tide, fishing vessels approach and enter the harbour in severe weather.

The town of Les Sables d'Olonne on the east side of the entrance is a large sophisticated holiday resort with a casino, many hotels and restaurants facing the sands. A narrow peninsula separates this from the fishing port with its market and cafés. Visiting yachts may not lie here, but Port Olona, a large marina, has been set up in the

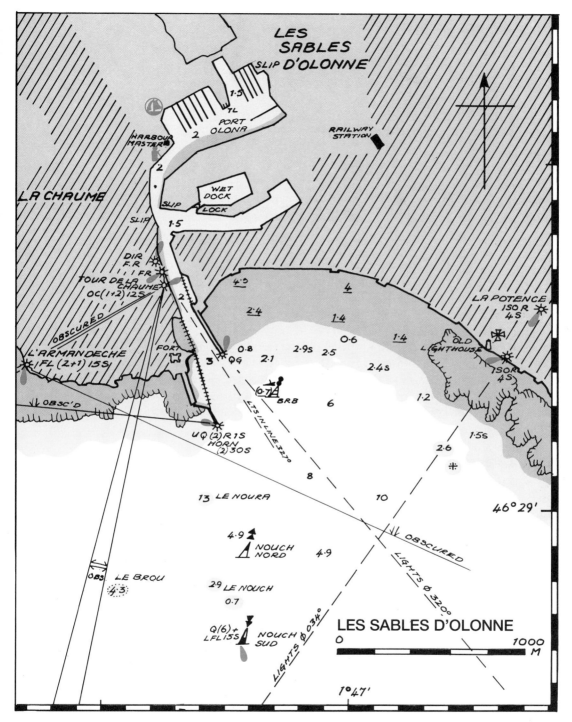

LES
SABLES
SLIP D'OLONNE

PORT OLONA

TL

2

HARBOUR MASTER

LA CHAUME

RAILWAY STATION

WET DOCK

SLIP LOCK

SLIP

2

1·5

DIR F.R.
1·1 FR.
TOUR DE LA CHAUME
OC(1+2) 12S

OBSCURED

L'ARMANDECHE
1 FL (2+1) 15 S

OBSC'D

FORT

3 QG

4·5

2·4

0·8 2·1

4

1·4

2·9S 2·5

0·6

0·7 BRB

6

LA POTENCE
ISO R
4 S

OLD LIGHTHOUSE

1·4

2·4S

1·2

ISO R
4 S

UQ (2) R 1S
HORN (2) 30 S

LTS IN LINE 327°

8

10

1·55

2·6

✳

OBSCURED

LIGHTS Ø 320°

13 LE NOURA

4·9

NOUCH NORD

4·9

46°29'

LE BROU

OBS

4·3

2·9 LE NOUCH

0·7

Q(6)+
LFL 15S

NOUCH SUD

LIGHTS Ø 034°

LES SABLES D'OLONNE

0   1000
              M

1°47'

MLWS 0.8m; MLWN 2.1m; −0020(sp), +0015(np) Brest, Index 0, MTL 3.1m
Based on French Chart No. 5611 with corrections (No. 6522 supersedes). Depths in metres; right hand
margin in cables

Les Sables d'Olonne, Port Olona Marina, Capitainerie with *Accueil* and fuel pontoon

dredged scouring basin further inland. This is a long way from the town by the ring road and the shops and restaurants of La Chaume on the west bank are more readily accessible.

Approach and entrance

The harbour lies about 1 mile to the SE of the Pointe de l'Aiguille, SE of which is the tall white lighthouse of l'Armandèche, with three tower blocks east of it and a radio mast to the north. On the east side of the harbour the hotels and other large buildings on the long curving front are also conspicuous when approaching from the south. Les Barges lighthouse, 1 mile offshore to the west is another aid to identification of the entrance.

From the W or NW, round La Petite Barge (card S) buoy, leaving it 200m or more to port; then steer 095° to identify Nouch Sud (card S) buoy and leave it also to port. Proceed eastwards until the entrance has been positively identified. The white lighthouse with red top on the head of the west breakwater should be conspicuous. Behind it the tall square crenellated tower of La Chaume is partially masked by an eight-storey building, but can be located to the left of the church spire. Approach the entrance with La Chaume tower in transit with the light tower on the east mole (white with a green top) bearing 320° and, if entering near low water, when the west breakwater head is abeam to port

Les Sables d'Olonne, looking into the entrance. Jetée des Sables head, far right. Jetée St Nicolas head, centre. L'Armandèche lighthouse, far left. La Chaume church spire is just left of the Jetée des Sables and La Chaume Light is on the tower just left of the church

alter to port to bring the WRW and RWR vertical stripe panels on the inner light structures in transit bearing 327° and follow this transit into the channel.

Approaching at half tide or over, in ordinary weather, attention to the leading lines is unnecessary and yachts can cross over the rocks and shoals to the south, and sail direct to the harbour entrance.

Approaching from the south, use the SE approach, sailing straight for the transit of the east mole head and La Chaume tower, bearing 320°. This leaves all the shoals to port, and the water is deep until within 400m of the harbour entrance; this approach should always be used in bad weather.

Berthing

Enter under power (sailing forbidden) past the fishing harbour to starboard, being wary of fishing boats leaving it at speed. Continue, as the channel curves to starboard, to the *accueil* pontoon of the marina on the port hand side and check in at the Bureau du Port to obtain a berth. Charges in 1988 were the most expensive on the coast.

Visitors may not use the fishing harbour and the wet dock can only be entered with prior permission from the port authority.

Facilities

Water and electricity are on the pontoons, as are showers and toilets. Fuel may be found at the *accueil* pontoon. There is also a 28-tonne travel lift, two slips, and all repair facilities. The marina was still developing in 1988 and the intention is to cater in the one complex for all the requirements of yachtsmen in the way of provisions, restaurants, chandlers, sailmakers and engineers.

The nearest outside banks, shops and restaurants are at La Chaume. There are excellent communications from Les Sables d'Olonne by train, bus and air.

Bourgenay

Charts: English BA 2648.
      French SHOM 6522 P. ECM Navicarte 1022.

High water: See Les Sables d'Olonne.

Tidal streams: 3 miles offshore: + 0200 to + 0500 Brest, WNW 0.5 to 1.3 knots. − 0400 to − 0000 Brest SE 0.4–0.9 knots.

Depths: 1m in the entrance, 1–2m at the pontoons.

Lights:
1. Fairway buoy, white with red vertical stripes, fluorescent orange sphere topmark. Fl W 10s.
2. Leading lights, 040° sync Q G 8M.
    Front; White hut on E breakwater. Green rectangle mark.
    Rear; Tall thin white column, white rectangle, green border.
3. W breakwater head; Fl R 4s, 9M. Red structure.
4. E mole head; Iso G 4s, 5M. Not visible to seaward.
5. W breakwater elbow; Fl(2)R 6s, 5M. Not visible to seaward.

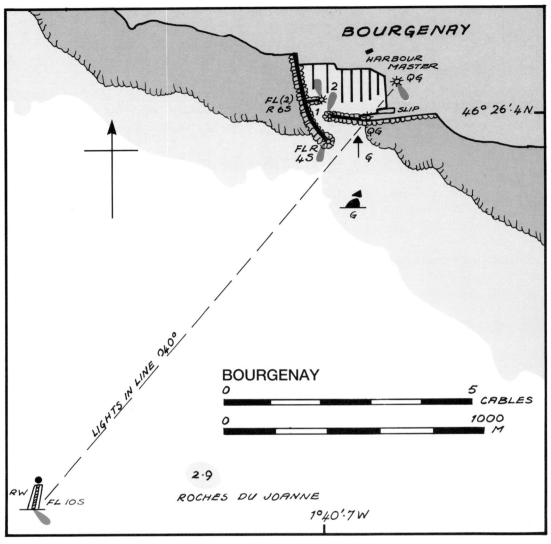

BOURGENAY

HARBOUR MASTER

QG

FL (2)
R 6S

2

1

SLIP

46° 26'.4 N

QG

FL R
4S

G

G

LIGHTS IN LINE 040°

BOURGENAY

0					5	

CABLES

0					1000	

M

2.9

RW

FL 10S

ROCHES DU JOANNE

1°40'.7 W

MLWS 0.8m; MLWN 2.1m; −0020(sp), +0015(np) Brest, Index 0, MTL 3.1m
Based on information provided by harbourmaster. Scale in metres approximate

This large and convenient marina some 6 miles SE of Les Sables d'Olonne was operational in 1986; the buildings were almost complete in June 1988 and the shops were being stocked. Behind the marina is a large holiday complex with boating lake and an old château with grey turrets which is now a convent, the conspicuous white topmark on the highest turret being, in fact, a statue of Notre Dame d'Espérance. The entrance is not easy to locate for the first time on a low lying, rocky and rather featureless coastline to the NW and a sandy beach to the SE, at the entrance to the river leading up to the town of

Bourgenay entrance. Entry involves a sharp turn to port. The rear leading mark, a thin white column, is centre picture. The outer breakwater head is marked with white paint (shoe shaped, pointing right)

Talmont. Entry should not be attempted in strong westerly winds but there is complete shelter inside.

Approach and entrance
It is essential first to locate the fairway buoy which is situated 1 mile SW of the marina. It is a metal framework buoy with RW vertical stripes and a fluorescent orange-red topmark. From the buoy the buildings behind the marina will be seen, bearing 040° with the rear leading mark, a tall thin white column.

The channel has been blasted out of a rocky, gently sloping seabed, with parts exposed at LW. Keeping the white column on 040°, approach until a green beacon can be seen to the right of a white patch marking the west breakwater head. A 90° turn to port is made to enter the marina followed by a 90° turn to starboard, fluorescent green and red chevrons, illuminated at night, indicating the turns. The water in the entrance can be confused during SW winds.

Berthing
The *acceuil* pontoon is on the inside of the E mole. Visitors should secure to it unless met by a marina launch and shown to a berth. There are 110 berths for visitors, maximum length 20m.

Facilities
Electricity and water are on the pontoons, as are showers and toilets. There is also a fuel berth, grid, slip and 15 tonne mobile crane. A café was open in 1988 and provisions were obtainable in the marina. There should now be a chandlery and engineers on site. If not the Capitainerie staff are very helpful in sending for assistance. There is a supermarket up the hill past the convent.

Taxis are available for the railway station or airport.

Charts: English BA 2641, 2746, 2648.

French SHOM 6521 P, 6333 P. ECM Navicarte 551, 1022.

High water: −0500 Brest, springs, +0010 Brest, neaps, Index 3, MTL 3.6m.

MHWS 6.0m; MLWS 0.8m; MHWN 4.8m; MLWN 2.4m.

Tidal streams: The streams, which are weak offshore, increase as the island is approached. The streams south of the island, in the Pertuis d'Antioche, are given under La Rochelle on page 285. North of the island, in the Pertuis Breton, where the harbours are, they are as follows: Off Pointe de Lizay at the north of the island, the flood runs ESE, the ebb WNW, spring rates 1½ knots. Off the mainland opposite, near the Pointe du Grouin du Cou, the turn is about half an hour after high water and low water and the rates about half a knot higher. Near the eastern end of the island the flood meets the north-going flood through the Rade de la Pallice, and the ebb splits similarly, leaving a zone of relatively weak streams off the NE of the island. The streams in the Rade de la Pallice do not exceed 1½ knots, springs.

Depths: See individual ports.

Lights: North coast:

1. Pointe du Grouin du Cou (mainland); Fl WRG 5s, 29m, 22–18–18M. White eight-sided tower, black lantern.
2. Les Baleineaux or Haut-Banc-du-Nord; Oc(2)W 6s, 23m, 13M. Pink tower, red top.
3. Les Baleines; Fl(4)W 15s, 53m, 27M. Grey eight-sided tower, red lantern.
   Radio beacon call BN 303.4 kHz 1/6 H+5.
4. Le Fier d'Ars, leading lights, 265° (1989);
   Front; Iso W 4s, 8m, 10M. White rectangle on grey framework.
   Rear; Dir Iso G 4s, sync, 12m, 13M. Green square tower on dwelling. Intens 263°–267°.
5. Ars en Ré, leading lights, 232°;
   Front; Q W, 5m, 9M. White rectangular hut, red lantern.
   Rear; Q W, 13m, 11M. Black rectangle on white framework tower, green top.
6. Le Rocha (mouillage extérieur) buoy (card N); Q W (Radar reflector).
7. Saint Martin de Ré, SE of entrance; Oc(2)WR 6s, 18m, 10–7M. White tower, red top.
8. Saint Martin de Ré, entrance channel; Fl R 2.5s, 7m, 4M. New beacon 1989.
9. Saint Martin de Ré, mole head; Iso G 4s, 10m, 6M. White column, green top.
10. La Flotte; Fl WG 4s, 10m, 12–9M. White round tower, green top.

The island, over 20km long, projects seaward west of La Rochelle which can be approached, either through the Pertuis d'Antioche on the south side of the island, or by entering the Pertuis Breton on the north side and proceeding on under the new road bridge joining Ile de Ré with the mainland. This spectacular curving bridge, nearly

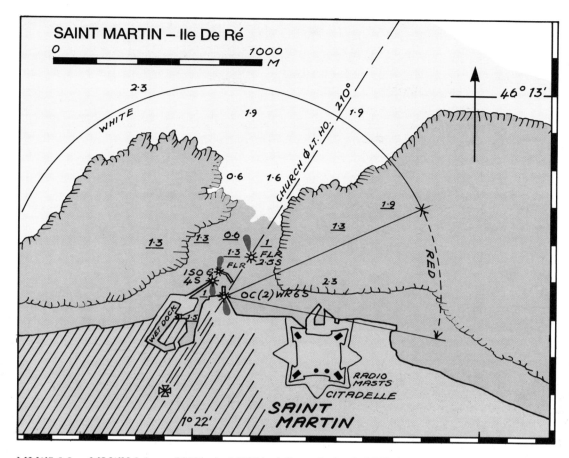

SAINT MARTIN – Ile De Ré

0   1000
                   M

46° 13'

210°

WHITE

CHURCH Ø LT. HO.

RED

2·3   1·9   1·9

0·6   1·6

1·9

1·3

1·3   1·3   0·6

1·3   FLR   1
     2·3S
FLR

2·3

ISO G   4S

1   OC (2) WR6S

WET DOCK   1·5

RADIO MASTS

CITADELLE

SAINT MARTIN

1° 22'

MLWS 0.8m; MLWN 2.4m; −0050(sp), +0010(np) Brest, Index 3, MTL 3.6m
Based on French Chart No. 157 with corrections (No. 6521 supersedes). Depths in metres; right hand margin in cables

2 miles long, with ample clearance for masts of any height, was opened in June 1988 and immediately flooded the island with cars, coaches and their contents.

The three ports, which are all in the Pertuis Breton, are a popular destination for a weekend sail from the mainland and support a substantial yachting activity of their own.

In the prevailing winds from the S and W the harbours are situated on the sheltered side of the island. This is useful to the cruising person, who can, in these winds, anchor off them while waiting to enter.

The Ile de Ré is a sandy island fringed in many parts by rocks, of which the most notable are the Banc du Nord extending from Les Baleines in the NW, and those off the Pointe de Chanchardon on the S and the Pointe de Chauveau on the SE. These are marked by light towers. The island is low and the scenery is like Holland, where windmills, now mostly converted into dwellings, and tall church spires rise high over the

267

land. The houses are as tidy as the Dutch ones. The island is a pleasant place in summer and much visited by holidaymakers.

Peaceful as it is today, the Ile de Ré has been the scene of much fighting and suffered greatly from the attacks of the English, and also during the religious wars. St Martin, the capital, is a fortified town with Vauban ramparts and a citadel, which was considerably damaged during the bombardment by the Anglo-Dutch fleet in 1696.

There are three harbours: St Martin, La Flotte and Fier d'Ars. All the harbours are tidal, but St Martin has a wet basin where yachts can lie afloat in complete shelter, in the centre of the old walled town with restaurants and shops close by.

Saint Martin

Depths: The near approach dries 1.6m, the inner harbour dries 1.5m. In the wet dock there is 3m at neaps, more at springs.

St Martin stands rather east of half way along the NE side of the Ile de Ré. The harbour consists of an Avant Port, not well sheltered by a mole and a jetty, connected with the drying harbour by a narrow entrance channel. From the drying harbour a channel to starboard leads through dock gates to the wet dock. There is active local yachting, as well as some fishing.

Approach and entrance

Approaching in the morning light the harbour is easily located, for the white lighthouse, the church tower and the citadel will be seen from afar. In the afternoon, with the sun in one's eyes, the walls do not stand out against the dark background and trees and the first

St Martin, drying basin and grid

St Martin entrance from the NE (1988). The outer approach is conveniently made with the lighthouse (left centre) and the ruined church tower in transit, bearing 210°. A wave-breaker was installed across the entrance in 1989. Leave it to port on entry

landmarks to be seen are the lighthouse and the church tower with ruined walls close to the right (see photograph).

There are extensive ledges of rock in and especially E and W of the approach, where they extend over $\frac{1}{2}$ mile seaward of the land. They are not so formidable as they appear at first glance on a chart, as the ones to the west farther offshore do not dry as much as the entrance channel and the ones to the east are marked by a beacon (card N).

The approach should be timed according to the draught of the yacht; between 3 hours before and 2 hours after high water should give 2.2m of water at the entrance on all tides. Convenient leading marks are the square church tower in transit with the lighthouse, bearing 209°, but it is not necessary to follow this line closely. When the church tower dips behind the trees, borrow to starboard and make the final approach with the church tower open of the trees and seen over the port hand side of the inner entrance (see photograph). Leave the mole head to starboard at a distance of less than 10m and steer straight for the centre of the channel leading in to the drying harbour. The channel to the dock gates will open up to starboard.

Approaching from the east, do not confuse the citadel, 600m E of the port, with St Martin itself; keep well to the north of the beacon (card N) on the Couronneau rocks unless the tide is well up, as rocks drying up to 1m lie to the north of the beacon and the 3m contour passes nearly 600m north of it. Thence bring the lighthouse and church into transit and steer as described above.

In 1989 a wave-breaker was constructed outside the entrance with a light (Fl R) on the west end (see chart). On entry, round the wave-breaker, leaving it close to port. Waiting pontoons are provided inside the western mole. Depths unknown.

By night
Make a position by Le Rocha buoy (**6**) and approach in the white sector of the St Martin light (**7**) bearing 200°. Note that the white sector extends from 124° to 245° and crosses

part of the outer ledges; it is not safe simply to enter in the white sector. On close approach bring the mole light (**8**) to bear 200° and steer so to the entrance, leaving the light close to starboard.

Mooring

There are quays in the drying harbour which dry 1.5m; vessels should not berth along the inner half of the west quay where there is a large grid, white patches along the top of the wall marking the positions of the rails. The swell gets into this harbour in onshore winds. It is better to moor either side of the wet dock entrance until the bridge and gate are opened and go into the wet dock.

The wet dock is completely solid with yachts during the summer weekends and the harbourmaster is magnificent at organizing departure and entry when the gate is opened. To be sure of a place, it is essential to arrive early and if possible secure to the wall by the entrance, leaving room for departing yachts to come out. Should there be no room, there are a number of white mooring buoys off the entrance and the Rade de St Martin povides an anchorage, sheltered from winds from west through south to south-east, in from 1.8 to 4m, inshore of La Rocha cardinal north buoy (*mouillage extérieur*) 2 miles to seaward. This is a recognized anchorage for big ships, and in offshore winds yachts can get closer in to anchor rather less than $\frac{1}{2}$ mile off the entrance in 2m sand and mud.

In daylight hours, near high water, the gate is opened and departure and entry are possible for at least one hour and usually 1 hour either side of HW, depending on the tidal coefficient. Times are posted at the Capitainerie and a clockface on the bridge shows the opening times each tide.

Facilities

Water is on the quay, showers and toilets are in the Capitainerie, and a fuel berth is outside the dock gate. There are also shipyard, chandler and engineers, slipway, grid and 9.5-tonne crane.

Bank, hotels, restaurants and all shops are close by. Taxis go to the mainland (a bus service is likely to have been established).

St Martin is a historic town of moats, walls and gateways, with a large church which has been only partly restored. At one period Ile de Ré was independent for customs purposes and St Martin was a prosperous port, carrying on a vigorous trade with America and distant parts; sailing ships loaded salt and wines and returned laden with woods, spices and other merchandise. It now has some signs of decay and is living on its past. The wet dock is now principally used by yachts, for which it is ideal, being clean and having every convenience at hand. The only disadvantage is that its popularity has led to overpopulation.

La Flotte

Depths: The approach and harbour dry 2m.

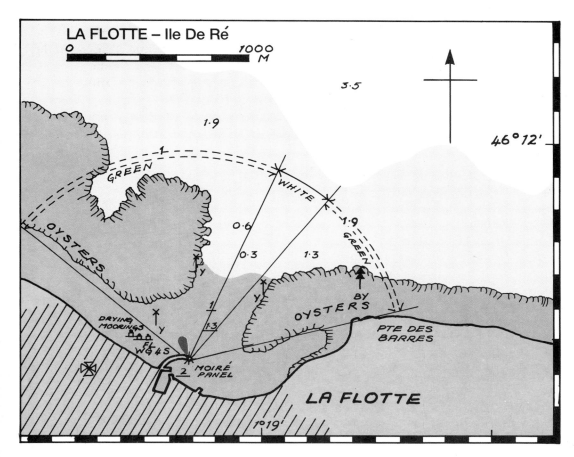

MLWS 0.8m; MLWN 2.4m; −0500(sp), +0100(np) Brest, Index 3, MTL 3.6m
Based on French Chart No. 157 with corrections (No. 6521 supersedes). Depths in metres; right hand margin in cables

La Flotte lies about 2 miles SE of St Martin; it is easily identified and the tall square church tower is conspicuous. The harbour is formed by two jetties, protected by a long curved outer mole. The narrow entrance faces east, across the shallow bay. Although there is no wet basin as at St Martin, the harbour is well sheltered, and is uncomfortable only in strong onshore winds. Pontoons were installed in 1988 along the walls in the upper half of the basin, providing 100 drying berths of which ten are reserved for visitors.

A fishing port, famous for lobsters, shrimps and sole, La Flotte is a compact town of

La Flotte, outer harbour with grid, right centre. Entrance to inner harbour, far left

short narrow streets and whitewashed houses with a beautiful church. It is less popular and more cheerful than St Martin. Except for the trouble of drying out, some yachtsmen may prefer it; yachts will be aground for long periods on each tide.

Approach and entrance

La Flotte is easy to locate in the bay ½ mile W of Pointe des Barres. It is approached by a channel with mud and sand bottom which dries 2m and lies between ledges of rock, extending up to ½ mile seaward, covered by oyster beds, marked by yellow beacons with diagonal cross topmarks.

Approach with the lighthouse bearing 215°. On this bearing (which it is not necessary to hold closely) the lighthouse will be in transit with a small belfry, not the main church tower. A beacon (card N) on the rocks off Pointe des Barres will be left about 600m to port. If approaching from the east, give a good berth to the beacon as the rocks extend outside it. Within 500m of the lighthouse, a vertical black and orange stripe will be visible day and night, defining the close approach on 215.5°. This ingenious Moiré Fringe system changes to an arrowhead pointing to the right if you are off course to port and to the left if you are off to starboard. If your error is great the arrowhead doubles. Change course in the direction indicated by the arrowhead and the vertical stripe will return when you are in the channel. Leave the breakwater head to starboard and steer for the narrow entrance between the jetty heads.

By night
As by day (light **10**) and Moiré Panel.

La Flotte outer breakwater, with the Moiré channel indicator to the left of the lighthouse

Mooring

The inner harbour is rectangular and dries 2m. Space for visitors is limited and it may be advisable to secure to the outer breakwater before entering and apply to the harbourmaster for a berth. It may be possible to lay alongside the breakwater and dry out in settled weather, but there is a grid at the root and fishing boats are moored with stern lines to the wall.

Outside the harbour to the west of the breakwater and inshore of the oyster beds is a line of white buoys on hard sand where vessels that can take the ground may moor. They may be reached by a close approach to the breakwater, turning to starboard inshore of the yellow beacon which marks the inner corner of the oyster beds. From here there is no problem getting ashore to the town, but the moorings are exposed to the not infrequent NW wind and the accompanying chop.

Deep draught yachts may anchor or use the white mooring buoys some $\frac{3}{4}$ mile offshore in 2m.

Facilities

Water and electricity are on the pontoons; moor bow to the pontoon and stern to a buoy. Water taps are on the quay. There are showers and toilets, two slips and a grid. Fuel is in St Martin, and there are some hotels, restaurants and shops in the town.

Fier d'Ars

Depths: The outer bar dries 0.4m, the outer anchorage has 2.6m. The second bar dries 1.5m, the main anchorage has 2m. The channel to the harbour dries out about 3m.

The Mer du Fier is a lake-like expanse of water, most of which dries at low tide. The word *fier* is said to be derived from the Scandinavian *fjord*, but the resemblance is remote. It is entered from the Pertuis Breton through a narrow channel some 5 miles east of Les Baleines. Though shallow, it is well sheltered and is the principal yachting centre of the island. The local boats are dinghies or of shallow draught to suit local conditions. Deep-keel yachts can lie afloat in the main anchorage off the Pointe du Fier, a delightful spot, or further out in a more exposed anchorage. It is possible to go up the channel to the harbour at tide time, but it is so crowded that it would be difficult to find a quayside berth for a yacht that cannot take the ground. The town is an attractive one; the local industries are making salt by evaporating sea water in salt-pans and cultivating oysters.

Approach and entrance

The approach is from the eastward and the channel lies between the ledges of rock extending from the island shore and the Banc du Bûcheron (called La Sablière on BA chart 2641), a big sandbank extending 2 miles to the east of Pointe du Fier.

Close with the land $\frac{1}{2}$ mile W of Pointe du Grouin (called Pointe de Loix on chart 2614). To the east will be seen Les Islattes tower (card N), to the west the wooded Pointe du Fier and the shore north of it. The approach is with the two leading marks on the Pointe du

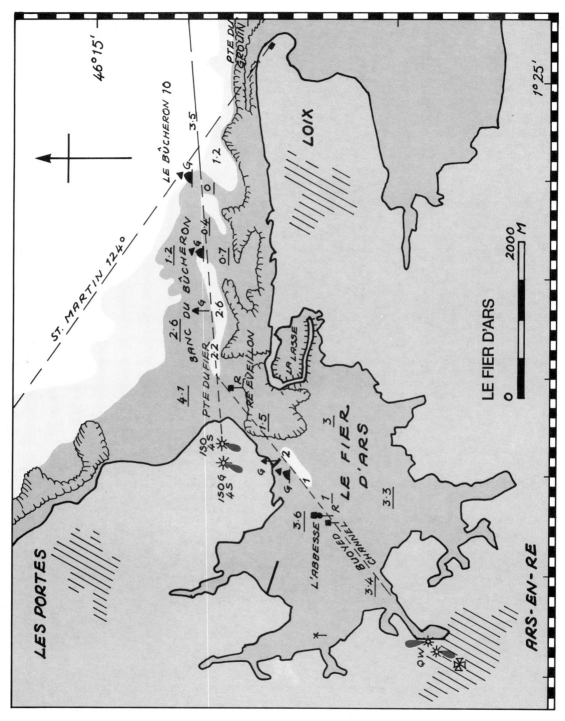

LES PORTES

ST. MARTIN 1240

LE BÛCHERON 10

46°15'

LE BÛCHERON 10

BANC DU BÛCHERON

4.1

2.6

1.2

G

1.2

G

0.4

G

0.7

2.6

3.5

1.2

0

PTE DU
GROUIN

PTE DU FIER

RE EVEILLON

R

2.2

1.5

LA LASSE

LOIX

ISO
4S

ISO G
4S

G

G

3.6

2

1

1

G

3

LE FIER
D'ARS

3.3

L'ABBESSE

R

1

BUOYED
CHANNEL

3.4

3

QW

ARS-EN-RE

1°25'

LE FIER D'ARS

0

2000
M

MLWS 0.8m; MLWN 2.4m; −0050(sp), +0100(np) Brest, Index 3, MTL 3.6m
Based on French Chart No. 6521 with corrections. Depths in metres; right hand margin in cables

Ile de Ré bridge. Opened June 1988

Fier in transit, bearing 265°. These marks/lights (**4**) are not at all conspicuous and must not be confused with the high tower of Les Baleines lighthouse, which stands out more clearly over the trees and well to the right of the alignment. The leading marks appear in a nick in the trees. The rear is a green square tower on a dwelling, the front mark is a grey metal framework tower with a white square board. It is on rails so that it can be moved as the channel shifts.

Approaching on the transit a buoy (Le Bûcheron, stbd) marking the end of the Banc de Bûcheron will be left to starboard. The Banc is tending to move southwards and a further starboard buoy and beacon close to the transit mark its present limit. In August 1988 it was reported that the beacon was missing and that a high tongue of sand extended right across the alignment. This tongue can be detected by a surface disturbance at HW. The alignment may be followed to a little W of the second green buoy when it is necessary to borrow to port and stay S of the line. It is possible that the front mark will have been moved and the beacon resited by 1990 to allow for this change. The channel shoals midway between the buoys, where it dries 0.4m; then it deepens again and just beyond the beacon is a narrow hole with up to 2.6m. This is the outer anchorage. Continuing on the transit for another $\frac{1}{2}$ mile Roche Eveillon beacon (port) will be seen. Just before the yacht reaches this beacon the leading-light/marks at Ars-en-Ré (**5**) might be located (transit bearing 232°). They are not easy to see by day and the conspicuous

275

black-topped church spire of Ars-en-Ré makes a better mark. When the spire bears 231° steer for it, leaving Roche Eveillon beacon 200m to port, over a rocky bottom which dries 1.5m. This course will run parallel to the shoreline of the Pointe du Fier, at the inshore end of which there is a landing slip. At this point begins the second deep pool forming the main anchorage; it has 2.6m and there are usually some boats anchored there. Beware of a rocky patch, awash at LWS towards the SE edge of the anchorage.

If proceeding to the harbour, leave the next two red beacons (L'Abesse and another) close to port and follow the buoyed channel, until it enters the canalized portion leading to the harbour itself. The channel and harbour dry 3m and the latter is very crowded with local boats.

By night
Make the initial approach with St Martin light (**7**) showing white, bearing more than 124°. Both leading lines are lit (**4** and **5**), but the pools will have to be found by sounding. The harbour is not accessible to strangers by night.

Anchorages
There are yacht moorings and an anchorage in 2m, $\frac{1}{2}$ mile E of Les Portes which is north of Le Fier d'Ars. The outer anchorage in Le Fier is exposed to the N and E, but is sheltered from S and W. Being outside the inner, shallower, bar there is more freedom to come and go, but it is a long way to the landing, with very strong tides.

The main anchorage has much better shelter, though it is somewhat exposed to the NE at high water. The tides also run hard here and the bottom is weedy. Land at the Pointe du Fier, which is a delightful strip of sand backed by woods.

The harbour is bordered by quays on each side, the width being 35m. It is shallow at the centre with deeper water along the quays. Hold well off the quays, since the foundations project. An inner harbour lies beyond a single dock gate, but this may be left open to help scour the channel.

Facilities
From the anchorages by Pointe du Fier it is necessary to walk 2 miles to Les Portes to reach the shops. A restaurant and shipyard are at the harbour. All shops, restaurants and buses in Ars-en-Ré, $\frac{1}{2}$ mile from the harbour.

Anse du Martray
This is an open anchorage on the south coast of Ile de Ré, off a sandy tourist beach, suitable in light NW to E winds.

Charts: BA 2641 or 2746, SHOM 6521 P or 6333 P, ECM Navicarte 551.

Approach and entrance
From a position $\frac{1}{2}$ mile E of Chanchardon tower (octagonal, black with white base: Fl RW

276

4s, 15m, 11–9M), steer north to a white mooring buoy and thence on about 355° towards an isolated white house at the E end of the sea wall. Use the church spires of Ars-en-Ré and La Couarde-Sur-Mer for fixing.

Anchorage
Run towards the white house until the depth of water and state of tide are suitable. The bottom is largely sandy, with a gentle gradient, but with a draught of 1.5m it is difficult to get within 400m of the beach.

Facilities
Land at the E end of the sea-wall, where there is a ramp. 100m to the E there is a campsite, with small supermarket, café, showers, toilets and launderette. The coast road leads W to Martray where there are seafood shops (oysters fr15 a doz in 1988) and a cycle track through the salt-pans or the road may be followed to Ars-en-Ré.

48 L'Aiguillon and Marans

Charts: English BA 2641, 2648.

French SHOM 6521 P. ECM Navicarte 551, 1022.

High water: −0050 Brest, springs, +0010 Brest, neaps, Index 3, MTL 3.6m.

MHWS 6.0m; MLWS 0.8m; MHWN 4.8m; MLWN 2.4m.

Tidal streams: For the streams in the Pertuis Breton see page 266. In Le Lay, leading to L'Aiguillon, the currents are about 1.5 knots springs. In La Sèvre Niortaise, leading to Marans, the streams are about 4 knots springs.

Depths: Le Lay dries in parts (0m at the entrance). The approach channel to La Sèvre Niortaise dries 0.1m. The canal to Marans and the port have more than 3m to accommodate coasters.

Lights: Le Lay and L'Aiguillon buoys are lit and there is a light on the Port du Pavé slip, but strangers should not attempt entry at night.

Six miles N of La Pallice, and to the NE of the Ile de Ré, two rivers flow between mud flats into the Pertuis Breton. The westernmost is Le Lay, leading to the town of L'Aiguillon. The eastern is La Sèvre Niortaise which leads from the Anse de l'Aiguillon to a lock, from which a canal leads to Marans. It is perverse that the town of L'Aiguillon is on a river which does *not* flow into the Anse de l'Aiguillon.

The entrances to both rivers, though sheltered at a distance by the Ile de Ré, are exposed to the S and W and, being shallow, are rough in winds from that quarter. Entry should only be attempted in fine weather or with offshore winds. Neither river is much visited by yachts and they provide an interesting excursion off the beaten track in suitable conditions. The scenery is similar to Holland or the Fens. The land is low and the rivers wind between training banks. The bird life is considerable, and with every variety of hawk in action along the poplar lined canal to Marans, one wonders how the white egrets, duck and other birds can survive.

L'Aiguillon

Caution

The coast outside and the river banks are devoted to the culture of mussels. These are grown on substantial timber piles which cover at HW and are very dangerous. The areas are marked by a line of yellow buoys outside the river and withies with branching tops inside. Withies with plain tops mark the oyster beds.

Entrance

The entrance to Le Lay river is not easy to locate from seaward. The low Pointe d'Arçay merges with the low shore NW of Pointe de l'Aiguillon and it is not until an incoming vessel closes with the land that that the course of the river opens up. Pointe de l'Aguillon is a long finger of sand which may be seen from a considerable distance if the sun is on it.

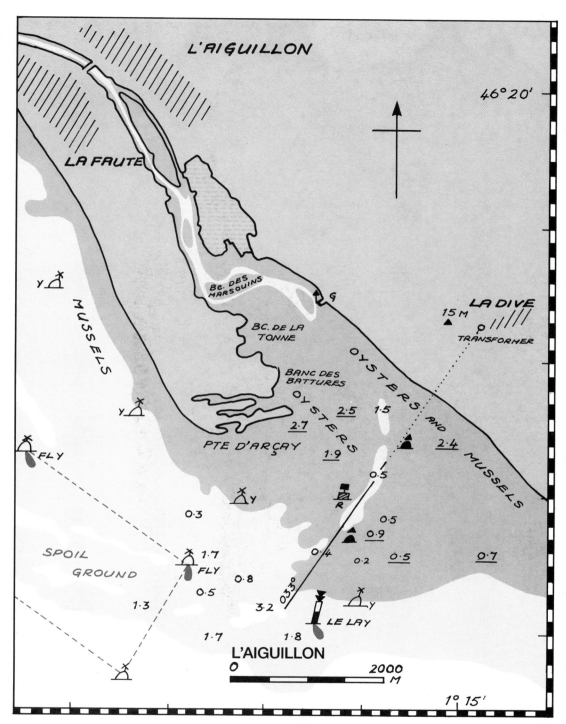

L'AIGUILLON

LA FAUTE

MUSSELS

BC. DES MARSOUINS

BC. DE LA TONNE

BANC DES BATTURES

PTE D'ARÇAY

OYSTERS

2·5

1·5

2·7

1·9

0·5

LA DIVE

15 M

TRANSFORMER

OYSTERS AND MUSSELS

2·4

0·5

0·9

0·5

0·7

0·3

FLY

SPOIL GROUND

1·7

FLY

1·3

0·8

0·5

3·2

1·7

1·8

Y

Y

Y

R

0·4

0·2

033°

LE LAY

Y

L'AIGUILLON

0   2000
                M

46°20'

1° 15'

MLWS 0.8m; MLWN 2.4m; −0050(sp), +0010(np) Brest, Index 3, MTL 3.6m
Based on French Chart No. 6521 with corrections. Depths in metres; right hand margin in cables

The anchorage and town of L'Aiguillon. The best water lay near the moorings

There is a large black beacon on the extremity. Pointe d'Arçay is low, but may be identified by the belt of low trees growing on it. Some 3 miles NW of Pointe de l'Aiguillon there is a curious land formation which looks like an inland island, and is conspicuous in the absence of any other break in the low coastline. This formation is named La Dive. It is now a farm, and has an electric transformer by it, adjacent to a conspicuous barn, but the buildings are erected on the site of a pre-Christian sanctuary.

The entrance to the river is with the transformer on La Dive bearing 033°. This course leaves the card S buoy (YB) about 600m to starboard, no. 1 buoy (stbd) 200m to starboard, no. 2 buoy (port) 200m to port and no. 3 buoy (stbd) 300m to starboard. Thence the channel swings steadily about 60° to port between oyster and mussel beds, until the river opens up and the distant town, with a prominent church tower, is seen ahead. The channel is marked by beacons; keep closer to those on the SW side, keep 10m away from beacons and withies throughout.

A low stone jetty will be passed and there are a few buildings on the starboard bank, ½ mile beyond the jetty. Here the channel swings round S of W and becomes very narrow so that it is better to proceed under power. There is a middle ground, the Banc des Marsouins, marked by beacons. The southern channel is very narrow and the northern one is to be preferred, though the deepest water is close to the middle ground and is also narrow. Keep to the E side of the next reach until opposite the last starboard hand mark before the Banc Cantin, at which point cross to the west bank; pass two port hand beacons which are amongst moored craft on the port side and then cross back to the E bank at the last starboard hand beacon on Banc Cantin. The yacht is then in the

Featureless entrance to Le Lay river and L'Aiguillon. Le Lay buoy (card S) marks the entrance

anchorage. The position of the best water changes from time to time, but the key to pilotage is to keep very close to one edge or the other of the channel, not midstream.

Anchorage and facilities
Anchor or arrange to borrow a mooring in the pool below the bridge. 2m may be found on sounding, but less water has been reported recently. Beware of the strong tide. Just below the bridge, on the starboard side, is a slipway and a number of small wooden jetties where local boats dry out on a muddy bottom. The visitors' berths on the port side may dry and make for an uncomfortable night.

A water tap is by the slip, but no fuel. Hotel, restaurants, shops and bus service are in the town. A short walk across the peninsula leads to good bathing at La Faute.

Marans
The tides run very hard in La Sèvre Niortaise, but it is desirable to enter well before high water, to ensure reaching the lock in time. On the Pointe de l'Aiguillon there is a large black beacon, with a topmark. Some $\frac{3}{4}$ mile to the SE of the beacon is L'Aiguillon fairway buoy (RW with solar panels and R ball topmark). Leaving this buoy close to port, make good a course of 038° for the smaller RW spar buoy at the entrance to the buoyed channel leading in to the river.

The Anse de l'Aiguillon is shallow, almost circular and about three miles wide. The mud flats on either side of the channel dry 4m or more and are covered with mussel beds, surrounded by piles. It is important to cross between the two RW buoys, which are nearly 2 miles apart, without deviating from the channel, and binoculars may be necessary to locate the second buoy. The channel dries 0.1m $\frac{1}{2}$ mile before the second buoy and 0.0m just beyond it, where the red and green channel buoys lead past the Port du Pavé slip and into the river.

The end of the slip is marked by a green beacon on a white pedestal and the channel leads between the moorings of a large fleet of mussel boats. The channel here had been dredged in 1988, but silting appears to be rapid after heavy rain. In the first reach after entering the river the flats cover at HW springs, but the plan shows where the channel lies in relation to the training banks. After this there are a few buoys marking shoals on the

Marans channel fairway buoy, with Pointe de l'Aiguillon Amer bearing 310°

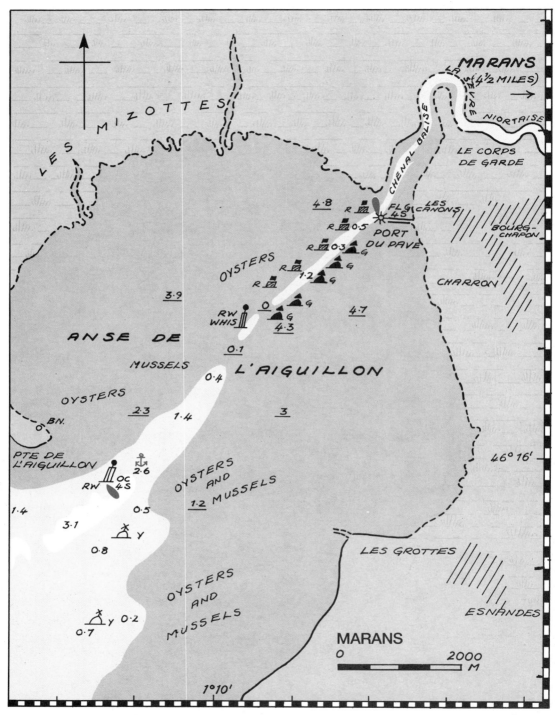

MLWS 0.8m; MLWN 2.4m; −0050(sp), +0100(np) Brest
Based on French Chart No. 6521 with corrections. Depths in metres; right hand margin in cables

Marans canal lock. The pontoon is short and submerges with two crew on it

bends, otherwise keep in the middle. About 1½ miles further up there is a landing on the starboard bank at Le Corps de Garde and more fishing boat moorings.

About 3 miles from the river entrance the yacht will reach the lifting bridge and the Brault lock giving access to the canal leading to Marans. There are two waiting buoys on the starboard side before the bridge. Do not lie to these on a falling tide with a strong westerly wind or you will be blown onto the bank!

The bridge is operated from the lock-keeper's cabin, with TV cameras to observe the road and river traffic. The bridge will be opened and the lock can be entered at highwater at the lock, during working hours, if boats are waiting. Departure is possible 1 hour before high water. The lock-keeper can be telephoned in advance (tel: 46 01 53 77).

The lock is enormous, being 104m long and 45m wide with gently sloping banks. There is a short pontoon on the port hand side to which a yacht may secure while waiting for the lock to be operated. Care must be exercised if the wind is blowing into the lock as it may be difficult to leave the pontoon. It may be simpler to remain under way, using the engine to keep in the middle of the lock. As you enter, the lock-keeper will hand you a form to record entry. At the upper end is a swing road-bridge.

The pretty tree-lined canal leads straight, for a distance of about 3 miles, to the port of Marans. Towards the end of the canal it appears to come to a dead end, but a channel opens up to starboard, through a pair of permanently open lock gates, into the port of Marans.

Anchorage and mooring
By far the best place is the Port of Marans. Go past the berths used by the coasters and

Marans basin, looking towards the canal. The boatyard at the far end specializes in wooden craft

moor or raft alongside another yacht on the wall on the starboard side, beyond a barrage to port.

It is possible to anchor at Le Corps de Garde, where some fishing boats lie, and there is a landing with access to Charron 1½ miles away. This is quite sheltered but the tide runs hard. Since one would only enter the river on the tide there does not seem to be much reason for stopping here rather than proceeding to Marans.

It is also possible to land at the slip at Port du Pavé, whence Charron is a walk of 1½ miles. This anchorage is exposed to the SW at high water. However, at neaps the extensive mud flats are only just covered at high water leaving a narrow channel between them. At neaps, therefore, the shelter is better than it looks. The depth here in the channel is only 0.6m, but at low water neaps there will be nearly 3m. So this anchorage is possible in settled weather at neap tides.

Facilities

At Marans
Water and electricity are available on the quay, fuel from the garage by the supermarket. There are shipyards for repairs, a crane and slip. A number of yachts winter in Marans.

A bank, hotels and a good choice of restaurants are in the town, with all shops. The excellent supermarket is on the main road out of town, 3 minutes walk after crossing the road bridge at the top of the port onto the north bank.

49 La Rochelle and Port des Minimes

Charts: English BA 2743, 2746, 2648.

       French SHOM 6334. ECM Navicarte 551, 552.

High water: −0035 Brest, springs, 0000 Brest, neaps, Index 3, MTL 3.7m.

  MHWS 6.1m; MLWS 1.0m; MHWN 4.9m; MLWN 2.5m.

Tidal streams: For the Pertuis Breton, see under Ile de Ré, page 266. In the narrows off La Pallice the flood runs N, the ebb S, spring rates $1\frac{1}{2}$ knots. In the entrance to the Pertuis d'Antioche, north of Pointe de Chassiron, the flood runs E, the ebb W, spring rates $2\frac{1}{4}$ knots; south of the Ile de Ré the streams turn about $\frac{1}{2}$ hour after HW and LW and are slightly weaker. The streams are weak in the harbour and its near approaches.

Depths: The approach carries 0.7m as far as Tour Richelieu; the buoyed channel has 0.2m as far as the towers. 1.3m can be found at some of the pontoons in the Bassin d'Echouage. 3m in the wet dock. 1–2m at the Minimes Marina pontoons.

Lights:

1. Le Lavardin; Fl(2)WG 6s, 14m, 11–8M. Black tower, red band two black spheres topmark.
2. Tour Richelieu; Fl(4)R 12s, 10m, 9M. Red eight-sided tower.

     Radio beacon, call RE, 291.9 kHz, continuous, 5M.
3. Leading lights, 059° sync Dir Q W at night, Fl W 4s by day. Obscured 061°–065° by St Nicolas tower.

       Front: 15m, 14M. Red round tower, white bands.

       Rear: 25m, 14M. White eight-sided tower, green top.
4. Port des Minimes, W mole head; Fl G 4s, 9m, 8M. White tower, green top.
5. Port des Minimes, E mole head; Fl(2)R 6s, 6m, 5M. White tower, red top.

La Rochelle, half way down the coastline of the Bay of Biscay, may be a convenient port of call for yachts bound to or from Spain or the Mediterranean via the Midi canal, or it may mark the farthest port in a cruise from England. There are few yachting centres south of it until the Gironde is entered, and beyond the Gironde, Arcachon is the only port in a long, sandy, featureless coastline, and it is not accessible in strong onshore weather.

Thus the geographical position of La Rochelle makes it important to yachtsmen, and it also offers all facilities. There is a large marina at Port des Minimes, with pontoon berths for 3,000. This has eased the congestion, but it is a long way from the shops and sights of the town. The entrance to the town harbour is shallow; once inside there is a wet dock where all can lie afloat and shallow draught yachts can lie in the Bassin d'Echouage. The entrance, between the two towers of St Nicolas on the east and La Chaine on the west, is impressive, and the historical old town is most attractive.

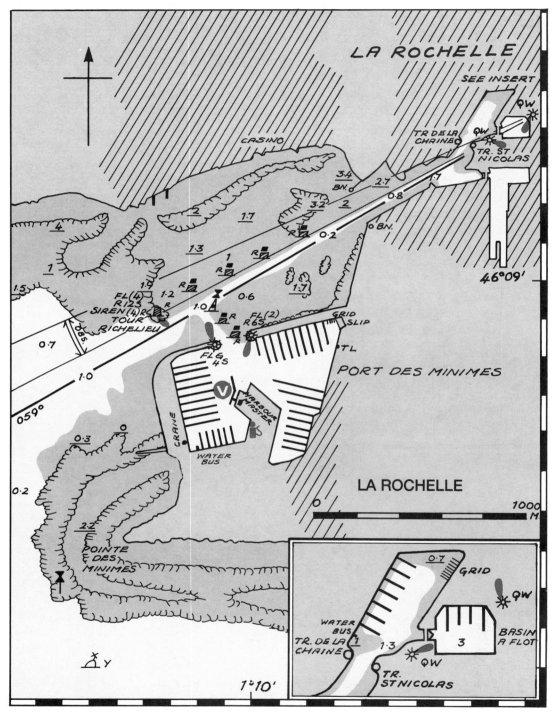

LA ROCHELLE

SEE INSERT

QW

TR DE LA
CHAINE

QW

TR. ST
NICOLAS

46°09'

CASINO

3.4
BN.

2.7

1.7

3.2

2

0.8

2

0.2

0.BN.

4

1.7

1.3

1

R

1

1.9

R

1.5

1.2

R

R

0.6

1.7

FL(4)
R 12S
SIREN(4)RC
TOUR
RICHELIEU

1.0

FL(2)
R 6S

GRID
SLIP

0.7

R

TL

1.0

FL.G
4.S

PORT DES MINIMES

059°

V

HARBOUR
MASTER

0.3

CRANE

WATER
BUS

LA ROCHELLE

0.2

2.2

1000
M

POINTE
DES
MINIMES

Y

1°10'

0.7
GRID

QW

WATER
BUS
TR. DE LA
CHAINE

1

1.3

BASIN
A FLOT

3

QW

TR.
ST NICOLAS

QW

MLWS 1.0m; MLWN 2.5m; −0035(sp), 0000(np) Brest, Index 3, MTL 3.7m
Based on French Chart No. 6468 with corrections (No. 6334 supersedes). Depths in metres; right hand
margin in cables

Final approach to La Rochelle. Minimes marina has been left to starboard. The yacht's mast is between the two towers and the leading marks are to the right of the right hand tower

Approach and entrance

The distant approach is either through the Pertuis Breton, on the north side of Ile de Ré, and thence through the Rade de la Pallice, or through the Pertuis d'Antioche on the south side.

Caution

A firing danger area exists to the south of the entrance, marked by yellow buoys with X topmarks. This area is prohibited during working hours on weekdays, except public holidays.

The near approach lies from a position about 1 mile S of Le Lavardin isolated danger beacon tower (BRB). In most conditions the red Tour Richelieu stands out against the

La Rochelle, pontoons in the inner basin. The entrance to the wet basin is beyond the fishing boats on the left

background of the port buildings. Coming from the south of Ile de Ré, leave Le Lavardin at least ½ mile to port, as spoil ground of varying depth lies to the SE of the tower. Coming from the Rade de la Pallice, after passing under the Ile de Ré bridge, the outer breakwaters of La Pallice commercial harbour can be left to port and the coastline followed at a distance of 500m until the Tour Richelieu has been sighted.

Steer for the red Tour Richelieu and identify the church and two towers of La Rochelle. Then steer for the towers bearing about 060° until the leading lighthouses can be seen. These are just to the right of the larger, right hand Tour St Nicolas. The front leading lighthouse is red with white bands and the rear lighthouse white with a green top. With the leading lighthouses in transit, bearing 059° steer up the channel, leaving Tour Richelieu close to port. If bound for Minimes Marina, the dredged entrance channel is marked by a cardinal W buoy and two red port hand buoys. Keep on the 059° transit until the turn in will leave the card W buoy close to port, thus avoiding a shallow patch on the starboard side of the entrance.

If bound for the old port, follow the transit, leaving four red channel buoys well to port. When close to the towers, bear to port and enter the harbour.

By night

Entry by night is easy with the leading lights (**3**) in transit bearing 059°. North of the line the leading lights can be obscured by the Tour St Nicolas. To enter Minimes Marina, make the turn to starboard (course 140°) 200m past Tour Richelieu. The cardinal W buoy and two port hand buoys marking the channel are unlit.

Mooring

In Port des Minimes, lay alongside the *accueil* pontoon opposite the entrance and obtain a berth from the Capitainerie. In 1988 there was a charge for the first night and the second night was free.

In the old port, *Bassin d'Echouage*, a visitor's pontoon berth with 1m depth might be obtained from the harbourmaster. At worst, yachts will take the ground at springs and remain upright in soft mud. Beware, however, of the open air disco which can continue until 0300 on a Sunday morning. There is no escape if your keel is fast in the mud!

La Rochelle approach channel. Minimes marina is to the right and the twin towers are behind the Tour Richelieu (red)

The inner wet basin, *Bassin Flot Intérieur*, is for yachts but space is limited and berths appear to be reserved for large, long-stay boats. Daytime entry is possible 2 hours before to $\frac{1}{2}$ hour after high water. At night the gate may be opened on application in advance to the Bureau du Port (telephone: 46 41 32 05). Yachts which arrive, or intend to leave, when the dock gates are closed should secure to a pontoon and visit the Bureau du Port to arrange a berth.

The quay between the dock and the Tour St Nicolas is reserved for fishing boats. The first half of the quay beyond the dock is reserved for the ferries to the islands and a large scrubbing grid lies along the second half. It is possible to use this grid, but prior inspection at low water is essential to select a suitable spot in which to lie.

Facilities

Every imaginable facility is available: banks, all kinds of shop, hotels and restaurants of every grade, yacht builders, chandlers, engineers and sailmakers. Bonded stores are available. French charts can be bought at a bookshop up the street under the old clock tower.

Port des Minimes has a fuel berth at the Capitainerie, water and electricity on the pontoons, showers and toilets, cranes and a travel lift. Restaurants, cafés, food shops, chandlers, sailmakers and engineers are available on site, making a visit to the town for supplies unnecessary. Except at lowest tides, a *bus de mer* runs approximately hourly to the Avant Port from the SW corner of the marina.

The town is very attractive and historically interesting. There is an airport and a good train service.

La Pallice

This is the large modern commercial port of La Rochelle. It has no facility for yachts, which are not welcome; nor has it any attractions for the yachtsman. No doubt it would be possible to use the port in an emergency. Entry is obvious from the large-scale charts.

Charts: English BA 2648, 2746.

French SHOM 6334. ECM Navicarte 551, 552.

High water: −0050 Brest, springs, +0010 Brest, neaps, Index 3, MTL 3.6m.

MHWS 6.1m; MLWS 0.8m; MHWN 4.9m; MLWN 2.4m.

Tidal streams: 3 miles NW of the island the SE stream begins −0520 Brest, the NW begins +0040 Brest, spring rates 1 knot. 1 mile SW of the island the SE stream begins −0530 Brest, the NW begins +0140 Brest, spring rates 2 knots.

Depths: An open roadstead or drying beach, depths as required.

Lights:

1. Chauveau (SE of Ile de Ré); Oc(2+1)WR 12s, 23m, 15–11M. White round tower, red top.
2. Ile d'Aix; Fl WR 5s, 24m, 24–20M. Two white round towers, red top, one for the light, the other supporting the red sector screen.
3. La Charente river entrance leading lights, 115°; dir. Q R.
   Front: 8m, 19M. White square tower, red top.
   Rear: 21m, 20M. White square tower, red top.
4. Aix SE; yellow by, X topmark, Fl Y 2.5s marking SE corner of oyster beds.

The Ile d'Aix lies about 8 miles south of La Rochelle and is a popular objective for a day sail, though the anchorage is sufficiently sheltered for a night stop in fine weather. It is pleasanter in the evening, after the day trippers have gone. The island is horseshoe shaped and measures about a mile at its maximum. Within this area is built a walled and moated village where Napoleon was imprisoned before he was taken to St Helena in *HMS Bellerophon*.

At the east side of the island a prison still exists, but there are no restrictions elsewhere. A few fishermen live on Ile d'Aix, together with people who seek the peace of an island, free of convention and so small that all parts are within earshot of the sea.

Ile d'Aix, Pointe de Coudepont right foreground. Looking SW towards the Pointe Ste Catherine

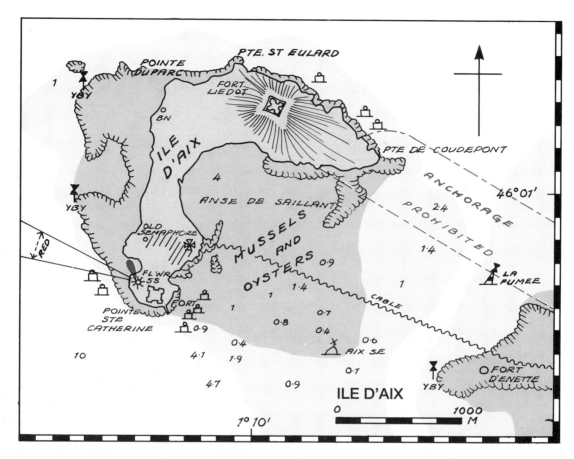

MLWS 0.8m; MLWN 2.4m; −0050(sp), +0010(np) Brest, Index 3, MTL 3.6m
Based on French Chart No. 3711 with corrections (No. 6334 supersedes). Depths in metres; right hand margin in cables

Approach

The approach is straightforward from any direction, but probably easiest from the NW. Two beacons (card W) mark the outlying rocks on the west side. The northern one should be given a berth of at least 500m, and the southern one at least 200m. When the two white towers, one carrying the light and the other the screen for the red sector, come in transit, bearing 110°, the island can be approached. The SW side of the island is fairly clean and can be passed at a distance of 200m.

There is a narrow, deep channel to the E of the island. From the north, leave the eastern point of the island at least 500m to starboard to avoid a rocky spur and steer 195° to leave two cardinal W buoys and the conspicuous Fort d'Enette to port, passing between a cardinal W beacon to port and a yellow buoy with X topmark, marking the SE corner of the Aix oyster beds, to starboard.

By night
From the NW, keep in the white sector of the Ile d'Aix light (**2**) until Chauveau light (**1**) turns from red to white, bearing 342°; steer 162° down this boundary, passing through the red sector of Ile d'Aix light. When this turns white again, steer on the leading lights for the Charente (**3**) bearing 115°. When Ile d'Aix light bears N steer 020°and anchor in 3m, or pick up a free mooring. There are liable to be yachts on moorings in this area.

Anchorage

Anchor 50–100m off the jetty and landing slip at Pointe Sainte Catherine, the south point of the island, going in as far as draught, tide and the need to keep clear of moorings allow. This anchorage is really sheltered only from the N and NE, but is partially sheltered from other directions by the mainland and Ile d'Oléron, so that it can be used in fine summer weather. The approaches are so well lit that there would be no difficulty in running for shelter to La Rochelle or elsewhere. The mud is very soft and the holding consequently poor.

It is also possible to anchor off the N or SW sides of the island on a calm day and several white mooring buoys are in position for short-stay visitors. The Anse du Saillant, a sandy bay on the east side of the island, is a delightful place in which to dry out. It is advisable to observe the obstructions at low water before venturing in from the south between the oyster beds and the rocky patches off the SE side of the island.

Facilities

Facilities are those of a village, with shops and a restaurant catering for the holiday visitors by ferry.

51 La Charente

Charts: English BA 2648, 2746, 2748.

       French SHOM 6334. ECM Navicarte 552.

High water: −0050 Brest, springs, +0010 Brest, neaps, Index 3, MTL 3.0m.

       MHWS 5.6m; MLWS 0.3m; MHWN 4.4m; MLWN 1.7m.

Tidal streams: Off the entrance the SE stream starts −0530 Brest, the NW starts +0130 Brest, spring rates 2 knots. In general streams in the river are about 2 knots, but where the river narrows they run up to 4 knots; they are affected by flood water. There is a bore on big spring tides; at such times the river should be avoided at all costs. At Rochefort the streams begin about 1 hr after HW and LW.

Depths: The approach is shallow, 0.4m, but there is more water in the river. Without the large-scale chart it should be treated as having 1m. Off Soubise there is 4m or more.

Lights: Two sets of leading lights and a line of lit starboard hand buoys lead into the river, after which there are no lights so that entry by night is not advisable.

Important note

No plan of the river is given in this book; those wishing to enter should have BA 2746 for the entrance or BA 2748 which shows the whole river up to Rochefort. ECM Navicarte shows the entrance and SHOM 6334 the river to Rochefort.

La Charente is an interesting river, away from the crowds, with a lot of bird life and some commercial traffic. The river lies between reedy banks, which have been reported to harbour mosquitoes on occasion. Rochefort is a historical town, an old naval base, well up the river for security from the British fleets. Today the remaining naval activity is all in 'stone frigates'. The wet basin is now full of local yachts, many for sale and some being worked on. Upstream of the wet basin is what is claimed to be the oldest hydraulically operated dry dock in the world, constructed in 1669. The original pumping apparatus was repaired in 1988.

    Masted vessels can go up to Tonnay and the river is navigable for motor yachts, and is said to be very attractive, for a considerable distance upstream to Saintes.

Approach and passage up river

The approach is straightforward at sufficient rise of tide. There are two pairs of leading lights to follow through the outer shoals, and a line of starboard hand buoys. Oyster beds are extensive outside the channel. When the river is entered it is sufficient to keep in midstream. There are beacons on the shore defining a succession of leading lines for the coasters. Many of the lines are marked at both ends, and the beacons for each line carry

La Charente river, lifting bridge with the old transporter bridge, preserved as an historic monument, behind Rochefort. Entrance to the wet basin for yachts

the same letter. It is better not to rely on them as the large-scale chart shows that, in some cases, the intersection is in shallow water, so that it is necessary to turn off one line before the next is reached. Entrance and exit should be made on the flood or at the high water slack. As soon as the ebb starts any sea outside produces breakers on the bar.

A few miles above Soubise is the lifting bridge at Martrou with the disused transporter bridge a short distance upstream. The bridge is operated for commercial traffic between 0515 and 2045 and for yachts 1 hour before to 1 hour after high water when the wet dock gate at Rochefort is open. There are waiting buoys for yachts on either side of the bridge (telephone: 46 83 08 95 or call VHF, Ch. 12 or 16).

Anchorage

At Soubise anchor on the S side of the river, as near the bank as possible, or arrange to borrow a mooring. The Yacht Club de Rochefort is on the north bank, downstream of Soubise and appears to be active, with landing facilities and a number of moorings along the south bank. There is a disused ferry slip at Soubise at which it is possible to land, but it is silted up with mud.

Upstream of Soubise, anchoring in the river is not recommended as the bottom is foul with old cables and the mud is very sticky. For a short wait on a rising tide it is preferable to stick the bows into the muddy bank.

At Rochefort it is possible to moor to the wall outside the wet dock gate, or to enter the dock when the gate is opened. The docks farther up are strictly commercial.

Facilities

At Soubise all shops and a hotel are in the village, 5 minutes walk. At Rochefort there are all the resources of a substantial town.

Charts: English BA 2746, 2648.

French SHOM 6334 P, 6335 P. ECM Navicarte 552.

Tides and depths: See under the ports.

This island, formerly somewhat of a backwater, looking back to the days when it was part of the realm of the kings of England, has now been connected to the mainland by a bridge. Consequently it is developing many of the characteristics of a standard French summer resort. The *quichenotte*, a starched bonnet designed to resist the attentions of the licentious British soldiery, is not now much worn. The name is a corruption of 'kiss-not'.

There are five harbours, for four of which descriptions follow. The fifth, La Cotinière, is on the west side of the island. The west coast has a bad reputation and yachts should stand well off except in calm conditions. La Cotinière is base to a substantial fishing fleet, riding on heavy moorings against the Atlantic swell, with a recently built mole providing some shelter.

In 1988–89 the marina Le Douhet, some $4\frac{1}{2}$ miles down the NE coast, originally built for local boats, was expanded to accept visiting yachts, with an improved entrance channel.

During the same period, a new marina was constructed at St Denis at the northern tip of the island. Both of these were visited by Paul Dane (RCC) in July 1989, making it possible for the editor to add a brief description to the present edition.

Boyardville has previously been the main yacht harbour, with limited accommodation for visitors in the wet basin, but with a good anchorage off the beach.

Le Château d'Oléron is a small port wholly occupied with oysters, a place of historical interest, in which the large number of fishing boats, backed by the walls of the old fortifications overlooking the harbour, make a picturesque scene. Yachts are no longer welcome in the port as they are expected to use the facilities provided for them elsewhere on the island. Entrance to Le Château is described in this edition in case the situation should change.

Le Coureau d'Oléron is an interesting place to explore, rather off the beaten track. The English chart BA 2648 is of too small a scale and 2746 and 2748 each cover only part of the island. The French ECM Navicarte 552 covers the area comprehensively and SHOM 6334 and 6335 overlap to cover the island and Le Coureau.

St Denis d'Oléron

Position: 46°02.2′N 01°22′W.

High Water: −0050 Brest, springs, +0010 Brest, neaps, Index 3, MTL 3.6m.

MHWS 6.2m; MLWS 1.0m; MHWN 5.0m; MLWN 2.4m.

Tidal streams: Outside SE begins −0430 Brest, NW begins +0100 Brest, spring rates 1.5–2 knots.

Depths: Access across the sill for 2m draught $3\frac{1}{2}$ hours either side of HW.

Lights: E Breakwater head Fl G, 6s.

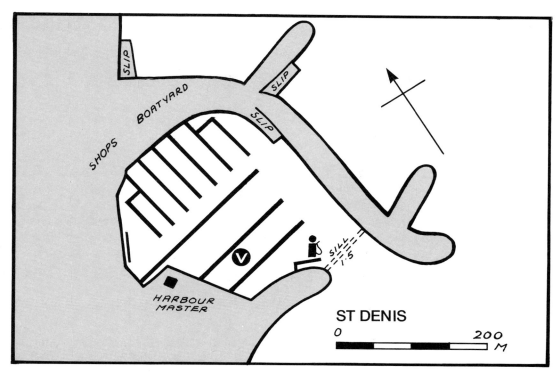

ST DENIS

0   200
M

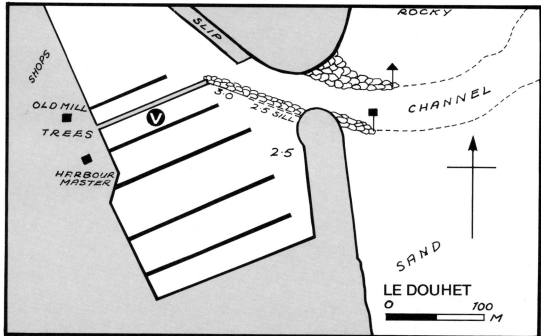

LE DOUHET

0   100
M

MLWS 0.8m; MLWN 2.5m; −0050(sp), +0010(np) Brest, Index 3, MTL 3.6m
Based on sketches provided by the harbourmasters. The scales in metres are estimated and further
information from visiting yachtsmen would be appreciated

Entrance

The marina has been built on a point NE of the town, where two piers (now removed) are shown on Chart BA 2746. Approach from the SE and, leaving a green beacon to starboard, cross the sill at the entrance.

Facilities

All the usual facilities are being provided and there are shops in the town. There are 670 berths in this marina.

Le Douhet

High water: −0050 Brest, springs, +0010 Brest, neaps, Index 3, MTL 3.6m.
   MHWS 6.2m; MLWS 1.0m; MHWN 5.0m; MLWN 2.4m.
Tidal streams: Outside SE begins −0430 Brest, NW begins +0100 Brest, spring rates 1.5–2 knots.
Depths: The sill is 2.5m above datum, giving a depth of 2.5m at the pontoons. No information is available about the depth in the entrance channel.
Lights: No information available (July 1989) but a Moiré Direction Panel, visible day and night (see La Flotte, Ile de Ré), should be situated on one side of the entrance channel.

The Port du Douhet lies midway between the Pointe de Chassiron and Boyardville. It was enlarged in 1989, an approach channel dredged and marked and pontoons installed to cater for 350 boats with berths for some 30 visitors.

Entrance

The entrance was observed in July 1988 (see photograph). There were rocky shoals drying 2.5m or more on either side, with a sand bank to the south. However, if the channel is adequately marked, entrance should not be difficult, on a course of 310°, when there is sufficient water over the sill, which is 2.5m above chart datum.

   After entering the channel, a turn to port will lead over the sill. Once inside, the Capitainerie and visitors' pontoons are to starboard.

Facilities

The usual facilities are being provided and provisions should be available.

Boyardville (La Perrotine)

High water: −0050 Brest, springs, +0010 Brest, neaps, Index 3, MTL 3.6m.
   MHWS 6.1m; MLWS 0.8m; MHWN 4.9m; MLWN 2.3m.
Tidal streams: Outside the SE begins −0600 Brest, NW begins +0100 Brest, spring rates 2 knots.
   There is some stream in the channel but it is not excessive.
Depths: The bar dries 2m. Yachts take the ground inside, but the channel does not completely dry. The wet basin has 2m.
Lights:
   1. La Perrotine mole head; Oc(2)R 6s, 8m, 7M. White metal framework, red top.

Le Douhet entrance, June 1988, before improvements were completed

The small port consists of a tidal river, La Perrotine, with a bar at the entrance, which dries. There is a long stone mole on the SE side of the entrance. Outside the wet dock there are only a few berths suitable for yachts which cannot take the ground.

Approach

The entrance lies about 2 miles, 200°, from the conspicuous Fort Boyard. A green (stbd) buoy lies in 11m, 800m NE of the mole head. 150m inside the buoy the bottom shoals almost vertically to the sand bank which dries 2m. The channel across the sand shifts. In July 1988 a bulldozer was moving sand out of the channel inside the mole. Between the mole head and the buoy the channel curved slightly to the north. From the buoy, steer for the mole head and, as the soundings decrease, alter to starboard and swing back in a gentle curve to leave the mole head about 40m to port. Thence keep close to the mole, say 10m off, until the side begins to slope as the river is entered. From here, cross over to steer starboard of mid channel, and be prepared for a sharp turn to starboard to enter the wet basin.

By night
It is not very practicable for a stranger to enter by night, unless there is very bright moonlight (see below for offshore moorings).

Mooring

The entrance to the wet dock is at its E corner; the gates open and close automatically about 2 hours either side of high water, a warning light indicating their movement.

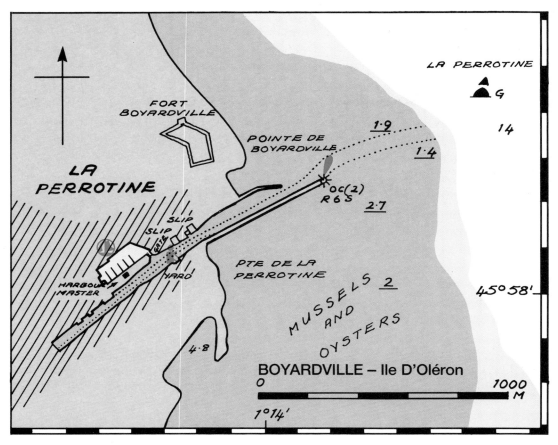

BOYARDVILLE – Ile D'Oléron

MLWS 0.8m; MLWN 2.5m; −0050(sp), +0010(np) Brest, Index 3, MTL 3.6m
Based on French Chart No. 3711 with corrections (No. 6334 supersedes). Depths in metres; right hand margin in cables

Visitors must be prepared to berth against the NE wall, which is piled so that a plank is useful. In 1989 the number of visitors' berths was increased from 40 to 60. There is little room to manoeuvre in the dock.

Yachts can lie in the river against quays above the marina entrance, the second from the sea end being recommended, or they can take the ground between the last quay and the bridge. The harbourmaster's office is on the wet dock quay. He is most obliging and his help should be sought. Yachts take the ground but do not dry out completely. The bottom is not level everywhere so care is needed.

Three quarters of a mile north of the mole is a line of visitors' moorings, a yellow buoy with X topmark at either end and one can anchor nearby in from 8m to 12m with due regard to the rapidly shoaling bottom. Both yellow buoys were lit in 1988 (Fl Y 2.5s), and late arrivers can locate a mooring without attempting to enter the harbour.

300

La Perrotine entrance from the E

Facilities

Water and electricity on the pontoons. Yacht yard, chandlery and fuel berth on the port hand entering the river. Showers and toilets are in the Capitainerie. Small supermarket and restaurants on the quayside. Some shops are in the small town, with a laundry which will do washing, drying and folding for a reasonable fee. There is an excellent bathing beach, and small clams can be collected at low water.

La Perrotine river at LW. The boat yard and fuel berth are on the right and a sharp turn to starboard, beyond the slip and outcrop of loose stones, is necessary to enter the Boyardville yacht basin at HW

Le Château d'Oléron

High water: −0040 Brest, springs, +0015 Brest, neaps, Index 2, MTL 3.5m.

MHWS 6.0m; MLWS 1.0m; MHWN 4.7m; MLWN 2.7m.

Tidal streams: Off the entrance the SSW stream begins −0500 Brest, the NNE at +0100 Brest.

Spring rates about 1¼ knots. There is no stream in the harbour.

Depths: The approach has a depth of 0.6m, the harbour dries 1.6m.

Lights:

1. Leading lights, 319°; sync Q R.

    Front; 11m, 7M. Red rectangle on low white tower.

    Rear; 24m, 7M. White tower, red top.

There is no yachting activity in this small oyster fishing port, but Le Château has the facilities of a holiday town, with the historical interest of the old fortifications.

Approach

The approach is made in the Coureau d'Oléron.

From the north

The shallows in the southern half of the Coureau are entirely covered by oyster beds. The channels are narrow and winding. Buoy hopping is the order of the day, with a careful lookout for withies and the beacons which are often located well into the shallows. Read the name on the buoy to confirm your position before proceeding.

From a position midway between Ile d'Aix and Fort Boyard, a course of 155° should lead nearly 5 miles to the cardinal west buoy 'Chenal EN' and will clear the dangers off the mouth of the Charente. Leaving 'Chenal EN' close to port, continue on 155° for 1.5 miles to leave 'Chenal ES' cardinal E buoy to starboard and 'Brouage' red (port) buoy (lit) close to port. From here on port hand beacons should be left to starboard, as the channel is marked for entry from the south. A course of 210° leads clear of Banc Lamouroux while the Banc de Charret beacon (black square topmark), well into the mud-flats to port, and a red beacon and the green buoy 'Agnas' to starboard, are located.

Steer for 'Agnas', leaving her close to port and, leaving two red beacons on the Grande Mortanne to starboard, make for the 'Mortanne Sud' cardinal S beacon marking the entrance of the channel to Le Château d'Oléron.

From the south

The channels look rather intricate and are subject to change. At low water an up-to-date chart is the best guide. If the rise of tide is sufficient to enter the harbour, it will be possible to pass safely over the shoals in midstream; note that the Banc d'Agnas dries up to 2.9m.

Entrance

Keep the Mortanne Sud card S beacon close aboard to starboard. Steer straight for the

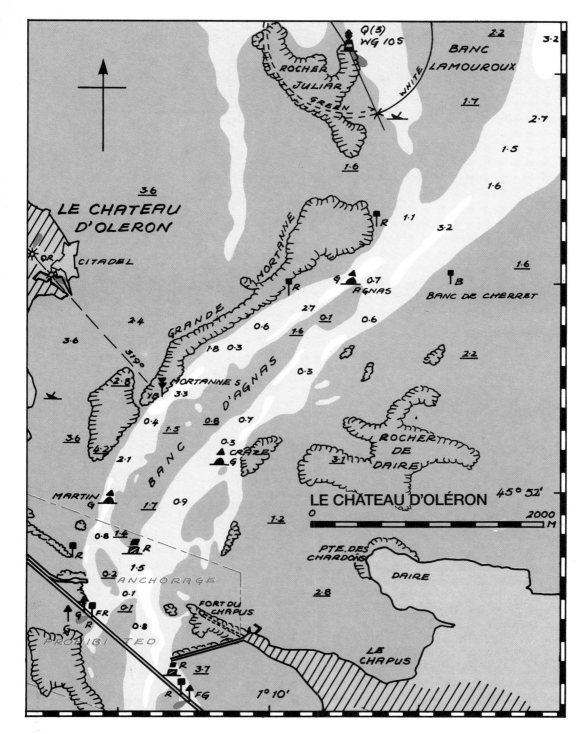

MLWS 1.0m; MLWN 2.4m; −0040(sp), +0015(np) Brest, Index 2, MTL 3.5m
Based on French Chart No. 6037 with corrections (No. 6335 supersedes). Depths in metres; right hand
margin in cables

303

leading light structures. The front mark is a tubby white cylindrical tank with a red board above it, the rear mark is an ordinary white light tower with a red top. The starboard side of the entrance channel is marked by a line of withies; leave these about 10m to starboard. The channel is 10m wide and is dredged to a depth of 0.8m.

By night
A stranger would not be able to navigate the Coureau d'Oléron by night. If he has reached the entrance channel by nightfall the leading lights (**1**) will take him up to the harbour.

Harbour
The best water is at the quay on the port side of the outer harbour, drying 1.6m. The bottom is soft mud. Here a yacht will be very much in the way of fishing vessels and must

The harbour of Le Château. The leading light structures are indicated. This side of the harbour is very busy; yachts should berth to starboard

take advice. The quay on the starboard side dries about 3m, bottom soft mud, near the seaward end, getting shallower near the shore. Here the yacht will be out of the way and this is the place to go. There are plenty of ladders and mooring rings.

There is an inner harbour. It has a serviceable dock gate, but this is not used. The inner harbour is therefore shallower and it is absolutely packed with fishing boats.

Facilities

Petrol and diesel are on the quay. There are no visible signs of water. There are chandlers near the harbour. All shops and restaurants are in the town, about 10 minutes walk. Municipal showers at the far end of the town. This is an interesting little harbour; the only difficulty is to find enough space without inconvenience to the busy fishermen.

La Boirie and Le Port de St Trojan

Moorings (1988)

Some 2 miles SE of the Pointe de Chassiron, at the northern tip of the island, yacht moorings will be found off St Denis d'Oléron. The area is shown on Navicarte 552 as 'La Boirie' with 'Les Bungalows' where there are many holiday houses along the shore. These moorings looked attractive from seaward and were recommended by a French yachts-man in Rochefort as were the moorings off St Trojan les Bains at the south of the island, below the bridge. There appeared to be much yachting activity at St Trojan in 1988.

BA 2746 is adequate for La Boirie, but a French chart should be used to avoid the oyster-beds when visiting St Trojan. The existence of a marina at St Denis may cause an alteration in the mooring arrangements off La Boirie.

53 La Seudre

Charts: English BA 2648.

French SHOM 6335. ECM Navicarte 552.

High water: −0030 Brest, springs, +0020 Brest, neaps, MTL 3.5m.

MHWS 5.8m; MLWS 1.2m; MHWN 4.7m; MLWN 2.4m.

Tidal streams: In the Coureau d'Oléron the tides vary considerably from point to point, but typically run up to 2 knots springs, except under the Oléron to mainland roadbridge, where they can reach 4 knots.

Depths: The channels of approach are shallow, one carrying 1.1m and the other drying 1m. The river is deep, typically about 7m. The canals to Marennes and Tremblade can be assumed to dry 2.5m.

Lights: Except for those on the bridges, the area cannot be considered to be lit.

La Seudre offers a secure anchorage near the southern end of the Coureau d'Oléron. The entrance is shallow and should not be taken near low water, but once inside the river is deep. The scenery is not exciting, as salt-pans lie for some distance behind either bank; in these an extensive and intensive oyster culture is carried on. Both La Tremblade and Marennes are pleasant towns in the season; the latter is farther both from the river and the inner end of its canal.

Approach and entrance

There are two entrance channels, La Soumaille to the north and La Garrigue to the south. Both channels are narrow and the stranger should take frequent soundings to ensure that he is keeping in the deep water.

An up-to-date French chart should be used as the configuration of the banks changes and at present there is no large-scale English chart available.

Chenal de la Soumaille

In 1988 the simplest way to enter this channel was across part of the Banc Bourgeois drying 1m. Coming from the north it is first necessary to pass under the road bridge joining Oléron with the mainland. 400m S of the bridge in mid-channel is a wreck, marked by a red beacon. The channel is buoyed for entry from the south and it is advisable to check their names as the buoys are passed. The preferred arches for passage under the bridge are marked by white squares with a red square or a green triangle.

Round the head of the old ferry pier on the mainland bank and, leaving a red (port hand) buoy to starboard, pass under the marked arch of the bridge to leave the next red buoy close to starboard. The next buoy to steer for, bearing 198°, is the green (stbd) Meule NW, to be left close to port. Meule SE (150°) is the next green buoy to leave to port, followed by a red (port) buoy, Trompe de Sot, (210°). Leave this and La Palette

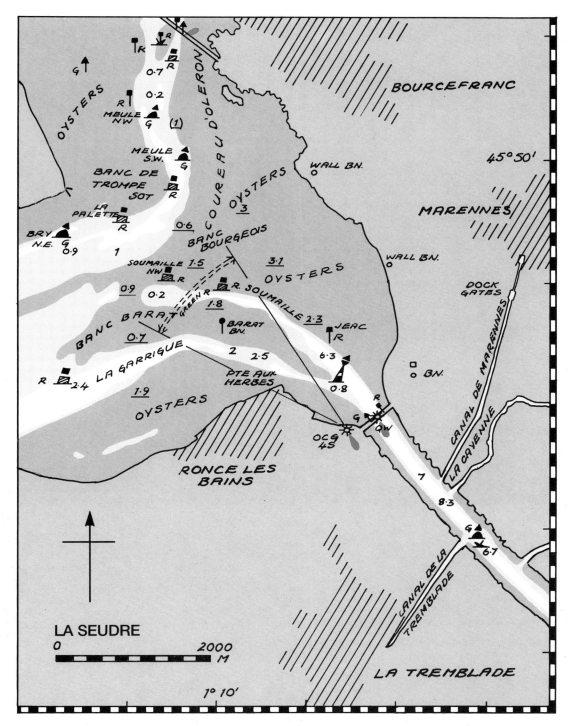

BOURCEFRANC

45°50'

MARENNES

WALL BN.
○

DOCK
GATES

WALL BN.
○

OYSTERS
3

BANC
BOURGEOIS
0·6

COUREAU D'OLERON

OYSTERS

3·1

OYSTERS

○ BN.

JEAC
R

6·3

CANAL DE MARENNES

LA CAVENNE

R
G

QW

R.SOUMAILLE
2·3

1·8

BARAT
BN.

OC G
4S

0·8

GREEN R

Soumaille
NW R

0·9   0·2

1·5

BANC BARAT

0·7

R   2·4   LA GARRIGUE

1·9

OYSTERS

2   2·5

PTE AUX
HERBES

RONCE LES
BAINS

7

8·3

G

6·7

CANAL DE LA
TREMBLADE

LA TREMBLADE

OYSTERS

BANC DE
TROMPE
SOT

LA
PALETTE
R

BRY
N.E. G
0·9

1

MEULE
S.W.
G

MEULE
NW   G
R   (1)

0·2

0·7

R

R
0·7

G

R

LA SEUDRE

0   2000
M

1°10'

MLWS 1.2m; MLWN 2.4m; −0030(sp), +0020(np) Brest, Index 1, MTL 3.5m
Based on French Charts Nos. 6335 and 6037 with corrections. Depths in metres; right hand margin in cables

Oyster floats near the entrance to the Marennes canal. The entrance to La Tremblade canal is on the opposite bank of the river

(port) to starboard and approach Bry NE green (stbd) buoy closely enough to read its name without passing it, as it will be left to starboard.

From Bry NE buoy the red buoy (port), Soumaille NW, marking the beginning of the Soumaille channel bears 115°. Steer to leave this buoy to port as you will now be passing up the channel. The southern end of Banc Bourgeois (drying 1m) will be crossed and, after Soumaille NW, the channel, which is narrow and steep to on its northern side, deepens to 2m and shortly after to 4.5m. The Seudre road bridge (clearance 15m) will be seen ahead, with Soumaille SE buoy (port), Le Jéac beacon (port) to be left to port and Saut de Barat card E buoy to be left to starboard before passing under the marked arch of the bridge.

Chenal de la Garrigue

The outer section of this channel is well buoyed on the port side; the first buoy is Galon d'Or (RW fairway buoy), inside the Pertuis de Maumusson at the southern end of Ile d'Oléron. It is followed by three port hand buoys and from the last of these, Barat, with extensive oyster beds to starboard, the channel continues towards the Barat beacon (red with sphere topmark) 1½ miles away (070°). Steer to keep a white wall beacon on the shore in transit with Barat beacon, bearing 067°. About 400m from the Barat beacon the channel turns to starboard. Steer to keep the Saut de Barat buoy (card E) bearing 107°; ½ mile before Saut de Barat the channel narrows and soundings are necessary to avoid straying into the shallows. The depth here should be 5m but reduces to 1.1m abreast the buoy, shortly after increasing to 7m or more below the bridge.

Anchorage and mooring
The best anchorages are near the disused ferry slips for Marennes (north bank) and La Tremblade (south bank). The former is called La Cayenne and is about $\frac{1}{2}$ mile downstream of the latter. Anchor near the side of the river and land on the ferry slip, carrying the dinghy ashore clear of the slip.

There are canals, which should be treated as drying 2.5m, leading to the villages of Marennes and La Tremblade. To get this depth it is essential to keep exactly in the middle of the channel. The canals are lined on each side by the boats and other apparatus for oyster culture.

At La Tremblade it is possible to berth alongside the stone quay to starboard just round the bend at the top end of the canal. Once round the bend the best water is on the starboard side; the bottom is soft mud. The water shoals rapidly once the far end of the quay is reached. There is not much room but visitors may be helped to find a berth. Although some yachts are based at the top of the canal, it is really better for a dinghy excursion, which is worthwhile if only to have it brought home how many oysters there are.

Looking up the Marennes canal to the wet basin

Marennes; the wet basin, from the gate

Marennes canal entrance

At the entrance to the Marennes canal, which lies just downstream of the ferry pier, there is a slight bend to starboard. The perches are high on the mud, but the best water lies roughly half way between them. At the upper end of the canal is a wet dock with 2.5m depth, the gates of which are open about 1 hour each side of high water. A power line with 16m clearance crosses the canal below the gate and another with 24m clearance crosses the dock. The dock is used by some 70 yachts and provides a convenient and pleasant berth if there is room. The oyster culture, though notable, is not quite on the scale of that at La Tremblade.

Facilities
At La Tremblade there are all shops and restaurants, a marine engineer and outboard specialist. At Marennes there are shops, cafés and a large hypermarket, which sells everything, at the rear of the post office, reached by a few minutes walk through pretty municipal gardens. There is a yacht builder at the wet dock, a 6 tonne crane, toilets, cold and hot showers, with a water tap and electricity on the quay.

54 Pertuis de Maumusson (passage notes)

Charts: English BA 2648.

       French SHOM 6335 P. ECM Navicarte 552.

High water: As Brest, Index 1, MTL 3.5m.

  MHWS 5.8m; MLWS 1.2m; MHWN 4.7m; MLWN 2.4m.

Tidal streams: The E stream begins about +0600 Brest, spring rate 3 knots, the W stream begins about −0100 Brest, spring rate 4 knots.

Depths: Variable but sufficient for yachts near high water.

Note: The information for this chapter comes principally from Mrs Tew, Mr Ian Tew and Mr P.C.Hordern.

The Pertuis de Maumusson, between the southern end of Ile d'Oléron and the mainland, has such a bad reputation that many people say that it cannot be used by yachts in any circumstances. Twenty years ago, discussions with local fishermen, and the experience of at least one yachtsman who used it, suggested that this was not true. Mrs Tew told the present editor that her husband went out through the Pertuis in a local fishing boat to reconnoitre and that, when they attempted the passage in their yacht, they missed the tide by 15 minutes. The rapid formation of the breakers made it essential for them to turn back.

Pertuis de Maumusson, a calm day. Fairway buoy with the first port hand channel buoy to the right and breakers to the left

Mrs Tew's advice today is that the passage should only be attempted in a well-found boat with a strong keel and that arrangements should be made to follow a local fishing boat, known to have a greater draught.

The passage is completely exposed to the Atlantic and, if there is any onshore wind or swell, the shallow and uneven bottom causes breakers to form right across as soon as the flood tide stops. The passage must, therefore, be made on the last of the flood, and at that only in calm weather or with an offshore wind, and in the absence of swell.

The bottom is sand, so the channel shifts and is said to be tending to get shallower. The buoys are not moved to follow all these shifts, though normally they indicate a line which will give enough water for a yacht at high water in smooth conditions. Only the local people know the current position of the deepest water in relation to the buoys; hence the need to follow a local fishing boat.

For the outward passage there is the opportunity to inspect the channel near low water if one arrives in good time, to see the state of the sea, and if necessary, to turn back with a favourable tide, since the passage should be taken before high water.

The inward passage must contain an unacceptable element of risk except in very good weather. The breakers, if they exist, cannot always be seen clearly from seaward; it is more difficult to identify the run of the channel and, if one gets into difficulty, it will be hard to retreat to sea with the tide carrying one in. It is the opinion of Colonel J. Tisserand, Président de la Station de Sauvetage de Royan, that a modern yacht should not attempt entry, whatever the conditions.

Finally, it must be emphasized that this passage is very *severe*, only to be attempted in very good weather by those who have experience of tidal race conditions and a robust boat. Adequate and reliable power is essential. The speed at which the breakers begin near high water is dramatic.

Charts: English BA 2910, 2916, 2664.

French SHOM 7028 P, 7029 P. ECM Navicarte 553, 554.

High water: +0010 Brest, Index 0, MTL 3.0m.

MHWS 5.2m; MLWS 0.9m; MHWN 4.1m; MLWN 1.9m.

Tidal streams: In the main entrance channel the flood E begins about −0500 Brest, spring rate about $2\frac{1}{2}$ knots, the ebb W about +0130 Brest, spring rates $3\frac{3}{4}$ knots. In the bay close to the port there is an eddy; the stream runs continuously southward, 1 knot during the flood, 3 knots during the ebb.

Depths: The estuary channel is deep. There is 1m or less at the entrance to Royan harbour. The marina is dredged to 2.5m.

Lights:

1. BXA light buoy; Iso W 4s, 8m. 8M. Whis.
2. La Coubre; Fl(2)W 10s, 64m, 28M. White tower, red top.
   Auxiliary light; Fixed RG, 42m, 10M. Sectors: 030°–R–043°–G–060°–R–110°. On same support.
   Radio beacon; call LK, 303.4 kHz, 1/6 min, 100M. Begins H+3 min.
3. Cordouan; Oc(2+1)WRG 12s, 60m, 22–18M. White conical tower, dark grey band and top.
4. Leading lights, 081.5°.
   Front: dir Oc W 4s, 21m, 22M. White frame structure.
   Auxiliary Q(2)W 5s, 10m, 3M. Same structure.
5. Palmyre; rear for 4. Dir Q W, 61m, 23M. 080.5°–082.5°. White radar tower.
   Rear for 6. Dir F R, 57m, 17M. 325.5°–328.5°. Same structure.
6. Leading lights, 327°:
   Front: Terre-Nègre; Oc(3)WRG 12s, 39m, 18–14M. White tower, red top on W side.
7. The channel buoys are: Port; red, flashing or occulting. Starboard; green, flashing, occulting or isophase, except for No.7, card N, Q W.

Royan entrance:

8. South jetty head; UQ(2)R 2s, 11m, 12M. Horn (2) 20s. White tower, red brick base.
9. New jetty, 20m from head; Oc(2)R 6s, 8m, 6M. White mast, red top.
10. North mole spur; Iso W 4s strip light.
11. East jetty head; Fl G 4s, 2m, 6M. White post, green top.

In the Second World War, according to information in the modern church of Notre Dame, the town of Royan was thought by the Allies to be a German base and consequently was bombed with heavy loss of life to the inhabitants. The buildings are all new and the unsymmetrical spire of the church stands up above the town as a landmark. Royan is now a holiday centre with a yacht harbour; it is twinned with Gosport. The

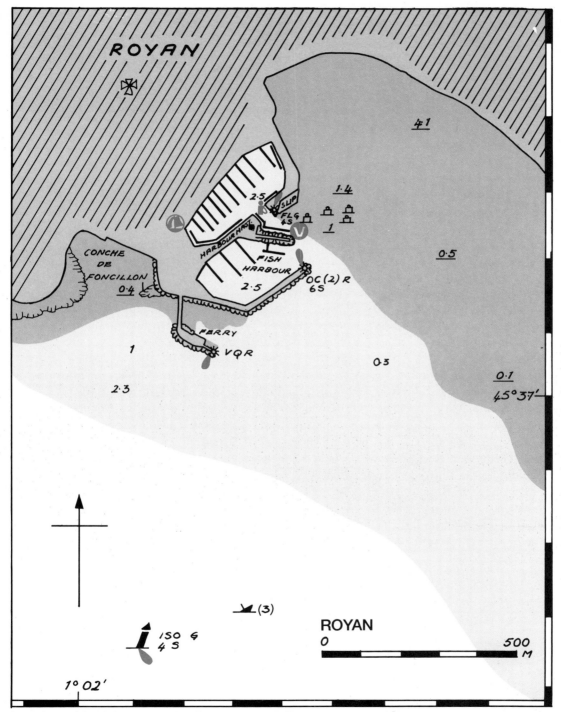

ROYAN

MLWS 0.9m; MLWN 1.9m; +0010 Brest, Index 0, MTL 3.0m
Based on French Chart No. 6141 with corrections (No. 7028 supersedes). Depths in metres; right hand margin in cables

315

Leading marks into the Gironde. The front structure is on rails to allow for changes in the channel

marina makes an excellent staging point for those entering or leaving the Gironde on the way to or from the Canal du Midi. Out of 630 berths, 60 are reserved for visitors. The harbourmaster is most helpful and will do his best to find a berth for a short stay in the busy season.

Approach

Entry to the Gironde should not be attempted in heavy weather, or in bad visibility. The shoals extend a long way seaward and the strong tides can make bad seas. A recently corrected chart is essential; the banks shift and not only does this entail frequent movement of the buoys, but also of the leading lights. In 1989 the starboard hand channel buoys nos 7a and 9 were north of the leading line of 081.5°, although there was still sufficient water (6m) for a yacht if she kept to the line.

The Banc de la Mauvaise (Banc de la Coubre on BA 2910) has an evil reputation which is well merited. Coming from the north keep at least 5 miles offshore. It is convenient to enter the channel 2 hours before high water and so to arrive at Royan before the tide turns. Make a position ½ mile west of the first two channel buoys, nos 1 and 2, and turn in on to 081° to steer between the buoys and pick up the leading line. The deep water channel is narrow for 3 miles and a yacht may prefer to sail a parallel course, but keeping south of the port hand buoy no. 6. After no. 7 (card N) it is wide and there is no problem in following the buoyed channel for Royan.

The town of Royan, with its white buildings and modern church, will be easily identified. The shore should be given a berth of 400m; on reaching Pointe du Chay, steer for the red and white light tower on the south jetty head, where the ferry berths.

From the SE, pass outside Banc de St Georges, leaving to starboard no. 12 (port hand)

Royan's new church is designed to represent a ship. The outer breakwater-head lighthouse is right of centre and the marina is behind the breakwater, extending towards the sunlit building in the far right of the picture

Royan yacht marina. The *Accueil* pontoon is at the entrance, the fuel berth end-on to the right and the Capitainerie further to the right

buoy at its NW end, or cutting the corner if tide and conditions allow. An alternative daylight course inside the Banc passes about 500m off Pointe de Susac and Pointe de Vallières; thence on 330° for the south jetty head, avoiding wrecks over which there is 3m, marked by a starboard buoy.

By night
The outer approach is as by day, remembering that buoys nos 7a and 9 (stbd) are north of the leading line. On passing no. 11 buoy (stbd, Iso G 4s), alter to starboard to follow the curve of the channel.

Entrance
On close approach leave to port the south jetty and the outer harbour mole. The marina entrance then opens up, the straight approach on a NW course leaving three mole heads to port and one to starboard. There is only 1m outside but the marina is dredged to 2.5m.

By night
Pick up the harbour lights (**8**, **9**, **10**, **11**) and leave to starboard a buoy (stbd, Iso G 4s) marking a wreck.

Mooring
On arrival, secure to the *accueil* pontoon on the port hand side in the entrance. Visit the Capitainerie to obtain a berth. If possible do not remain on the *accueil* pontoon as the excursion boats sometimes have trouble with their departure manoeuvres.

St Georges de Didonne, upstream of Royan. The lighthouse is not in use. A marina is proposed behind the breakwater, right centre

Facilities

All the facilities of a sophisticated holiday town are here: water and electricity are on the pontoons, showers and toilets in the Capitainerie and elsewhere, fuel berth below the Capitainerie, slipway, grid, crane, which could be used for dismasting if proceeding into the Canal du Midi, 26 tonne travel lift. All shops, chandlers, restaurants, banks and hotels close by, many in the arcade overlooking the marina. There is a railway station and airport, and a ferry runs from the south jetty to Port Bloc.

St Georges de Didonne

Work is in progress (March 1989) on the construction of a yacht harbour at St Georges de Didonne some 1½ miles upstream of Royan. This should provide a very pleasant out-of-town berth and it is hoped that it will be completed in time for the 1990 season.

The Gironde

Although outside the scope of this book, the following notes may be helpful. There is a well-marked ship channel to Bordeaux. The tide runs so hard that, with a reasonable turn of speed, a yacht can make Bordeaux on a single tide. It is also possible to stop at a number of places, such as Pauillac and Blaye, on the way up. At Bordeaux there is a marina to starboard just above the suspension bridge, and it is also possible to enter the docks, a little further up to starboard, from two hours before HW until HW. There are cranes for dismasting both at the marina and at the docks.

318

56 Port Bloc

Charts: English BA 2910, 2916, 2664.

  French SHOM 7028 P. ECM Navicarte 553, 554.

High water: +0010 Brest, Index 0, MTL 3.1m.

  MHWS 5.3m; MLWS 1.0m; MHWN 4.2m; MLWN 2.0m.

Tidal streams: The SE stream begins at −0530 Brest, the NW at +0130 Brest, spring rates $3\frac{3}{4}$ knots.

Depths: The approaches are deep. There is 2m to 2.5m in the harbour.

Lights:

1. Pointe de Grave; Oc WRG 4s, 26m, 19–15–15M. Square white tower, black corners and top.
2. Buoy 13B (stbd); Oc G 4s, 7m, 5M.
3. N exterior mole head; Q W, card N beacon.
4. N landing stage; Fl G 4s, 8m, 6M. White tower, green top. Lit by day in poor visibility.
5. S landing stage; Iso R 4s, 8m, 6M. White tower, red top. Lit by day in poor visibility.

Port Bloc, a small harbour just behind Pointe de Grave, is a convenient passage harbour. It is used by the ferries to Royan and by the buoy maintenance vessels, but is otherwise a long way from anywhere. Pleasantly situated among the pine trees, it is reasonably sheltered, though some swell is said to enter in bad weather. Verdon to the SE is being developed as a major marina and, when completed, will affect the facilities on this side of the Gironde estuary.

Port Bloc, looking SW into the entrance

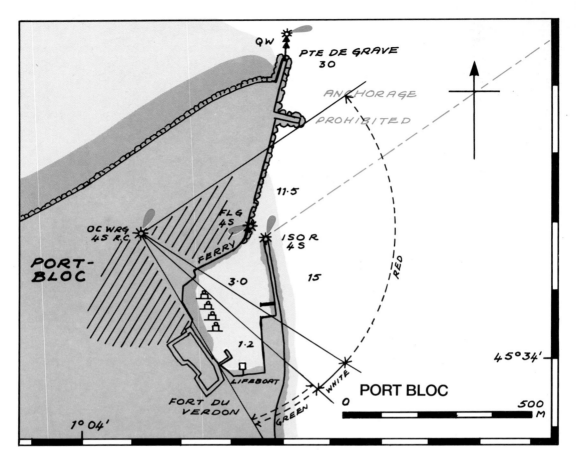

MLWS 1.0m; MLWN 2.0m; +0010 Brest, Index 0, MTL 3.1m
Based on French Chart No. 6141 with corrections (No. 7028 supersedes). Depths in metres; right hand margin in cables

Approach and entrance

For the outer approach, and notes on the Gironde, see Chapter 55. By night the final entry into the river can be made with La Palmyre red light in transit with Terre Nègre light, astern, bearing 327°.

The main concern in the final approach is to avoid being set on to the mole off Pointe de Grave, or swept up the river, depending on the tide. The harbour entrance faces NE, nearly parallel with the shore. The entrance is not very easily made out until it is close to, but it is only about 600m to the south of the extreme tip of the Pointe de Grave.

Approach on a SW course, from buoy no. 13B (stbd), and enter between the light structures, white with red top to port and white with green top to starboard. The ferries occupy the whole of the entrance, so if one is on the move stand off until the entrance is clear.

Port Bloc, looking N. The ferries would be strong competitors if a cup were offered for the world's ugliest ship

Anchorage and mooring
There is a line of white mooring buoys running down the centre of the harbour in a north–south direction. The eastern or seaward side of the harbour is for the use of the ferries, the buoy vessels and the lifeboat. Yachts berth between the mooring buoys in 2–2.5m, or, if a berth is available, at the pontoon at the top of the harbour. There is little space for visitors. The depth between the moorings and the shore to the west is given as 0m and it may be possible, but uncomfortable, for shallow draught vessels to anchor well south of the ferry slip.

Facilities
Water, showers and toilets, and a scrubbing slip are available but not much else at present. There is a café and there are frequent ferries to Royan. There is also a railway with train services to Bordeaux.

Tide Tables

From the Nautical Almanac take the time and height of HW Brest. Note that in Nautical Almanacs Brest is in Time Zone −0100. From the chapter heading for the port (or the caption to the plan of the port) take the time of local high water as compared with Brest, the Port Index, and the mean tide level (MTL).

1. Calculate the time of local high water (HW Brest ± difference for the port).
2. Calculate the interval between local HW and the time when the height is required.
3. Along the top of the tide table, below, find the column with the nearest height of HW Brest.

Brest HW m		5.5	5.6	5.7	5.8	5.9	6.0	6.1	6.2	6.3	6.5	6.6
Tide index		0	1	2	3	4	5	6	7	8	9	10
Total index		0	1	add 2	3	4	5	6	port 7	8	9	10
0h 00		0.8	0.9	0.9	1.0	1.1	1.1	1.2	1.3	1.4	1.5	1.6
20		0.8	0.8	0.9	1.0	1.0	1.1	1.2	1.3	1.3	1.4	1.5
40		0.8	0.8	0.9	0.9	1.0	1.1	1.1	1.2	1.3	1.4	1.5
1h 00		0.7	0.8	0.8	0.9	0.9	1.0	1.1	1.1	1.2	1.3	1.4
10		0.7	0.7	0.8	0.8	0.9	0.9	1.0	1.1	1.2	1.2	1.3
20		0.6	0.7	0.7	0.8	0.8	0.9	1.0	1.0	1.1	1.2	1.3
30		0.6	0.6	0.7	0.7	0.8	0.8	0.9	1.0	1.0	1.1	1.2
40		0.5	0.6	0.6	0.7	0.7	0.8	0.8	0.9	0.9	1.0	1.1
50	Add to MTL (m)	0.5	0.5	0.6	0.6	0.7	0.7	0.7	0.8	0.9	0.9	1.0
2h 00	Interval from local HW	0.4	0.5	0.5	0.5	0.6	0.6	0.7	0.7	0.8	0.8	0.9
10		0.4	0.4	0.5	0.5	0.5	0.6	0.6	0.6	0.7	0.7	0.8
20		0.3	0.4	0.4	0.4	0.4	0.5	0.5	0.5	0.6	0.6	0.7
30		0.3	0.3	0.3	0.3	0.4	0.4	0.4	0.4	0.5	0.5	0.5
40		0.2	0.2	0.2	0.3	0.3	0.3	0.3	0.3	0.4	0.4	0.4
50		0.1	0.2	0.2	0.2	0.2	0.2	0.2	0.2	0.2	0.3	0.3
3h 00		0.1	0.1	0.1	0.1	0.1	0.1	0.1	0.1	0.1	0.1	0.1
10												
20		0.1	0.1	0.1	0.1	0.1	0.1	0.1	0.1	0.1	0.1	0.1
30		0.1	0.1	0.1	0.2	0.2	0.2	0.2	0.2	0.2	0.2	0.3
40		0.2	0.2	0.2	0.2	0.3	0.3	0.3	0.3	0.3	0.4	0.4
50		0.3	0.3	0.3	0.3	0.3	0.4	0.4	0.4	0.4	0.5	0.5
4h 00		0.3	0.3	0.4	0.4	0.4	0.5	0.5	0.5	0.5	0.6	0.6
10		0.4	0.4	0.4	0.5	0.5	0.5	0.6	0.6	0.6	0.7	0.7
20		0.4	0.5	0.5	0.5	0.6	0.6	0.6	0.7	0.7	0.8	0.8
30		0.5	0.5	0.5	0.6	0.6	0.7	0.7	0.7	0.8	0.8	0.9
40		0.5	0.6	0.6	0.6	0.7	0.7	0.8	0.8	0.9	0.9	1.0
50	Subtract from MTL (m)	0.6	0.6	0.7	0.7	0.8	0.8	0.9	0.9	1.0	1.0	1.1
5h 00		0.6	0.7	0.7	0.8	0.8	0.9	0.9	1.0	1.1	1.1	1.2
20		0.7	0.7	0.8	0.8	0.9	1.0	1.0	1.1	1.2	1.3	1.4
40		0.8	0.8	0.9	0.9	1.0	1.1	1.2	1.2	1.3	1.4	1.5
6h 00		0.8	0.9	0.9	1.0	1.1	1.1	1.2	1.3	1.4	1.5	1.6

4. Note the corresponding Tide Index, add the Port Index (see opposite), and locate the column headed by the total.

5. Run down this column to the correct interval from local HW, calculated in (2) opposite, and read off the correction to the MTL.

6. Add or subtract this to or from the MTL (opposite), as indicated in the margin, to obtain the rise of the tide above chart datum.

6.8	6.9	7.1	7.3	7.5	7.7	7.9						
11	12	13	14	15	16	17						

index

11	12	13	14	15	16	17	18	19	20	21	22	
1.7	1.8	1.9	2.1	2.2	2.3	2.5	2.7	2.9	3.1	3.3	3.5	oh 00
1.6	1.8	1.9	2.0	2.2	2.3	2.5	2.6	2.8	3.0	3.2	3.4	20
1.6	1.7	1.8	1.9	2.1	2.2	2.4	2.5	2.7	2.9	3.1	3.3	40
1.5	1.6	1.7	1.8	1.9	2.1	2.2	2.3	2.5	2.7	2.9	3.1	1h 00
1.4	1.5	1.6	1.7	1.8	2.0	2.1	2.2	2.4	2.6	2.7	2.9	10
1.3	1.4	1.5	1.6	1.8	1.9	2.0	2.1	2.3	2.4	2.6	2.8	20
1.2	1.3	1.4	1.5	1.6	1.7	1.9	2.0	2.1	2.3	2.4	2.6	30
1.1	1.2	1.3	1.4	1.5	1.6	1.7	1.8	2.0	2.1	2.2	2.4	40
1.0	1.1	1.2	1.3	1.4	1.5	1.6	1.7	1.8	1.9	2.0	2.2	50
0.9	1.0	1.1	1.1	1.2	1.3	1.4	1.5	1.6	1.7	1.8	1.9	2h 00
0.8	0.9	1.0	1.0	1.1	1.2	1.3	1.3	1.4	1.5	1.6	1.7	10
0.7	0.8	0.8	0.9	0.9	1.0	1.1	1.1	1.2	1.3	1.4	1.5	20
0.6	0.6	0.7	0.7	0.7	0.8	0.9	0.9	1.0	1.0	1.1	1.2	30
0.4	0.4	0.5	0.5	0.6	0.6	0.7	0.7	0.7	0.8	0.9	0.9	40
0.3	0.3	0.3	0.4	0.4	0.4	0.5	0.5	0.5	0.5	0.6	0.6	50
0.1	0.1	0.2	0.2	0.2	0.2	0.2	0.2	0.2	0.2	0.3	0.3	3h 00

Add to MTL (m)

												10
0.1	0.1	0.2	0.2	0.2	0.2	0.2	0.2	0.2	0.2	0.3	0.3	20
0.3	0.3	0.3	0.3	0.4	0.4	0.4	0.4	0.5	0.5	0.5	0.6	30
0.4	0.4	0.5	0.5	0.5	0.6	0.6	0.6	0.7	0.7	0.8	0.8	40
0.5	0.6	0.6	0.7	0.7	0.7	0.8	0.9	0.9	1.0	1.0	1.1	50
0.7	0.7	0.8	0.8	0.9	0.9	1.0	1.1	1.1	1.2	1.3	1.4	4h 00
0.8	0.8	0.9	0.9	1.0	1.1	1.2	1.2	1.3	1.4	1.5	1.6	10
0.9	0.9	1.0	1.1	1.1	1.2	1.3	1.4	1.5	1.6	1.7	1.8	20
1.0	1.0	1.1	1.2	1.3	1.4	1.5	1.6	1.7	1.8	1.9	2.0	30
1.1	1.2	1.2	1.3	1.4	1.5	1.6	1.7	1.8	2.0	2.1	2.2	40
1.2	1.3	1.4	1.5	1.6	1.7	1.8	1.9	2.1	2.2	2.3	2.5	50
1.3	1.4	1.5	1.6	1.7	1.8	2.0	2.1	2.2	2.4	2.5	2.7	5h 00
1.4	1.5	1.6	1.8	1.9	2.0	2.2	2.3	2.5	2.6	2.8	3.0	20
1.6	1.7	1.8	2.0	2.1	2.2	2.4	2.6	2.8	2.9	3.1	3.3	40
1.7	1.8	1.9	2.1	2.2	2.3	2.5	2.7	2.9	3.1	3.3	3.5	6h 00

Subtract from MTL (m)

Index